THE 5 RATIONAL STEPS FOR MANAGING IT INVESTMENTS

HOW-TO GENERATE MAXIMUM
BUSINESS VALUE FROM IT

SOLOMON BABA

Copyright © 2012 Solomon Baba
All rights reserved.

ISBN: 1475127391
ISBN 13: 9781475127393

Library of Congress Control Number: 2012906131
CreateSpace, North Charleston, SC

*This book is dedicated to the memory of my late parents
Mr James Baba and Mrs Rachael Baba*

DISCLAIMER

Although the author took proper care in writing this book, no warranty is given by the author as to the accuracy and completeness of the information contained therein, and neither the author, nor the publisher shall be responsible or liable for any loss or damage whatsoever arising by virtue of such information or any advice contained within this book.

All trademarks, registered names, and so forth acknowledged in this book are the property of their respective owners.

CONTENTS

Forward	*ix*
Preface	*xi*
Acknowledgements	*xiii*
The Journey Begins: The Five Rational Steps	*1*
Introduction	3
Step One: IT Governance	17
How-to Make Effective IT Alignment and Investment Decisions	
Step Two: IT Solutioning	89
How-to Formulate IT Strategy and Design Solution Architectures	
Step Three: IT Execution	161
How-to Select, Fund, and Deliver IT Programmes and Projects	
Step Four: IT Operationalization	191
How-to Source and Provision High Quality IT Services	
Step Five: IT Benefiting	211
How-to Harvest the Expected Benefits of IT Services in Full	
About the Author	*239*
Index	*241*

FORWARD

Five Rational Steps...to understanding, managing and optimising one of the most vital assets in your business.

This book has been written from the author's experience, both as a practicing technology consultant who originated the rational steps as a consulting approach and from extensive research of the key literature on the subject.

The author has identified key themes and threads from extensive study of the related research areas that impact IT investment. He has woven these threads into five themes which together help the reader identify what to do to manage their IT investment projects successfully and generate maximum value.

The author recognises the need to combine the theoretical and practical into the feasible and understandable. The rational steps provide justified and referenced checklists of what to do for each aspect of IT investment. It may not promise to provide the answer as to what IT to invest in and how much value should you expect, but it will force you to consider the components of IT value for your business and the aspects you should think about. It will also help you identify where you are in the process and what factors you might want to consider for your specific technology situation.

As information technology is pervasive, this book should appeal to all levels of an enterprise. Readers at board level interested in generating maximum value from IT will find it valuable for laying out a feasible process for developing an IT investment management strategy, whilst enterprise and solution architects should include its tenets in their architecture strategy and roadmaps. Programme and project managers will be keen to explore mechanisms that may help them understand the investment contribution of their projects. Above all the humble man of the business will find it invaluable in helping them understand what all the IT fuss is about and why information technology is a vital element in keeping their business competitive if the relative value of supporting IT is managed and optimised.

Although technology may change and move on, this book should provide a useful and companionable guide as to how to identify what information technology investments to make and how to manage them to enable a successful and competitive business.

Dr Vaughan Michell BSc MBA D.Phil C.Eng
Henley Business School
United Kingdom
09 May 2012

PREFACE

The insight in this book comes from four years' extensive research to identify the critical factors for managing IT investment initiatives successfully and generating maximum value and from my more than a decade's work experience gained from working for a multinational corporation (MNC) as an enterprise and solutions architect. Most of the research for this book was done during my postgraduate degree programme at the Informatics Research Centre (IRC) of the Henley Business School at the University of Reading in the United Kingdom (UK).

This book is written for people who occupy the following roles in any organisation: Board of Directors (BoDs); Chief Executive Officers (CEOs); Chief Information Officers (CIOs); Chief Enterprise Architects (CEAs); Enterprise Solutions Architects (ESAs); Business Analysts (BAs); Chief Governance Officers (CGOs); IT Portfolio, Programme, and Project Managers; IT Services Portfolio, Delivery, and Operations Managers; and Business Change Managers.

By using the IT investment management methodology or framework presented in this book, each of the stakeholders mentioned above will be able to do the following accordingly:

- BoDs and CGOs will be able to govern how their enterprises invest in IT effectively.

- CEOs will be able to generate maximum business value from their investments in IT.

- CIOs will be able to manage how they invest in IT and improve their conversion effectiveness.

- CEAs will be able to identify the right strategic IT investment initiatives/opportunities and ensure that strategic IT solutions are consistent with existing enterprise architecture and standards.

- ESAs will be able to translate strategic IT investment initiatives into technically feasible strategic IT solutions.

- BAs will be able to assess the financial and business feasibility of strategic IT solutions and develop robust business cases for prospective solutions.

- IT Portfolio Managers (ITPMs) will be able to select and fund strategic IT investment programmes or projects with the best potential value.

- IT Programme/Project Managers will be able to execute strategic IT investment programmes or projects successfully in order to deliver strategic IT capabilities or services.

- IT Services Portfolio Managers (ITSPMs) will be able to make effective IT sourcing decisions and manage their portfolio of strategic IT services throughout their entire life cycle.

- IT Services Delivery/Operations Managers will be able to deliver strategic IT services at the right level of quality and cost.

- Business Change Mangers will be able to harvest the expected benefits of strategic IT services in full.

ACKNOWLEDGEMENT

I would like to thank my brothers and sisters, uncles and aunties, friends, former colleagues at Oracle, the Informatics Research Centre (IRC) staff of the Henley Business School at the University of Reading, and most especially Dr. Vaughan Michell for his insightful contributions and for writing the forward of this book. I would also like to thank Grace Henry B. for her wonderful support throughout the periods of writing this book. Lastly, I would like to thank the staff of Capgemini UK: David Pepperell (vice president and head of technology consulting) and Cameron Spence (enterprise architect) for their contributions.

CHAPTER 1

THE JOURNEY BEGINS:
THE FIVE RATIONAL STEPS

INTRODUCTION

'The companies that manage their IT investments most successfully generate returns that are as much as 40% higher than those of their competitors'.

—Peter Weill[1]

It is widely reported that the information assets of an enterprise can account for more than 50 percent of its capital investment.[2] The 2009/2010 information technology (IT) Spending and Staffing Benchmarks study conducted by the research firm Computer Economics Inc. corroborated these reports to some extent by stating that 'the median organization spent 1.5 percent of its revenue on IT in 2009—the same level as reported in 2008.'[3] So, if the information asset, which includes information and information technology, is that important as indicated by the magnitude of enterprises' investments in acquiring it, why is it that most enterprises do not have a system for managing their most important IT process—that is, how to invest in IT and generate maximum value? According to a 2007 Forrester Research report, 'Given IT's importance, making the right IT investment decision is critical to organizational success. Yet our research indicates that many do not have formal IT investment processes.'[4]

Keep in mind that investment is the act of investing money in something, which includes the investment process, the money invested in something, and the thing invested in—that is, the result of the act of investing[5] such as an IT system. This implies that managing IT investments involves managing the processes for investing in IT, managing the enterprise resources that are invested in IT, as well as managing the IT systems or enterprise applications that result from the IT investment processes and the commitment of enterprise resources. In addition, keep in mind that the terms: *model*, *system*, *method*, *framework*, and *process* are used interchangeably throughout the remainder of this book.

In *The Execution Premium*, Robert S. Kaplan and David P. Norton justified the need to have systems for managing the important processes or assets of an enterprise:

> THESE DAYS, successful companies seem to have a system for everything. From acquiring new customers to managing customer relationships, from quality management to performance measurement, industry leaders have realized that having systematic processes in place reduces risk, prevents oversights, and assures the best chance of delivering results.[6]

Similarly, Mark Morgan, Raymond Levitt, and William Malek in *Executing Your Strategy* corroborated that having systems for carrying out important processes is critical to achieving enterprise success. The reason why most executives fail to execute their strategies and to deliver on their promise to shareholders, they asserted, is that executives lack a *systematic method* for identifying and implementing the right initiatives or key action programmes to deliver on that promise.[7] Finally, Robert J. Benson, Thomas L. Bugnitz, and William B. Walton in *From Business Strategy to IT Action*, confirm that, 'with the right management frameworks and management practices, companies can successfully control the growth of IT costs and at the same time improve the business bottom-line impact of those costs and investments.'[8]

The IT units of enterprises that do not have an effective system for managing how they invest in IT and generate maximum value—those that do not have an IT investment management process—are usually perceived as cost centres instead of able contributors to company's profit because they are often not able to generate maximum value from their IT investments. These enterprises typically show the following symptoms:

1. Their IT investment decisions are often ineffective because they have no formal means of ensuring that they are making the right IT investment decisions. This could also mean that they have no

means of encouraging the desired behaviour in the use of IT or the means for ensuring that their resources are used responsibly and allocated appropriately.

2. They have *low conversion effectiveness*. In other words, they require more time and resources than their competition to convert their IT investments into business value and are, therefore, less able to generate the same value from the same level of IT investments as their peers,[9] which could also mean that they are less able to maximise their investments in IT.

3. They are not always sure they are *doing the right things*, as they have no means of ensuring that their investments in IT are supporting or enabling the achievement of their strategic objectives. Put another way, their IT investments are usually not aligned with their business priorities. And if they are sure they are doing the right things, they are not sure they are *doing them the right way*.

4. Their IT investment projects are often *not well done*; they often run late, are over budget, and lack the required functionalities.[10]

5. They are usually not sure they are provisioning the right IT services at the right level of quality and cost to support the delivery of the business services that create value for their customers.[11]

6. Their plans for realising the benefits of their investments in IT and their plan for reviewing their IT investment projects following their implementation are often not done well (if they have a plan at all), and, as a result, the IT units of such enterprises are not sure they are getting the benefits they expected from their IT investment projects.[12]

Numerous for-profit and not-for-profit organisations have made efforts to develop systematic processes for managing how they invest in IT and generate maximum value in the form of standalone frameworks, systems development life cycle and project management methodologies, and bodies of knowledge; however, their availability alone is not sufficient, the examples of which include:

1. COBIT (system for IT governance)
2. IBM BSP (system for strategic IT planning)
3. TOGAF (system for enterprise architecture documentation, analysis, and solution design)
4. PRINCE2 (method for portfolio, programme, and project management)
5. DSDM (method for rapid application development)
6. ITIL (systematic process for IT services management)
7. Val IT (system for IT benefit realisation)

The problem is not the availability of individual systems or methodologies for managing IT investments, but rather the lack of integration (i.e., no consideration for each other or lack of proper handoffs) between pockets of systems, frameworks, and methodologies, which makes it very difficult to use them collectively in managing IT investments throughout their entire life cycle. Robert J. Benson et al, in *From Business Strategy to IT Action*, supported this idea by stating that, the reasons why enterprises are not able to control their on-going IT costs and generate maximum from their investments in IT is because their business and IT planning processes, IT investment decision processes, performance measurement processes and so forth are poorly connected.[13] Finally, the IT Governance Institute (ITGI), assert that enterprises that want to generate maximum value from their investments in IT must be able to choose the best IT investments from a portfolio of proposed IT applications or solutions and manage them throughout their entire life cycle—from concept to benefit realisation and retirement.[14]

Evolution of Rational Framework or System

Due to the apparent limitation of existing systems, this book presents a comprehensive rational system or framework to integrate disparate systems and methods so that they are aligned and synchronised with each other, helping enterprises to manage their IT investment initiatives or opportunities throughout their entire life cycle and generate maximum value. The rational framework exhaustively integrates pockets of isolated global best practice IT investment management systems that cover the domain of IT capabilities required to manage IT investments successfully and generate maximum value, which are:[15]

1. IT governance system
2. Strategic IT planning method and enterprise architecture management (EAM)
3. IT portfolio, programme, and project management (ITPPPM) methodologies
4. Software development life cycle method
5. IT sourcing and funding models
6. Enterprise change management framework
7. IT services management (ITSM)
8. IT benefit realisation management

These eight (8) vital IT capabilities are integrated and aligned to form a coherent and systematic process for managing the entire life cycle of IT investments. Many enterprises do not manage their IT investments well because they lack a system that integrates these eight IT capabilities.

Rational IT Investment Management (RITIM) Principles

The rational system or steps for IT investment management was developed based on the following global best practice IT investment management principles:

1. *Adopt a capability-oriented approach that supports the development of new IT solutions* as we now have software vendors referring to their software packages as IT solutions rather than what they are: software applications. Enterprises must adopt a capability-oriented approach in order to distinguish between the so-called IT solutions (which are only *part* of the solution) and the ability of enterprises to solve their problems using IT (which *is* the solution). A capability is the right mix of competent, well-trained people, redesigned business processes, software applications, and other resources required to solve enterprise problems or to achieve enterprise objectives. Adopting a capability orientation also helps to ensure that the IT capabilities delivered by enterprise IT align with business priorities.[16] According to Forrester Research, 'Capabilities are the fundamental elements that make up a business; they are the building blocks of business execution.'[17]

2. *Manage IT as an investment, not as expenditure.* IT investment is like any other type of investment in enterprise change carried out by enterprises to generate value,[18] earn an income, grow the enterprise, boost enterprise results, develop a new capability, and solve enterprise problems.

3. *Understand the three perspectives of IT investment.* First, it is the *act* of investing money in IT—that is, the *process* of making investment decisions. Second, it is the *money* invested in IT, and, third, it is the thing invested in—IT assets—which are the end result of the act of investing.[19] In summary, IT investment is the act of investing (the investment process), the capital invested, and the result of the act of investing (the resulting IT assets).

4. *Manage IT as investments that deliver IT capabilities, rather than IT solutions or systems.*[20] A follow-up to the first principle, this principle helps to send home the point that in order to generate maximum value from IT, an enterprise must effectively leverage or exploit the capabilities that IT delivers.[21] The availability of capability—that is, the ability to do something—will not yield any results until that ability is put to good use. (For example, a person can have

THE JOURNEY BEGINS:

the ability to run a marathon, but if he or she does not run in the marathon, he or she cannot win the marathon.)

5. *Adopt a process-centric approach to governing and managing investments in IT.* Process is everything; without a well-defined process for doing a thing, the way that thing is done cannot be continuously improved upon or optimised, nor can it be standardised. In addition, adopting a process-centric approach encourages process ownership, which then enables process accountability.

6. *Include all the steps or the full scope of activities required to achieve value from IT.* Enterprises should manage their investments in IT throughout their entire life cycle—from conception to retirement.[22]

7. *Design effective and transparent IT governance architecture to direct and control IT investment processes.*[23,24] Enterprises should select the right combination of IT governance building blocks—style, organisational structure filled with competent people, process, information, and systems—for making effective IT investment decisions.

8. *Adopt a portfolio approach to managing investments in IT, one that has a different risk and return profile.*[25] Balance this portfolio to align it with the business strategy and to meet the desired mix of short- and long-term benefits.

9. *Categorise portfolios of IT investments into those that are mandatory, or those that are infrastructural and regulatory driven, and those that are discretionary or non-mandatory.*[26] Discretionary IT investments are further categorised into those that are required to run, grow, or transform the enterprise, or into those required to deliver strategic, informational, or transactional capabilities or services.

10. *Adopt a service-oriented approach to managing and to developing new IT capabilities.*[27] The development of new IT capabilities should enable the provisioning of any or all of the following: strategic, informational, transactional, and infrastructural IT services.

11. *Renew mind-sets and focus on IT's contribution to enterprise outcomes and performance.*[28] Managers can do this by linking IT capabilities delivered through IT investment programmes to the IT services they enable or support, linking IT services to the business services they support or enable, and, finally, linking business services to business outcomes. In summary, managers should link IT capabilities to IT and business services, link business services to business outcomes, and link business outcomes to business value.

12. *Be cognizant that enterprise change management is the single biggest challenge to introducing new IT systems.* At the same time, be aware that enterprise change management significantly affects the realisation of value from IT investment programmes or projects. Because real benefits only arise when either IT investment is supplemented by other enterprise changes or enterprise changes drive combined investments in IT and other resources.[29]

Rational System for Managing the Life Cycle of IT Investments

The systematic process or rational system for managing the life cycle of IT investments—sometimes called the IT investment management (ITIM) process—consists of five (5) sequential and iterative steps or capabilities models (see Figure 1.0) for managing how enterprises invest in IT and generate maximum value from IT or for converting IT investments into value. The rational system or framework was developed based on twelve (12) global best practice rational IT investment management (RITIM) principles outlined in the previous section of this book.

THE JOURNEY BEGINS: 11

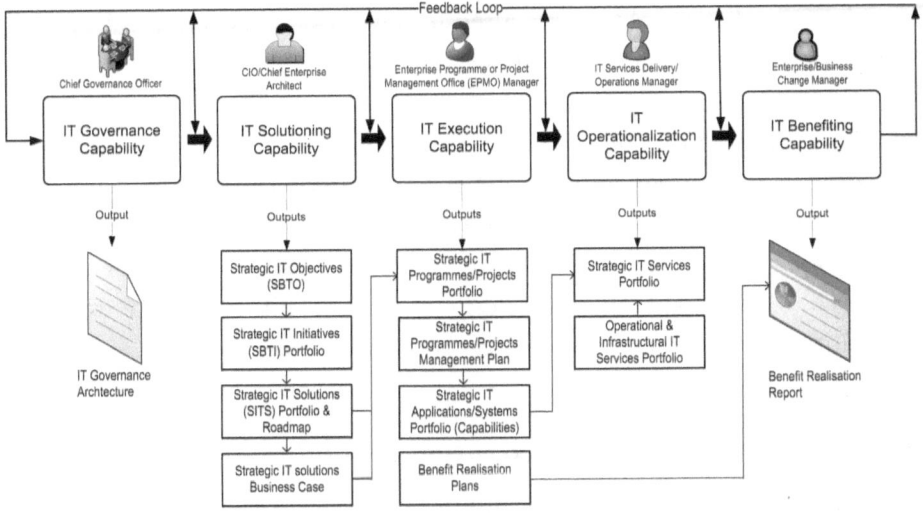

Figure 1.0 Rational System or Steps for IT Investment Management (ITIM)

Rational Step 1: Develop IT Governance Capability

Developing IT governance capability is the first of the five rational steps for IT investment management (ITIM) that enterprises must take in order to manage their investments in IT successfully and generate maximum business value. This capability represents the ability of enterprises to select the right styles, structures, processes, and communication mechanisms (i.e., design and implement effective IT governance architecture) for making effective IT alignment and investment decisions.

Rational Step 2: Develop IT Solutioning Capability

Next, enterprises need to develop IT solutioning capability, which is the ability of enterprises to formulate IT strategy aligned to their business strategy—that is, the ability of enterprises to specify strategic IT objectives (the *what*) and to identify the right strategic IT initiatives (the *how*) that should be executed to develop the capabilities required to achieve strategic IT objectives.

IT solutioning capability also includes the ability to translate the outcome of IT strategy formulation (i.e., strategic IT initiatives) into the architecture of technically feasible IT solutions needed to develop the IT capabilities required to deliver *strategic IT services*. In other words, IT solutioning also involves designing the architecture of enterprise solutions, or enterprise solution architecture (ESA).

Rational Step 3: Develop IT Execution Capability

IT execution capability is the ability of enterprises to execute the business-aligned IT strategies (i.e., the strategic IT investment initiatives or opportunities) formulated at the IT solutioning step. Put another way, it is the ability of enterprises to evaluate, select, fund, and deliver strategic *IT investment solutions-cum-projects* with the best potential to help enterprises achieve their strategic IT objectives. In fewer words, IT execution capability is one of the critical capabilities required by an enterprise to convert its strategic IT investment projects into a thing of immense value.

Rational Step 4: Develop IT Operationalization Capability

IT operationalization represents the ability of an enterprise to translate the strategic IT capabilities or systems delivered at the IT execution step into a business-relevant portfolio of *strategic IT services* or *operational IT systems* that will be used to support or enable the delivery of business services. This capability also includes the ability of an enterprise to maintain the usability, availability, protection, and continuity of those IT systems and services throughout their economic life cycle.

Rational Step 5: Develop IT Benefiting Capability

Finally, IT benefiting capability is required to realise the benefits expected from strategic IT investment projects or services in full.

Research has found that the degree (maturity level) of an enterprise's ability to carry out the five rational steps efficiently and effectively—that is, to convert IT investments into enterprise/business value (called conversion effectiveness)—will determine the value the firm gets from its investments in IT. Peter Weill and Marianne Broadbent, in *Leveraging the New Infrastructure*, affirmed that 'the firm with better conversion effectiveness produced systems faster and more cheaply and had better operational and financial performance.'[30] They also asserted that the competence required to translate IT investments into enterprise/business value varies significantly between different firms, which implies that conversion effectiveness is necessary and sufficient for using IT to create sustainable competitive advantage.

NOTES

1. Ross, J. W., & Weill, P. (2002, November). Six IT Decisions Your IT People Shouldn't Make. *Harvard Business Review*, 1-10, p. 2.
2. Nolan, R., & McFalan, F. W. (2005). Information Technology and the Board of Directors. *Harvard Business Review*, 1-11, p. 1.
3. Marks, N. (2010). The Pulse of IT Governance. *Internal Auditor*, 33-37.
4. Symons, C., Cullen, A., Orlov, L., & Belanger, B. (2007). *Making The Right Investment Decisions: Best Practices for IT Steering Committees*. US: Forrester Research Inc. p. 1.
5. Masse, P. (1962). *Optimal Investment Decisions*. US: Prentice-Hall.
6. Kaplan, R. S., & Norton, D. P. (2008). *The Execution Premium: Linking Strategy to Operations for Competitive Advantage*. US: Harvard Business Press.
7. Morgan, M., Levitt, R. E., & Malek, W. (2007). *Executing Your Strategy: How to Break it Down and Get it Done*. US: Harvard Business School Press, p. 2.
8. Benson, R. J., Bugnitz, T. L., & Walton, W. (2004). *From Business Strategy to IT Action: Right Decisions for a Better Bottom Line*. US: Wiley, John & Sons, p. 3.
9. Weill, P., & Broadbent, M. (1998). *Leveraging the New Infrastructure: How Market Leaders Capitalize on Information Technology*. US: Harvard Business School Press, p. 249,
10. Weill, P., & Ross, J. W. (2004). *IT Governance: How Top Performers Manage IT Decision Rights for Superior Results*. US: Harvard Business Press, p. 218.
11. Hunter, R., & Westerman, G. (2009). *The Real Business of IT: How CIOs Create and Communicate Value*. US: Harvard Business Press, p. 45.
12. Weill & Broadbent, *Leveraging the New Infrastructure*, p. 250.
13. Benson et al, *From Business Strategy to IT Action*, p. 5.
14. IT Governance Institute. (2005). Optimising Value Creation From IT Investments. *IT Governance Domain Practices and Competencies*. US: IT Governance Institute, p. 10.

15 Cameron, B., DeGennaro, T., & Leaver, S. (2009). *Forrester's Best Practices Framework for BT Leadership Maturity: Use Our Self-Assessment To Accelerate Your BT Transformation*. US: Forrester Research Inc., p. 8.
16 Scott, J., Cullen, A., & An, M. (2009). *Business Capabilities Provide The Rosetta Stone for Business-IT Alignment: Capability Maps Are a Foundation for Business Architecture*. US: Forrester Reseach, Inc., p. 3.
17 Ibid., p. 2.
18 Weill & Broadbent, *Leveraging the New Infrastructure*, p. 23.
19 Masse, P. (1962). *Optimal Investment Decisions*. US: Prentice-Hall.
20 IT Governance Institute. (2007). *COBIT 4.1*. US: IT Governance Institute, p. 12.
21 IT Governance Institute, *Optimising Value Creation From IT Investments*, p. 10.
22 IT Governance Institute. (2008). *Enterprise Value: Governance of IT Investments, The Val IT Framework 2.0*. US: The IT Governance Institute, p. 11.
23 Hunter & Westerman, *The Real Business of IT*, p. 5.
24 Weill & Broadbent, *Leveraging the New Infrastructure*, p. 253.
25 Ibid., p. 244.
26 Broadbent, M., & Kitzis, E. (2005). *The New CIO Leader: Setting the Agenda and Delivering Results*. US: Harvard Business School Press, p. 137.
27 Peppard, J. (2003). Managing IT as a Portfolio of Services. *European Management Journal, 21*(4), 467-483, p. 467.
28 Hunter & Westerman, *The Real Business of IT*, p. 4.
29 Ward, J., & Elvin, R. (1999). A New Framework for Managing IT-enabled Business Change. *Information Systems Journal*, 197-221, p. 198.
30 Weill & Broadbent, *Leveraging the New Infrastructure*, p. 72.

CHAPTER 2

THE FIRST RATIONAL STEP: IT GOVERNANCE
HOW-TO MAKE EFFECTIVE IT ALIGNMENT AND INVESTMENT DECISIONS

IT GOVERNANCE

Companies that effectively govern information technology garner profits that are 20% higher than those of other companies pursuing similar strategies.[1]

IT governance capability is the first of the five rational capabilities for IT investment management (ITIM) that enterprises must develop in order to manage their investments in IT successfully and generate maximum business value. This capability embodies the ability of an enterprise to design an effective IT governance architecture by selecting the right styles, structures, processes, and communication mechanisms that enable or support the development of IT governance system required for making effective IT governance decisions.

IT governance is the first rational step for ITIM because getting the right people into the right seats to make effective IT governance decisions is the first, and the most important step enterprises must take in order to manage their IT investments successfully and generate maximum value. Peter Weill and Richard Woodham concurred by stating that 'an effective IT governance structure is the single most important predictor of getting value from IT.'[2] In *Good to Great*, Jim Collins affirmed this supposition by stating that executives who succeeded in taking their companies from 'good to great' had to first figure out the *who*—to get the right people into the right seat—and then figure out the *what* (i.e., to set the vision and formulate strategies for realising the vision).[3]

In *Execution*, Ram Charan, Larry Bossidy, and Charles Burck also stressed the significance of 'having the right people in the right place'[4] to successfully execute strategies and, subsequently, to generate maximum value from IT investments. Similarly, the US General Accounting Office

(GAO) stated that the creation of investment awareness through the establishment of an investment board to provide oversight for the governance of IT investment management processes is the *first* critical maturation step required to move to the next stage of IT investment management capabilities development.[5] In addition, Marianne Broadbent and Ellen S. Kitzis, in *The New CIO Leader,* pointed out that creating clear and appropriate IT governance is the *first* step in the processes that allow enterprises to reap the benefits of their IT investments.[6]

So, if the development of IT governance capability is the *first* step for managing IT investments successfully and generating maximum value, what then is IT governance, and why is it so important to IT investment management and value maximisation?

What is IT Governance?

Consider first the definition proposed by Peter Weill and Jeanne W. Ross in *IT Governance,* 'Specifying the decision rights and accountability frameworks to encourage desirable behavior in the use of IT.'[7] In other words, IT governance is the process of clearly stating who has the professional obligation to make certain IT decisions, and the development or availability of the right mechanisms for holding them accountable for the outcome of their decisions. The goal is to ensure that IT objectives are achieved in a controlled and predictable fashion. The IT Governance Institute (ITGI) in the *Control Objectives for Information and Related Technology (COBIT) 4.1* documentation released in 2007 stated that:

> IT governance is the responsibility of executives and the board of directors, and consists of the leadership, organisational structures and processes that ensure that the enterprise's IT sustains and extends the organisation's strategies and objectives.[8]

ITGI also pointed out that IT governance enables organisations to take advantage of their information and IT to maximise benefits and revenues, make the most of opportunities, and gain advantage over their competitors.[9]

The third and newest IT governance definition comes from Deloitte Inc., a global professional services firm. Deloitte defined IT governance as

> the organised capacity to guide the formulation of IT strategy and plans, direct development and implementation of initiatives and oversee IT operations in order to achieve competitive advantage for the organisation.[10]

Finally, this book defines IT governance as the act of directing and controlling the IT alignment and investment processes of an enterprise in order to make effective IT governance decisions that will help to manage IT investments successfully and generate maximum value. Enterprises can increase their ability or develop the capability to make effective governance decisions by designing and using the right IT governance architecture (the arrangement of archetypes or styles, organisational structures, processes, and communication mechanisms) to make effective IT governance decisions and manage IT-related risks.

Forrester Research provided a succinct summary of all the definitions of IT governance presented in this book:

> At its most basic definition, IT governance is the process by which decisions are made around IT investments. How decisions are made, who makes the decisions, who is held accountable, and how the results of decisions are measured and monitored are all parts of IT governance.[11]

Ryan Peterson, a professor of information systems management at Instituto de Empresa in Spain and a leading authority on governance, asserted that enterprises must develop the following three key capabilities in order to govern its IT investments effectively: *structural* IT governance capability, *procedural* IT governance capability, and *relational/communicational* IT governance capability.[12]

Why Do Organisations Need Strong IT Governance?

Given the importance of information and information technologies (i.e., information assets and resources), developing an excellent capability for directing, controlling, and providing oversight for IT investments are critical to the success of private and public organisations alike.

It is widely reported that investments in information resources and assets can account for more than 50 percent of organisations' capital spending.[13] The 2009/2010 information technology (IT) Spending and Staffing Benchmarks study conducted by the research firm Computer Economics Inc. corroborated these reports to some extent by stating that 'the median organization spent 1.5 percent of its revenue on IT in 2009—the same level as reported in 2008.[14] The importance of information assets is evident from the magnitude of organisations' investment in its acquisition. As a result, IT investments can no longer be governed using ad hoc, fragmented, or inconsistent approaches; enterprises need to develop an excellent IT governance system to govern how they invest in IT in order to generate maximum value.

The many failures and disappointments with IT-enabled enterprise transformation efforts is also another important reason why enterprises need to develop excellent IT governance capability. According to the Standish Group in its 2009 chaos report, only 32 percent of IT projects that are the key vehicles for delivering IT-enabled enterprise transformations succeeded—that is, only 32 percent of IT investment projects are delivered on time, within budget, and with the required functionalities,[15] which implies that the remaining 68 percent of IT investment projects failed.

The massive failure of IT investment projects adds to the list of reasons why enterprises must develop or improve their ability to govern their IT investments effectively in order to reduce their failures, as project failures often lead to business disruptions, customer defection, decrease in shareholders' value, and other undesirable side effects, including staff and senior executives losing their jobs.

A typical example of the negative effect of IT investment project failure is the downward spiral ($3 billion in a single day) of Oxford Health Plans' market capitalisation that resulted from the announcement the company made about the IT system's problems that led to general errors in the way it processes its billing and claims.[16] Another example is the case of Cigna, a global health service company, in which a badly implemented customer relationship management (CRM) system led to poor customer service at the end of 2001; Cigna lost 6 percent of its health care customers (membership fell from 13.3 million to 12.5 million at the end of 2001).[17]

In addition to the apparent significance of IT to enterprise success, and the fact that IT investments consume a large portion of organisations' capital spend, and the dismal failure of projects that result from such investments being the reasons why organisations must develop effective IT governance capability. Peter Weill and Jeanne W. Ross in *IT Governance* gave another very important reason why enterprises need to develop excellent IT governance capability. In their study of the IT governance practices of over 250 for-profit and not-for-profit organisations in twenty-three different countries, they found that 'good governance design allows enterprises to deliver superior results on their IT investments.'[18] From the same research, they also found that high-performing organisations govern their IT investments differently from low-performing organisations, which led them to conclude that 'effective IT governance is the single most important predictor of the value an organisation generates from IT.'[19] Therefore, good IT governance does pay off.

The bottom line? It is *IT investment management*, which includes IT governance, that matters in extracting strategic business value from IT—not the general availability of IT assets.

So, if good IT governance pays off, and it is indeed the single most important predictor of the business value an organisation can generate from its investments in IT, why is it that most organisations today are still struggling with putting good IT governance in place to help them generate maximum value from their investments in IT? As indicated by the large number of IT investment project failures, the reason for this is obvious. Recall the IT Governance Institute's definition of IT governance, which states that IT governance should be the responsibility of executives and board of directors. Yet, most boards in enterprises today 'remain largely in the dark when it comes to IT spending and strategy.'[20] The boards in most organisations fall prey to imitating the best practices of other firms, and only a handful understands the strategic relevance of IT to their firm's strategies.[21]

While it may seem that the board committees in erring organisations are incompetent, this is not so. Certainly, board committees understand their role with regard to other areas of corporate control; the problem is the lack of a comparable body of knowledge, best practices, standards, and systems for IT governance.[22] Because of this, board members in most enterprises most often lack the fundamental knowledge needed to ask intelligent questions about IT investment benefits and risks, which leads to lack of board oversight for IT. A lack of oversight for IT activities is detrimental to the firm, as it puts the firm at risk as would the failure to audit the books of the firm.[23] Because of this challenge, a primary focus of this book is to provide the body of knowledge, standards, and systems for IT governance.

Due to the lack of relevant capabilities to effectively govern how they invest in IT, the board of most companies have relinquished their IT investment governance responsibility to executive review boards, project management offices,[24] or CIOs.[25] But it is only the enterprises that create board-level committees of equal significance as the audit, compensation, and governance committees to assist the CEO, CIO, senior management, and the board in driving technology decisions that may put costly projects under control and carve out competitive advantage from the use of technology.[26] Although creating a board-level committee is critical to governing IT investments effectively, it is only one of the essential components of effective IT governance system. In order to govern their IT investments effectively, organisations must design an IT governance architecture that consists of board-level committees—people, styles or archetypes, and structures—and other critical elements of IT governance such as processes and communication mechanisms, and use the architecture to develop IT governance system—that is, to implement the IT governance architecture. According to Forrester Research, designing and implementing good IT governance requires a framework or architecture with structure, process, and communication as its building blocks.[27]

Designing IT Governance Architecture and Developing IT Governance System

Designing IT governance architecture is the deliberate process of arranging the critical building blocks of the IT governance capability or system to create an organisation capable of making effective IT decisions—that is, one that reflects how the organisation intends to exploit IT to achieve its objectives. A well-designed IT governance architecture enables the development of a strong IT governance capability or system, which in turn enables enterprises to make better IT alignment and investment management decisions.[28]

IT Governance Architecture Building Blocks

IT governance capability building blocks, also called governance mechanisms,[29] are the key components from which enterprises develop their IT governance capability or system or implement a particular IT governance style.[30] Enterprises need to orchestrate the right combination of building blocks to develop their abilities to make effective IT alignment and investment decisions; these building blocks consist of the styles, organisational structures filled with competent people, procedures, and communication mechanisms.[31,32]

1. IT Governance Styles

    IT governance styles identify the types of collaborations that exist between the people in the business, corporate, and IT units of an organisation for the sake of making IT governance decisions.[33] IT governance styles also specify or determine who should be consulted for input into IT governance decisions, who should be responsible for making decisions, and who should be informed about the decisions that were made.[34]

    Numerous literature has identified six types of IT governance styles for making IT decisions: *business monarchy*, *IT monarchy*, *IT duopoly*, *federal system*, *feudal systems*, and *anarchy*.[35,36] Business monarchy is a centralised IT governance style where all the decisions concerning IT investments in an enterprise are delegated to senior-level business executives or a selected group of senior-level business executives, which may also include the CIO. In the IT monarchy governance style, IT decisions are made by the CIO alone or by a group of IT executives (usually in the form of IT steering committees). In the IT duopoly governance style, IT executives and one group of business unit leaders or process owners make all the IT decisions; this style is popularly referred to as a two-party arrangement. In the federal IT governance style, senior-level executives and line-of-business (also called operating groups) leaders or their representatives (business process owners and end users), together with the IT unit, collaborate to make IT decisions. In the feudal IT governance style, strategic business units (SBUs) or business process leaders have the authority to make IT decisions based on the needs of their unit or processes. Finally, in the IT anarchy governance style, lower-level business processes owners and individual end users have the sole right to make IT decisions; this style of IT decision making is the most decentralised of all the other styles.[37,38]

2. IT Governance (Decision-making) Structures

IT governance structure, the most visible of the four (4) IT governance capability building blocks,[39] is the formal manner by which IT-savvy business executives and business-savvy IT executives are grouped together by governance style of the enterprise to make IT alignment and investment decisions.[40,41,42] According to Broadbent and Kitzis in *The New CIO Leader*, 'Different governance styles invoke different combinations of business and IT executives at different organizational levels.'[43] MIT research scientists Peter Weill and Jeanne W. Ross corroborated this assertion when they stated that 'different archetypes rely on different decision making structures.'[44] These groupings or combinations of people (i.e., IT governance structures) are referred to as IT committees, teams or councils, and so forth. Typical variants of IT governance styles and their corresponding structures are as follows:[45,46]

- *Business Monarchy Decision-Making Structures*: Executive or senior management committee, business needs committee, enterprise or

IT investment committee, IT investment review board (ITIRB), strategic IT investment council, or capital investment approval and budgets

- *Federal Decision-Making Structures*: IT audit committee

- *IT Monarchy Decision-Making Structures*: IT strategy committee and IT architecture committees/review board, which identify and enforce strategic IT standards, and IT leadership teams composed of heads (strategy, architecture, operations, and so forth)

- *IT Duopoly Decision-Making Structures*: IT steering committee composed of executives, business and IT management, IT councils, process organisations, and business/IT relationship managers

- Feudal: SBU or functional business unit leaders

- Anarchy: No structure

3. IT Governance—alignment and investment—Processes

   IT governance consists of two main processes. The first is the IT investment management process, shortened to IT investment process. The second is the IT alignment process. IT governance processes are the formal processes—the series of steps—designed to direct and control the way enterprises make IT investment and alignment decisions. The objective is to ensure that IT decisions are consistent with the strategic business objectives; existing enterprise IT architecture and standards; and IT principles in order to generate maximum value from IT. The IT governance process also encourages stakeholders' involvement in making and implementing governance decisions.[47]

   Typical IT investment processes include the following:

   - IT strategy formulation
   - IT portfolio management
   - IT programme/project management

- IT services management
- IT benefits realisation

Here are some typical IT alignment processes:[48]

- Formal enterprise IT architecture and standards compliance and exception
- Technology research and adoption (technology refresh process)
- Infrastructure renewal
- IT principles development and renewal

4. IT Governance Communications

IT governance communications represents the medium for gathering and disseminating information related to the entire IT governance architecture or framework and the information that resulted from the IT alignment and investment decisions made by the enterprise to relevant stakeholders. IT governance communications also facilitates collaboration between IT governance stakeholders[49] who might be the board of directors, executive management, business management, IT management, employees, or shareholders.

In summary, enterprises can design their IT governance architecture using the rational IT governance capability model depicted in Figure 2.0. Enterprises must follow five (5) steps in order to design an effective IT governance architecture.

The first step requires enterprises to determine who will be the owner or who will be accountable or responsible for IT governance efforts such as the design and implementation of IT governance architecture, communication of IT governance decisions and processes, and execution of IT governance processes across the enterprise.[50]

According to the IT Governance Institute (ITGI), 'IT governance is the responsibility of executives and the board of directors.'[51] Peter Weill and Jeanne W. Ross in *IT Governance* also agreed that the board of an enterprise is ultimately responsible for governing the entire enterprise, including IT, but the board will delegate this responsibility to the chief executive officer (CEO) or chief information officer (CIO), or to a group.[52] Forrester Research, however, recommended that enterprises create governance-specific positions such as a *chief governance officer* and relationship managers to implement IT governance programs.[53]

Enterprises also need to identify the types of IT investment and alignment decisions that must be made in order to generate maximum value from IT investments.[54] Once the decisions that must be made are identified, enterprises can then map out the right governance styles for making those decisions and specify the organisation's structures and processes for making those decisions.[55] Last, enterprises must determine the right tools, means, or metrics for measuring, monitoring, and communicating the outcomes of IT governance decisions to concerned stakeholders.

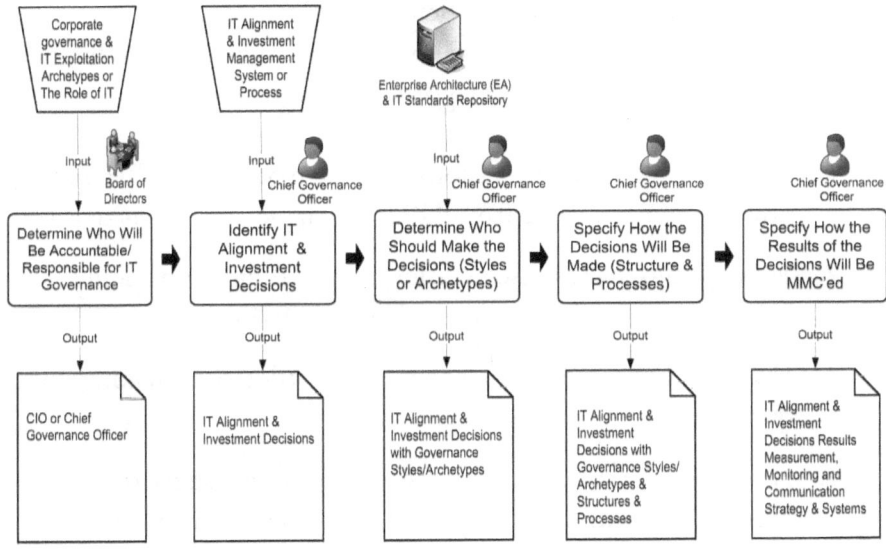

Figure 2.0 Rational IT Governance Capability Model

How to Design IT Governance Architecture and Develop IT Governance Capability

In order to generate business value from their IT investments that surpasses that of the competition, enterprises must develop the ability to govern their IT investments better than their competition or become better at making IT governance decisions, as the ability to govern IT investments effectively has significant bearing on the value generated from the investment. According to Weill and Ross, 'Effective IT governance is the single most important predictor of the value an organisation generates from IT.'[56] However, in order to develop an effective IT governance capability or system, enterprise must first design an IT governance architecture or mechanism best suited to the role of IT in the enterprise, or best suited to the way the enterprise intends to exploit IT to achieve its objectives[57] because 'well-designed, well-understood, and transparent mechanisms promote desirable IT behaviors.'[58]

A well-designed or effective IT governance architecture must be able to answer the following critical IT governance questions:[59,60]

1. What IT governance decisions must be made that will help to generate maximum value from IT? (governance decisions question)

2. Who should make these decisions, or who should be held accountable for them? (people and structure question)

3. How will these decisions be made? (decision-making process question)

4. How will the results/outcomes of these decisions be measured, monitored, and communicated? (performance assessment and tools/systems question)

The goal of this chapter is to help enterprises develop the capability required to answer the IT governance questions above using the rational IT governance capability model.

What IT Governance Decisions Must Be Made?

According to Weill and Ross, enterprises need to make five (5) IT governance decisions that are closely connected to each other.[61] Add the other IT governance decision introduced in this book—IT exploitation/role decision—to make it six (6) decisions in all:

1. IT exploitation archetype/role (not part of Weill & Ross's list)
2. Enterprise IT principles
3. Enterprise IT architecture
4. Enterprise IT infrastructure
5. Enterprise application needs
6. IT investments

The first decision concerns *IT exploitation archetype*, which include determining top management expectations regarding the role IT will play in the achievement of enterprise objectives or how the enterprise desire to use IT to achieve its objectives.

Enterprise IT principles, which include setting guidelines for making decisions on how the enterprise will use IT to achieve its objectives—that is, setting decision-making guidelines that are consistent with the selected IT exploitation archetype, is the second IT governance decision.

The third decision concerns *enterprise IT architecture*, which includes determining the most appropriate enterprise IT architecture design, standards, and policies that will help to guide the making of technical choices consistent with the integration and standardisation requirements of an enterprise.

The fourth is the *enterprise IT infrastructure* decision, which requires enterprises to decide which IT infrastructural or platform services will be shared among their strategic business units (SBUs), and those that will be left under the control of the SBUs.

Identifying the business need for strategic IT applications, be it packaged or custom applications software (*enterprise applications needs*), is an enterprise's fifth decision. In this book, this IT governance decision is concerned with determining the best strategic IT planning method to adopt that will enable an enterprise to identify the *right* portfolios of strategic IT initiatives-cum-solutions in which to invest.

The sixth and final IT governance decision is the IT investments decisions, which are concerned with determining the optimal level of enterprise investments in IT and how to select the best strategic IT initiatives-cum-solutions from the portfolio of *right* strategic IT initiatives-cum-solutions to fund. Peter Weill and Jeanne Ross further stated that these five key decisions (excluding IT exploitation archetype) are strongly related and should be linked for effective governance.[62]

In spite of the comprehensiveness of the IT governance decisions identified by Peter Weill and Jeanne W. Ross above, the identified governance decisions do not cover the entire economic life cycle of IT investments. Judging by the initial definition of investments presented in this book, three (3) critical IT governance decisions are missing. IT investment was defined as the act of investing enterprise money or capital into IT (i.e., the IT investment decision), the money invested, and the results of the act of investing (i.e., the IT systems invested in). Based on this definition, the following key decision areas are missing from the governance decisions identified by Peter Weill and Jeanne Ross:

1. How business-aligned IT strategy will be executed—that is, how strategic IT applications with the highest potential to create value will be *selected* among other alternatives and delivered to the enterprise—called IT execution decisions[63] or enterprise project management (EPM) decisions, which consists of portfolio, programme and project management decisions[64,65] together with enterprise (business and technology) change management decisions.[66] See chapter four of this book.

2. How the resulting IT systems will be translated into operational IT services used to create value for the enterprise—called IT services

management or operationalization decisions[67] (see chapter five of this book).

3. How the benefits of IT investments will be realised from the provisioned IT services and how the IT services will be retired when the cost of maintaining the investment exceeds the benefit—called IT benefiting decisions. These decisions are important because they are a key differentiator between a successful and failed IT investment programme or project[68] (see chapter six of this book).

IT execution decisions are mainly concerned with choosing the right programme and project management approach and life cycle methodology (e.g., project in a controlled environment [PRINCE2] or project management body of knowledge [PMBOK] to adopt). In addition, an organisation must also decide which software development life cycle (SDLC) methodology or commercially available off-the-shelf (COTS) application implementation methodology to adopt. Furthermore, the IT execution decisions should also include specifying how new IT systems will be introduced into the enterprise and how the effects of the accompanying changes will be managed.

IT operationalization decisions involve how the enterprise intends to source, develop, secure, operate, service, and maintain the IT infrastructure services or capability required to run the application software delivered as a result of its IT investments; it also involves how and where the newly delivered application software will be deployed, operated, and maintained. Examples of IT operationalization decisions might include deciding on whether the new application software or IT systems will be hosted and serviced on the premises, deployed in the cloud, or in a collocated data centre.

Finally, IT benefiting decisions involve how the benefit of the IT investment projects will be realised; these decisions also concern specifying how or when the IT systems will be retired.

To simplify, the five (5) IT governance decisions identified by Weill and Ross and the four (4) additional IT governance decisions identified in this book have been merged into five (5) main IT governance decisions based on the commonalities between them:

1. IT exploitation archetype/role
2. Enterprise IT principles
3. Enterprise IT architecture
4. Enterprise IT infrastructure
5. IT investment decision-making process,[69] which includes the following:
    i. IT investment decision-making process accountability
    ii. IT funding governance
    iii. IT sourcing governance
    iv. Enterprise applications needs decisions or IT solutioning governance
    v. IT investment portfolio, programme, and project decisions or IT execution governance
    vi. IT operationalization governance
    vii. IT benefits realisation decisions or IT benefiting governance

IT Exploitation Archetype/Role Decisions

Chief executive officers (CEOs) must state in clear terms the values they hope to generate from their investments in IT, which implies that the enterprise expectations for IT must be very clear in order for IT to succeed.

IT exploitation archetype is the way in which top management uses IT to achieve enterprise objectives—that is, top management's expectations for IT.[70] Forrester Research suggested three types of IT exploitation archetypes. The first archetype is the *solid utility*, where the enterprise's expectation for IT is the provisioning of cost effective and highly reliable solutions with continuous cost reduction. The focus of this type of business enterprise is on building reliable IT infrastructure that will enable them to keep the lights on.

The second archetype is the *trusted supplier*, where the enterprise's expectation for IT is successfully delivering IT projects based on the requirements and priorities of the business units. The focus of this type of enterprise is creating a strong project delivery discipline that will enable the enterprise to do and deliver the right projects. The third archetype is the *partner player*, where the enterprise's expectation for IT is the creation of unique and competitive solutions for its customers, suppliers, and internal users, coupled with being a trusted supplier.

Enterprises choosing the solid utility and trusted supplier archetypes are said to be operationally focused; they expect to use IT to achieve operational objectives, and their CIOs typically report to the CFO or COO. On the other hand, enterprises choosing the partner player archetype are said to be strategically focused; they expect to use IT to achieve strategic objectives; mostly the executive team governs the IT organisation in this type of enterprise.

Further corroborating the significance of IT archetypes, Weill and Ross asserted that enterprises with effective IT governance had clearer objectives for their IT investments.[71] In addition, they found that organisations with explicit objectives find it easy to govern their IT investments. Moreover, out of all the characteristics of top governance performers, having clear objectives for IT investments is the most difficult goal to achieve; thus, top IT governance performers often select the most important objectives to be the foundation of their governance architecture design.

Enterprises can use IT to achieve two main types of objectives. The first is strategic objectives, which focuses on the strategic use of IT to create and sustain a competitive advantage or to support future business strategies, usually through the use of IT to implement one or more of the following business strategies:[72,73]

- Cost leadership: using IT to lower costs
- Strategic alliance strategies: using IT to exploit relationships with suppliers and extend geographic reach
- Product differentiation: using IT to innovate and grow the business
- Vertical integration strategies: using IT to facilitate integration

The second is operational objectives, which is using IT to support or improve enterprise operations. Typical examples include the use of IT to accomplish one or more of the following operational objectives:

- Raise the level of service delivered to customers
- Enhance the quality of information provided to management
- Enable a complete and single view of customer information
- Better the quality of products and services offered to customers
- Reduce time to market for new products and services

Finally, IT exploitation archetypes or the primary role of IT in an enterprise helps to determine the right IT governance architecture design.[74] According to research carried out by two notable research scientists at MIT, in enterprises where the primary role of IT is strategic—that is, to support or enable the achievement of strategic objectives—business monarchies were used to make IT principles decisions, and federal IT governance style and corresponding structures were used to make enterprise IT infrastructure and architecture decisions.[75] However, in enterprises where IT's role is primarily operational—that is, to achieve operational objectives through helping to save costs or through other enterprise improvement initiatives—IT principles decisions were made using business monarchy IT governance style, while IT investment decisions were made using the IT monarchy governance style.

Enterprise IT Principles Decisions

Following the determination of top management expectations regarding the role that IT will play in the achievement of enterprise objectives—that is, the determination of enterprise's IT archetype, the enterprise must now articulate the principles that will guide how IT governance decisions will be made, and ensure they are consistent with the expectations that top management have for IT.

Deciding how to exploit information and IT assets to achieve objectives is one of the most important decisions an enterprise must make, as enterprises that properly articulate their basic philosophy for using IT to achieve their goals seem to be more effective at using IT.[76] According to the Open Group, 'Information technology (IT) principles provide *guidance* on the use and deployment of all IT resources and assets across the enterprise.'[77] The Open Group further stated that the sole objective of articulating IT principles is to ensure the productivity and cost-effectiveness of information and information technology. Davenport et al further emphasised this point by stating that the main aim of IT principles is to help enterprises make quick IT investment decisions that are free from disputes, as well as to ensure those decisions will help to further the enterprise's strategy.[78] Therefore, if having the right principles to guide how the enterprise invests in IT is important to achieving success with IT, what then are IT principles?

According to Davenport et al, 'Principles are simple, direct statements of an organization's basic beliefs about how the company wants to use IT over the long term,'[79] simply put, IT principles are the 'high-level statements about how IT is used in the firm.'[80] A typical example of an IT principle that helps an enterprise to identify the right stakeholder to be accountable or responsible for realising the business value of IT investment projects might read, 'The user-sponsor of a systems project will be responsible for the business success of the system.'[81] Another IT principle that helps an enterprise select a vendor might read, 'The IS department will maintain a shortlist of supported products in each technology category. Users may purchase other products at their discretion (subject to spending approval limits), but IS will not support them.'[82]

Enterprise IT Architecture or Blueprint Governance Decisions

Following IT exploitation archetype and IT principles decisions, the enterprise's third most important governance decision is IT architecture decisions; this decision must precede decisions concerning the development of the IT infrastructure upon which key enterprise applications must run.

Rockart et al.[83] identified four (4) challenges that must be addressed by the IT unit in developing and supporting the IT infrastructure that provides the foundation for enterprise applications to run. Two of the four challenges include developing the architecture that describes the future shape of IT infrastructure and specifying the IT standards for executing the architecture.

Two academicians from the University of Oxford also supported this view. A core IS capability for exploiting information technology, they said, is 'creating the coherent blueprint for a technical platform that responds to current and future business needs.'[84] So, if the decisions about the development of an effective IT architecture blueprint and the actual development of the blueprint are important to developing a robust platform for enterprise applications, what then is IT architecture? And how should enterprises go about developing this architecture?

In *Leveraging the New Infrastructure*, Peter Weill and Marianne Broadbent defined IT architecture as 'an integrated set of technical choices used to guide the organisation in satisfying business needs.'[85] They also stated that enterprise IT architecture is the composition of all the policies and rules that provide the technical guidelines for directing and controlling the use of IT or for making technical IT decisions and for providing technical directions for IT evolution. Architecture, they argued, should be subjected to constant reviews. They also pointed out that the most common goal of IT architecture is to help enterprises to achieve compatibility or to enable seamless integration between application software built on different platforms—that is, to integrate disparate IT systems and to support the execution of IT strategies or the achievement of IT objectives in line with the enterprise's objectives for IT.[86] To further the understanding of IT architecture, Jeanne W. Ross, a research scientist at the MIT Sloan School of Management, stated that IT architecture is 'the organizing logic for applications, data and infrastructure technologies, as captured in a set of policies and technical choices, intended to enable the firm's business strategy'.[87]

Although the two definitions presented above capture the essence of IT architecture, they do not state in specific terms what enterprises should expect as the deliverable of an IT architecture initiative; aside from the documentations of IT policies and rules, because of this inherent limitation, this book has developed its own definition of enterprise IT architecture. The foundation for this new definition is based on the fact that '[a]rchitecture in IT normally means high-level design.'[88] For this reason, enterprise IT architecture is defined as the high-level design or blueprint[89] of the current enterprise IT capability that conforms to or depicts the data, application, and technology principles, standards, policies, and choices of the enterprise.

Enterprises develop IT architecture in order to support the improvement or transformation of their current IT capabilities or to support the development of new IT capabilities,[90,91] which in turn helps to support or enable the development of business capabilities required to create or deliver business products and services.

In *IT Architectures and Middleware*, Chris Britton and Peter Bye proposed a definition similar to the one presented in this book.[92] They defined IT architecture as the overarching high-level design of application architecture, infrastructure architecture, security architecture, and other technical architecture that describe the IT capabilities of an enterprise. They also stated that the goal of designing IT architecture is to ensure that all the technical parts—the application, infrastructure, security, and so forth—are perfectly fitted together so that no part is left out or neglected during IT solutions design.

Enterprises must be able to make three (3) key IT architecture governance decisions in order to manage their IT investments effectively and set the precedence for generating maximum business value from IT. Decisions about the following should be made:

- Application platform framework to adopt
- Application infrastructure software (also called application platform or middleware) to adopt
- Enterprise IT standards or policies that will guide IT architecture development

1. Application Platform Framework (Software Development Standard) Decisions

An enterprise's first IT architecture governance decision is the application platform framework decision. At this juncture, enterprises must decide on the framework to adopt for the software application development/programming platform (also called application development frameworks or programming models) together with the corresponding programming languages[93] best suited to achieving their objectives for IT or for meeting the enterprise's IT expectations.

Based on the prevailing technical environment, enterprises will have to decide between the two commonly available application platform frameworks: the Java Platform, Enterprise Edition (JEE) specification[94] or the Microsoft .NET Framework.[95] Enterprises must choose one of these application platforms as the preferred framework for developing their core/mission-critical and non-core enterprise applications, or enterprises can decide whether to stick to just one of the platforms, although this is hardly practicable.[96] Following its application platform framework decision, an enterprise can go a step further to determine the best application development framework that will be used to develop applications that will run on chosen application platform standards—JEE or .NET or both. A common application framework for the .NET platform is Microsoft Visual Studio. For JEE or the Java platform, Oracle Application Development Framework (ADF), Apache Struts, Spring Framework, NetBeans, Eclipse, and so forth are available.

2. Application Platform Infrastructure Software Decisions

After deciding the application platform frameworks and application development frameworks to be adopted, enterprises must decide on the best application platform infrastructure (also called application infrastructure, applistructure, or middleware) to be the technology (software) platform for hosting, managing, and integrating their enterprise applications.[97,98]

The type of vendor or open-source application platform infrastructure (middleware) to choose depends entirely on the enterprise's earlier application platform frameworks decisions. According to Microsoft

Corporation, the Microsoft application infrastructure consists of Windows Server AppFabric (for deploying and managing web and composite applications), Windows Azure AppFabric (for deploying and managing applications in the cloud), and BizTalk Server (for connecting disparate IT systems built on the .NET framework) developer framework.

Therefore, if an enterprise should choose for example Microsoft .NET as its preferred application platform framework, then the choice of application infrastructure vendor will be limited to only Microsoft. However, if Oracle/Sun JEE is chosen as the preferred application platform framework standard, then the enterprise may choose from a wide array of vendors that support the Java-based platform framework (e.g., Oracle, IBM, and Information Builders) and other open-source options such as JBoss and Apache Tomcat.

Please note that an enterprise's choice of application platform framework standard will affect the selection of the right commercial-off-the-shelf (COTS) applications like ERP, CRM, and other key enterprise applications, as COTS applications from vendors, such as SAP or Oracle, are themselves built on or around an application platform framework and infrastructure/middleware standard. Therefore, when an organisation buys any of these applications, it also buys either the SAP or Oracle applications platform framework. If the organisation has not made up its mind on the application platform framework/middleware on which to standardise its applications, it will find itself with disparate middleware standards dominating its IT architecture landscape, which will cause numerous integration challenges.

3. Enterprise IT Standards Decisions

Following application platform framework and infrastructure decisions, enterprises must then decide on the rest of the data (i.e., shared data definitions, standards for ownership, and origin of data), applications (i.e., standards for application communication/interoperation and standards for user interface), and technology (i.e., standard hardware and software products) standards, to which the enterprise IT architecture must conform.[99] The specification of IT standards is the basis for architectural governance because specifying IT standards limits technology choices and reduces the number of platforms for enterprises to manage, ultimately leading to significant cost savings. It also facilitates seamless integration between enterprise applications.[100,101] In addition, specifying IT standards reduces the redundancy and complexity that results from the large number of vendor applications carrying out similar business functions in the enterprise.

After these three critical decisions have been made, enterprises can implement their enterprise IT architecture blueprints to deliver a standardised and flexible technology foundation (also called IT infrastructure)—routers, switches, servers, operating systems, databases, middleware, application development tools, security, mail servers, and so forth—for strategic IT capabilities development.[102,103]

Enterprise IT Infrastructure Decisions

IT infrastructure, the shared technology foundation for other IT capabilities development, includes both the technical and human elements required to deliver quality IT services.[104] This foundation consists of all the centrally shared and standard IT services and applications, such as corporate networks, help desks, shared customer data, hardware servers, computer data storage devices (storage area networks and network-attached storages), e-mail servers, as well as shared and standard applications, such as enterprise resource planning (ERP) and customer relationship management (CRM) systems.[105,106]

Enterprises must decide on the standardisation and sharing requirements for new IT infrastructure capabilities development; they must also decide if these capabilities should be located at the business unit level or managed centrally for enterprise-wide utilisation. These decisions are crucial because developing an effective IT infrastructure capability is a critical factor that determines the time-to-market for new strategic IT initiatives (also called strategic agility); as such, IT infrastructure decisions can significantly enable or impede strategic IT initiatives.[107]

IT Investment Decisions Process

According to Forrester Research, 'Given IT's importance, making the right IT investment decisions is critical to organizational success.'[108] However, in order to make the right IT investment decisions, enterprises must establish a formal decision-making process. Despite the fact that, the availability of formal processes for making IT investment decisions is necessary, it is not a sufficient condition form making the right IT investment decisions. The sufficient condition for making the right IT investment decisions dictates that an enterprise should have the ability to govern how it makes these decisions. That is, an enterprise should have the ability to effectively direct and control the processes for making these decisions.

In order to effectively manage IT investments and generate maximum value, enterprises must make certain governance decisions prior to investing in IT. These decisions concern the investment of enterprise capital on information assets, which starts when IT-related problems are identified or when the opportunities to use IT to solve business problems are discovered. These decisions are often referred to as *business application needs identification* decisions, and it ends with the approval and funding of an IT investment project.[109] These decisions further extend to decisions regarding the rest of the life cycle of IT investments—IT investment project delivery decisions, the operations and maintenance of IT systems, decisions about the realisation of business benefits from the resulting IT systems and, finally, the decision to retire the IT systems.

Classification of the IT Investment Decision Process

IT investment decisions consist of two (2) main high-level decision stages: the *pre*-IT investment decision stage and the *actual*-IT investment decision stage.[110] The *pre*-IT investment decision stage further consists of three (3) sub-stages, starting with the *initiation stage* (where IT investment initiatives are identified or business applications needs decisions are made),[111] the *development stage* (where IT investment initiatives are analysed and proposals are generated), and the *management stage* (where investment proposals are guided through the enterprise approvals cycle by the solution owner).

On the other hand, the actual IT investment decision stage has only one sub-stage, which is the approval stage where the responsible stakeholders approve the requested IT investment opportunities and allocate funding, following the evaluation and prioritisation of IT investment proposals or business cases.[112,113,114]

This book regards the decisions made at the *pre*-IT investment stage as belonging to a category of IT investment decisions called *IT solutioning decisions*—the decisions about finding the right solutions to IT-related business problems. And regards the decisions made at the *actual*-IT investment decision stage as belonging to a category of IT investment decisions called *IT execution decisions*—the decisions pertaining to IT investment evaluation, approval, prioritisation, and funding.

Based on the understanding that IT investment is both an act (the investment process) and the result of the act of investing (the resulting IT assets), IT investment decision stages will now be extended to include a third stage: the *post*-IT investment decision stage. This is the stage where the approved IT investment projects are developed or implemented and delivered as IT systems and consequently deployed by the IT unit and translated to business-relevant IT services for end users to exploit, and eventually retired when benefits no longer outweigh operation costs.

This book regards some of the decisions made at the *post*-IT investment decision stage as belonging partly to the earlier mentioned category of IT investment decisions called *IT execution decisions*, and the remainder of the decisions made at the *post*-IT investment decision stage as belonging to the category of IT investment decisions called: *IT operationalization decisions* and *IT benefiting decisions*.

The new classifications are IT solutioning decisions (where business applications needs decisions are made), IT execution decisions (where IT investment evaluation, approval, prioritisation, funding, and delivery decisions are made), IT operationalization decisions (where IT operations and maintenance decisions are made), and IT benefiting decisions (where IT benefit realisation and retirement decisions are made). Identified IT solutioning decisions belong to the pre-investment decisions stage, while IT execution decisions belong partly to the actual-investment decision stage and partly to post-investment decision stage; finally, both IT operationalization and IT benefiting decisions belong to the post-investment decisions stage. The identified IT investment decisions perfectly align with the five rational steps for IT investment management (ITIM), which are:

1. IT governance
2. IT solutioning
3. IT (strategy) execution
4. IT (systems/services) operationalization
5. IT (systems or services) benefiting.

Due to this alignment, the ITIM framework integrates the key IT investment decisions—pre-investment decisions, actual-investment decisions, and post-investment decisions—enterprises must make in order to manage their investments in IT successfully and generate maximum business value.

Newly Classified IT Investment Decision Process

In view of the new classification of the IT investment decision process presented in this book, with the addition of three new ones—accountability, funding, and sourcing decisions—enterprises now need to make seven (7) major decisions concerning the governance of the IT investment decision process:

1. IT Investment Decision Process Governance Accountability

By determining who will be accountable for the design, implementation, enforcement, improvement, and performance of the IT investment decision-making process or IT investment management process, this decision will enable enterprises to make subsequent IT investment decisions that will lead to the generation of maximum value from their investments in IT.

2. IT Funding (Investment) Governance Decisions

Making effective IT funding decisions is critical in generating maximum value from IT investment projects. According to MIT researchers Peter Weill and Jeanne W. Ross in *IT Savvy*, 'IT funding decisions are important because as systems are implemented, they become part of your firm's legacy.'[115] Without a working funding model (or governance architecture) to enable enterprises to make effective IT funding decisions, they asserted, it is nearly impossible to generate maximum value from IT investments.[116]

Although IT funding decisions are usually applicable to all the IT investment projects that enterprises will undertake and are not specific to any particular category of IT investment projects, be it strategic, tactical (informational and transactional), or infrastructural, the focus of this book is on making funding decisions for strategic IT investment projects.

Enterprises need to make three critical IT funding decisions that are categorised in this book as the *how*, *what*, and *from*. The first decision is the *how* decision, where enterprises must determine how much of their money to invest in IT. In other words, enterprises must decide on the percentage of their capital or operating expenditure (CAPEX or OPEX) or the percentage of their revenue or gross domestic product that is appropriate for investing in IT as a whole.[117,118] Determining the optimal level of investments in IT, however, is not an easy decision.[119]

The second decision is the *what* decision. Enterprises must determine the percentage of the IT budget that is appropriate for investing in a particular category of IT investments, which in this case are strategic IT investment initiatives. However, if or when the opportunities to invest in IT exceed the allocated budget, the enterprise must develop a mechanism for selecting the best IT investment opportunities to fund; this mechanism is popularly referred to as IT portfolio management (see chapter four of this book).

The third decision is the *from* decision. Enterprises must decide where the funding for IT investments will come from. They must decide if the fund will be sourced internally, from corporate through IT budget and organisational unit funding, or from external sources such as financial institutions, external IT service providers, and vendor financials.[120,121]

Determining the appropriate sources of funding is critical for IT investment projects because the source of fund will impact the cost of delivering projects and, consequently, on the ROI that is achievable from the investment.[122,123]

An enterprise must develop an appropriate model for guiding IT investment funding decisions for *specific* strategic IT investment initiatives, one that is aligned with its overall strategy for the enterprise and incorporates all the variables required to make an effective IT funding decision. The funding decisions for specific strategic IT investment initiatives that result from the use of the IT funding model are referred to as the funding strategy.

IT funding decisions for specific IT investment initiatives are best made at the IT solutioning step—the step where IT investment initiatives are identified and where the solution architecture of the initiatives are designed. At this stage, the conceptual business cases of IT investment initiatives are evaluated in the form of financial and business feasibility analysis.

3. IT Sourcing Governance Decisions

Given the potential challenges and costs associated with the management of IT and the dynamic nature of today's enterprise environment, enterprises must be able to *govern* how they make *IT sourcing decisions* in order to generate maximum value from their investments in IT. According to Linda Cohen and Allie Young in *Multisourcing*, 'Effective sourcing governance is more important to long-term sourcing success than any other factor'.[124]

In *Making IT Happen*, James D. McKeen and Heather A. Smith pointed out that IT sourcing decisions really come down to identifying *what* IT services to source internally or externally, knowing *where* to source them from, and determining *how* to best source the IT services that will support or enable the delivery of their business services.[125,126]

An enterprise can choose to transfer the management of its entire IT function to an external service provider (single outsourcing) or choose to retain the entire IT function management in-house (insourcing); it can also choose to provide its "core" IT services in-house and selectively outsource its non-core services to an external IT services provider—the first form of selective outsourcing.[127,128]

An enterprise can also choose to selectively source for the right IT services, which might be a mixture of core and non-core IT services, from the optimal set of internal (insource) and external IT service providers (outsource)—the second form of selective outsourcing.[129]

If an enterprise decision is to outsource some of its IT services, the enterprise must identify the candidate IT services to be outsourced,[130] choose evaluation criteria,[131] evaluate and select the best external IT services provider,[132] and decide when to outsource them, while also providing the justification for the outsourcing decision. All of these action plans and more are akin to formulating an IT sourcing strategy.[133]

Conversely, if an enterprise decision is to retain total control of its entire IT function or to provide some of its core/non-core IT services internally (i.e., to insource), occasionally the enterprise will also need to decide whether to build or buy new enterprise applications (software) to create new IT services. After deciding to build (custom develop) new applications in-house, an enterprise must decide where the new application will be deployed, such as in the cloud (i.e., hosted as a service at a remote location) or on the premises (i.e., hosted on the enterprise's own IT infrastructure).[134]

The decision to buy enterprise applications software has two implications. First, the decision can imply that the enterprise has decided to buy a commercial off-the-shelf (COTS) application software available in a box to be configured, customised, and deployed on its premises using in-house IT personnel or external system integrators hired on a short-term, contract basis (called body shopping).[135] Second, the decision can imply that the enterprise has decided to lease application software available as a service over the network, which is an IT service accessed through a secured public network connectivity to the application software vendor's own computing infrastructure (called public cloud); this type of sourcing is called netsourcing.[136]

If the decision is to build new applications in-house and deploy them in a public cloud in adherence to the enterprise IT architecture blueprint and standards, the enterprise must decide in advance which enterprise cloud computing company will be its preferred cloud service provider (called the IT service provider selection decision).

Furthermore, if an enterprise decision is to buy COTS applications software in a box or in the cloud (hosted remotely), the enterprise must decide in advance which COTS vendors or service providers will be on the list of its preferred partners and what processes will be used to evaluate and select the right IT service provider on the preferred list.[137]

In conclusion, bearing in mind all these numerous IT sourcing decisions, there is the need to formulate enterprise-wide IT sourcing principles or policies and enterprise IT architecture to guide IT sourcing decisions consistent with their sourcing strategy (that is aligned with the business strategy) and IT standards on a day-to-day basis. In *Multisourcing*, Linda Cohen and Allie Young concurred that enterprises need to have 'a solid sourcing strategy that effectively links sourcing decisions to business strategy.'[138]

MIT research scientists Jeanne W. Ross and George Westerman affirmed that the availability of IT architecture or the enterprise's ability to define, maintain, and govern IT architecture is critical to successful IT sourcing, especially selective outsourcing (also called multisourcing), because the availability of standardised IT architecture enables enterprises to integrate IT services sourced from multiple providers.[139] Ross and Westerman also stated that 'successful selective outsourcing ultimately involved defining standardized architectural components to provide a foundation for the "plug and play" of applications and infrastructure services,'[140] a point that further stresses the significance of making effective enterprise IT architecture and standards decisions previously discussed in this book.

Enterprises should make sourcing strategy an essential component of the strategic planning processes,[141] which can be achieved by creating specific sourcing strategy for the strategic IT initiatives-cum-services that were identified as part of the IT solutioning process, and by ensuring that the specific sourcing strategies are aligned to the business sourcing strategy.[142]

4. IT Solutioning Governance Decisions

The main goal of these decisions is to ensure that enterprises are able to identify the right strategic IT initiatives-cum-solutions (or strategic enterprise applications) that should be executed in order to develop the IT capabilities required to achieve their strategic IT objectives. In order to achieve this goal, an enterprise must first choose the most appropriate IT solutioning (also called strategic IT planning) methodology to adopt, which will enable the identification of the right strategic IT solution opportunities or strategic enterprise applications. The identification of the *right* strategic IT solution or enterprise application is the sole reason why enterprises formulate IT strategies.

Prior to formulating an IT strategy, organisations must decide on the right enterprise architecture (EA) framework and tools that will be used for documenting and analysing the architecture of the enterprise—that is, business and IT capabilities—to identify opportunities to improve and transform the enterprise through the use of IT. The key objective of the EA chosen by the enterprise is to facilitate, support, and enable the IT solutioning method adopted by the enterprise.

The selected EA framework will also be used to design the architectural blueprint of strategic IT solutions—that is, to translate the strategic IT initiatives identified as part of the output of the IT strategy formulation process into technically feasible strategic IT solutions; this will ensure that the strategic IT initiatives-cum-solutions *are done the right way*. According to Gartner Inc., IT project management (a component of IT execution decisions, and the fourth rational step) must leverage the output (e.g., solution architecture and other artefacts) of the selected EA framework for the completeness and quality of its deliverables.[143] This clearly demonstrates that selecting the right EA framework is critical to the success of both IT strategy formulation and execution.

IT solutioning decisions also include determining the criteria that will be used to assess the financial and business feasibility of newly architected IT solutions (called IT solutions feasibility assessment decisions).[144] Enterprises will also need to make the necessary IT sourcing and funding decisions that are specific to each identified strategic IT solution (discussed above as IT investment governance decisions two and three).

5. IT Execution Governance Decisions

From the research carried out during the writing of this book, four (4) main IT execution governance decisions were found to be critical in selecting and executing the best strategic IT solutions-cum-projects (i.e., decisions that will ensure enterprises are doing the right things and doing them well). These decisions must be made prior to investing in IT. The first decision is choosing the right process and criteria for evaluating, selecting, prioritising, and funding new strategic IT investment opportunities—that is, strategic IT solutions-cum-projects that will deliver maximum value to the enterprise.[145,146]

Next, enterprises must determine the weight to assign to each of them since all criteria are usually not equally important. The second decision is determining how best to direct and control the execution of strategic IT investment programmes. The third decision involves selecting the right IT programme and project management methodologies that will be the enterprise standard for managing and delivering IT investment programmes and projects that achieves the strategies of the enterprise. And the fourth decision is identifying the best approach to adopt in managing the changes that will emerge from the outcomes of IT investment projects.[147]

The first IT execution decisions enterprises must make concern an effective approach for managing the increasing portfolio of new strategic IT investment initiatives or an effective approach for evaluating and selecting the best strategic IT investment opportunities (also called IT portfolio management decisions). These decisions are usually concerned with choosing the right combination of financial criteria—return on investment (ROI), net present value (NPV), internal rate of return (IRR), payback, and non-financial criteria—strategic alignment, architecture and standards compliance used in evaluating and selecting the best strategic IT investment projects to fund.[148,149,150] A business case reflects the criteria that the enterprise chose to use in evaluating and selecting the best strategic IT investment project.

The same criteria are also used to assess the continued achievability (i.e., to assess the probability of IT projects to deliver the desired IT systems), desirability (i.e., to assess the cost/benefit/risk balance of the project), and viability (i.e., to assess the probability of the strategic IT investments delivering the expected benefits) of IT investment projects throughout their life cycle.[151,152] This continued assessment helps enterprises to decide whether to stop or change an on-going strategic IT investment project. The criteria are also used to assess whether operational IT systems should continue to be operated, upgraded, or retired.

Regarding the selection of the right criteria for evaluating potential IT investment opportunities, Edmund W. Fitzpatrick, in *Planning and Implementing IT Portfolio Management*, gave a seemingly genuine but unrealistic recommendation. Fitzpatrick recommended that enterprises use the same set of IT investment evaluation criteria and approach linked to enterprise strategic goals for all of their proposed and existing IT investment proposals, which makes it possible to compare investment proposals from different parts of the enterprise and to improve the mix of proposed and existing IT investments.[153]

However, it is practically impossible to standardise IT investment evaluation criteria for all IT investments, as enterprise investments in IT are driven by varying objectives, such as the need to cut cost, comply with regulations, create a sustainable competitive advantage, or support other investments across the enterprise, and so require different evaluation criteria and approaches.[154,155,156]

One possible solution to the challenge mentioned in the preceding paragraph is to classify proposed IT investment projects into three IT investment categories.[157] The first category comprises IT investments required to run the enterprise. The second category comprises investments required to grow the enterprise. And the third category comprises IT investment projects required to transform the enterprise. Alternatively, the proposed IT investment opportunities can be categorised into four categories: strategic, informational, transactional, and infrastructural.[158] Richard Hunter and George Westerman discussed categorisation in *Real Business of IT*:

Using specific categories ensures that proposals can be compared apples to apples, and it allows project sponsors to readily understand how to adjust initiatives to deliver a more attractive mix of benefits and risks.[159] After choosing a categorisation scheme, enterprises can then define the criteria used to evaluate new IT investment opportunities in each category.[160,161]

An enterprise's next strategic IT portfolio management decision is to determine the right categories of strategic IT investment projects—that is, a portfolio of strategic IT investments to commit enterprise resources that will generate the highest return at an acceptable level of risk. In other words, enterprises need to create the best combination of strategic, operational (transactional and informational), and infrastructure IT investment projects or the right mix of run, grow, and maintain investment opportunities to approve and fund.[162,163] Although enterprises must do this in order to make effective IT investment decisions, research has indicated that 'creating the right mix of investments to properly use limited resources while providing the maximum business benefit is the ultimate challenge for IT leaders.'[164]

IT programme management, an enterprise's second IT execution governance decision, involves determining whether directing, controlling, and delivering strategic IT investment programmes and projects require the setting up of an enterprise programme management office (EPMO) or portfolio, programme, and project office (P3O) to provide a support structure.

The third IT execution governance decision is IT project management (the planning and delivery decisions), which involves determining the right project management (PM) and software development life cycle (SDLC) methodologies and tools to adopt to ensure successful delivery of IT investment projects.[165,166]

According to Kathy Schwalbe in *Information Technology Project Management*, a major factor affecting the successful delivery of IT investment projects is that most of the enterprises encountering problems delivering their projects have yet to adopt a project management methodology; as a result, they are not following any standards or guidelines in executing their projects.[167] She then advocated that enterprises should adopt standard guidelines and enforce their usage.

In addition to standardising the right IT project management and software development methodology, IT execution decisions are also concerned with determining the best way to procure and identify the right service providers for application software, IT infrastructure, training, systems integration capabilities, and so forth.

The fourth IT execution governance decision is enterprise change management, which is concerned with assigning accountability for the enterprise's changes associated with IT investment projects.

6. IT Operationalization Decisions

IT operationalization decisions should be a follow-up to the previous decisions made by enterprises concerning whether to build or buy package applications and deploy them on the premises. Enterprises will better manage the life cycle of their IT investments if they are able to decide how best to support their internally deployed and operational IT systems in advance—akin to formulating the strategic IT systems-cum-services support strategy. According to Murrell G. Shields in *E-Business and ERP*, enterprises must decide on the best strategies for supporting new enterprise applications after the systems have been deployed and fully operational or in production.[168] Shields itemised three options for formulating IT support strategies: the use of the internal IT unit's resources and staff to support the on-going operations of new applications, the augmentation of internal IT resources and staff with that of external contractors, and the outsourcing of the activities required for the on-going operations and support of new applications to external IT service providers.

Therefore, the decision to buy or build new enterprise applications should be followed by appropriate decisions concerning how the on-going operation and maintenance of the application will be performed and how the support for the newly deployed application will be provided. If an enterprise decides to build new applications and deploy them internally, instead of buying packaged applications, the enterprise must first decide who will provide this support. Then, it must decide the most appropriate way and place where the support services will be provided, which will guarantee the achievement of its service level agreement (SLA). The achievement of the service level agreement specified for strategic IT systems helps to facilitate the utilisation of the system, as IT applications (services) that are properly supported will experience less disruption or downtime, which, consequently, contributes to the generation of maximum value from IT.[169]

An enterprise can choose to provide this support from a decentralised location situated within the premises of the application owners—for example, in the form of a help desk within the line of business. Alternatively, an enterprise can choose to provide support for its application software from a centralised location—that is, situated where the deployment infrastructure (data centre) is located—in the form of systems operations and support within the IT unit's facility.

If an enterprise decides to buy the package application instead of developing its own applications internally, then the enterprise must also decide on the most cost-effective way to support the new application both internally and externally (by the service provider) that will meet the service level requirement (SLR) and not jeopardise the application's ROI.

Apart from providing support, the enterprise also needs to decide on other courses of action to take and the IT resources needed to meet the service level requirements (SLRs) specified for new IT services before committing to the SLAs. Enterprises must also determine the courses of action to take and the IT resources that will be needed to meet their requirements for continued service delivery or business continuity (BC) requirements, especially those enterprises where the maximum availability of IT systems is critical to its operations.[170] Under these circumstances, the management of business continuity becomes an important component of IT governance.

In addition, enterprises must decide on the tools, templates, and resources that will be used for monitoring IT service delivery performance (i.e., for monitoring the availability of IT services within the agreed upon scope and level of quality) and provide general oversight of IT services outsourcing vendors activities.

Finally, enterprises must determine the best way to secure IT services and the appropriate delivery method to adopt in training the users of the systems or the consumers of IT services, the application administrators, and the services support personnel. Enterprises can choose from the following combination of options on or off the premises: instructor led in-class, instructor-led online, self-paced online, and webinars/CD-ROMs. An enterprise must choose a delivery approach that is best suited to achieving its IT training or staff capability development objectives.

7. IT Benefiting Governance Decisions

Following the development or implementation, delivery, deployment, operationalization, and utilisation of strategic IT systems or services, enterprises must determine who should be accountable or responsible for developing and executing the plan and process for harvesting the benefits expected from IT investments—that is, to appoint a benefit realisation manager, sometimes referred to as a business change manager (BCM).[171] This is important because managing the harvesting of benefits from completed strategic IT investment projects is critical to generating maximum business value from the investments.[172]

Following the appointment of a business change manager, he must decide when to begin the benefit delivery review; determine how often the benefit delivery review is conducted and audited; and determine when it should be completed.[173]

Enterprises must also determine who should be responsible for deciding whether to continue to operate/maintain, change/upgrade, or retire/abandon enterprise applications following the outcome of the benefit delivery review process.

Who Should Make IT Governance Decisions?

Following the seven (7) main IT governance decisions that enterprises must make in order to govern IT effectively and generate maximum value from IT investments, enterprises must decide who (which governance structure) should be accountable or responsible for making these decisions, whose input should be sought in making these decisions, and who should be consulted before the decisions are made.

In order to identify who should make these decisions, enterprises must first select the IT governance styles or archetypes that are best suited for making each of these decisions[174] and then identify the governance structures that are congruent with the selected governance styles, all of which translates to identifying who should make governance decisions. The aforementioned steps and advice is what this book calls the process for designing effective IT governance architecture or frameworks,[175] which helps to answer the question, 'Who should make IT governance decisions?'

Who Should Make IT Principles Decisions?

According to the research carried out by Peter Weill, the IT duopoly governance style was used by 36 percent of the enterprises surveyed to make IT principles decisions, while 27 percent of the enterprises used business monarchy. Eighteen percent of them used IT monarchies, and 14 percent of the enterprises used the federal governance style.[176] Weill suspected enterprises favoured duopolies in making IT principles decisions because taking the lead in setting IT principles strengthens the alignment between IT and business strategies. Weill also suspected that enterprises seemed to favour IT duopolies in making IT principles decisions because it helps to win the buy-in of IT into business principles. The other reason why duopolies might be favoured is that duopolies allow business executives to use the information about current or future IT capabilities to influence the development of business principles.

Who Should Make IT Architecture, Standards, and Infrastructure Decisions?

More than 70 percent of the enterprises surveyed by Peter Weill made use of the IT monarchies governance style in making IT architecture decisions; put another way, they translated IT principles, standards, and policies into IT architecture.[177] This act indicates that business executives from these enterprises considered IT architecture decisions to be more of a technical issue rather than a strategic business issue, and that they are less qualified to contribute to or make IT architecture decisions. As a result, only the IT team is charged with developing and managing the enterprise IT architecture and for communicating the architectural blueprints/artefacts to the whole organisation.

Just like IT architecture decisions, IT units only often make the decisions about the standardisation and sharing requirements for new IT infrastructure capabilities development. The IT monarchies governance style was used by nearly 60 percent of enterprises to make IT infrastructure decisions.[178] The success of IT infrastructure decisions is measured by how well IT supports and anticipates the enterprise application requirements of strategic business units in order to enable the development of future IT capabilities or enterprise applications.

Who Should Make IT Investment Decisions?

Seven (7) IT investment decisions were identified in earlier sections of this book; they consist of the following: accountability, funding, sourcing, solutioning, execution, operationalization, and benefiting decisions.

Who Should Be Accountable for the IT Investment Decision Process?

The CIO should be accountable for making this decision; however, he or she may choose to delegate this responsibility to the chief enterprise architect (CEA), who will now be responsible for making decisions concerning the conversion of IT investments into business value—that is, decisions related to the design, implementation, enforcement, improvement, and performance of IT investment management processes.

Who Should Make IT Funding/Investment Decisions?

Most enterprises make IT funding decisions using three main IT governance styles almost equally, which are business monarchy (30 percent), federal style (27 percent), and IT duopoly (30 percent). These styles are used to make decisions that help the enterprise to determine how much of its scarce resources to invest in IT, as well as to determine the best means of obtaining this funding, bearing in mind the cost of funds, which has a direct impact on the return on IT investments. Peter Weill and Jeanne W. Ross in *IT Savvy* gave an example of BT's CEO forming an IT board that consists of thirteen business and IT executives to make IT funding/investment decisions.[179]

Who Should Make IT Sourcing Decisions?

Business monarchy is the best IT governance style for making decisions about the outsourcing of the entire enterprise's IT function.[180] IT monarchy is probably the best IT governance style for making selective IT outsourcing decisions. In reference to IT monarchy, Jeanne W. Ross and Peter Weill pointed out that 'selective outsourcing decisions are usually best left to the IT unit.'[181]

Who Should Make IT Solutioning Decisions?

In order to make IT solutioning decisions, 36 percent of the 256 enterprises studied by Peter Weill used the federal IT governance style, while 27 percent of the enterprises used the IT duopoly governance style to make strategic enterprise applications needs decisions.[182] The IT duopoly governance style seems to be the most probable choice for making EA development decisions, since these decisions are concerned mainly with determining the most appropriate business and IT architecture modelling, analysis, and transformation framework, methodology, and tools. IT duopoly also seems to be the best IT governance style for making IT solutions feasibility assessment decisions.

Who Should Make IT Execution Decisions?

Enterprises mostly use three IT governance styles—business monarchy, federal, and IT duopoly—to make IT portfolio management decisions, and they will probably use the IT duopoly governance style to make IT programme or project management and change management accountability decisions.[183]

Who Should Make IT Operationalization Decisions?

IT operationalization decisions that consist of IT support, service level, and business continuity decisions are probably best made using the IT monarchy and federal governance styles due to their technical nature, wide-user orientation, and enterprise-wide implication.

Who Should Be Held Accountable for IT Benefiting (Benefits Measurement & Realisation) and Retirement Decisions?

Jeanne W. Ross and Peter Weill point out in their article 'Six IT Decisions Your IT People Shouldn't Make' that, business executives are the best candidates to assign the responsibility for the realisation of benefits from IT investment initiatives.[184] They also indicated the success of IT investments require the sustained commitment of the business managers who will use and benefit from the resulting IT systems. After which they concluded that the IT function should be responsible and accountable for IT investment project *management* success. In other words, IT should be responsible for delivering IT investment projects on time, within budget, and with the required functionalities—the necessary conditions for generating maximum value from IT investments. And only business executives should be held accountable for IT investment project success. That is, they should be responsible for carrying out the business and technology (enterprise) changes that are necessary for generating value from IT investments and for harvesting the expected value—the sufficient conditions for generating maximum value from IT.

However, the results of the study carried out by the IT Governance Institute revealed that 43 percent of enterprises assign the responsibility for measuring the value delivered by IT investment projects to both business units and IT departments, while 21 percent assign the responsibility to business units only and 15 percent to IT departments only.[185] The remaining enterprises assigned responsibility based on circumstances.

Finally, Hunter and Westerman advocated for the establishment of a harvest steering group to realise the benefits of IT investments; furthermore, the group should consist of business sponsors, key internal users, the CFO or CFO designate, and IT operations staff.[186]

In summary, from all the different points of view above, the following stakeholders appear to be common to all: business executives, IT units or operations staff, and key users or business process owners. This composition closely resembles the federal IT governance style or archetype.

Who Should Be Consulted About IT Governance Decisions? (Who Has Input Rights?)

The most common IT governance decisions input rights is a broad-based one that involves many people across the enterprise; consequently, more than 80 percent of enterprises use the federal IT governance style to provide input rights in the making of business-centric IT decisions such as IT principles, enterprise application needs identification, and IT investment. On the other hand, IT duopoly is used to seek input for technical IT governance decisions such as IT architecture, standards, and infrastructure.[187]

How Will These Decisions Be Made?

After identifying IT governance decisions that must be made by enterprises in order to govern and manage IT investments effectively and generate maximum value, and after identifying who should make these decisions, an enterprise must then decide *how* these decisions will be made. The "*how*" question involves specifying the processes that will be used to guide the decision makers in the course of making their decisions—that is, the IT investment management (ITIM) processes (also called IT investment decision-making processes). The high-level processes that should be used by enterprises to make IT governance decisions are IT solutioning, IT execution, IT operationalization, and IT benefiting. Subsequent chapters of this book will explain these processes in detail.

How Will the Results of These Decisions Be Measured, Monitored, and Communicated?

The old management adage that says, "You cannot manage what you don't measure" still holds true today. In *The Real Business of IT*, Hunter and Westerman affirmed this adage but from a different perspective, stating 'what is not measured can't be improved.'[188] Unless a thing is measured, there is no way of telling if the key attributes, characteristics, or properties of that thing (e.g., height, temperature, quantity, size, volume, weight, and so forth) are increasing, stable, or decreasing. To measure a thing is to find out the current state of the key attributes, characteristics, or properties of that thing.

Enterprises usually seek to measure the attributes, characteristics, or properties of an object so that they can compare the results of their measurement to the previous results of the measurement of that object obtained at an earlier or later point in time (internal benchmarking). Or, they can compare their results to the results of the measurement of a similar object taken elsewhere (external benchmarking).

Following this tenet, enterprises measure the current performance of their IT function or services; these are the results from IT governance decisions relative to their own past performance or to the performance of the IT functions or services of their peers to identify areas that need improvement.[189,190] According to Hunter and Westerman, there is no way the CIO and the executive team can assess the performance—providing competitively priced units of IT services at any given level of quality—of the IT function without comparing the performance of the IT unit against that of their peers.[191] Comparing an enterprise's IT functions or services performance to that of its peers or to its own past performance, Hunter and Westerman argued, helps the whole enterprise to assess or understand the degree of IT performance.

The most appropriate and effective way to monitor the outcome of IT governance decisions is through the automation of all the IT investment decision processes that enterprises follow to make decisions. Following the monitoring of IT decision results using automated IT investment management applications, the use of enterprise portal, electronic mail, and other

IT-enabled communication tools were found to be the most effective means of communicating the results of IT governance decisions and other governance-related information to relevant stakeholders across the enterprise.

How Will the Results of IT Principles Decisions Be Measured?

Enterprises can measure the results of IT principles decisions by capturing and comparing the time to market—that is, the time it took to conceive and deliver IT systems and the cost of integrating the newly delivered systems to existing systems for those IT investment projects that are executed in line with their IT principles and those that are not. The enterprise can then use this information to ascertain the effects of IT principles on IT investments. Thomas H. Davenport, Michael Hammer, and Tauno J. Metsisto pointed out that the time and effort spent on discovering the common ground between IT and business managers or to make IT decisions directly impacts the time to market for new IT investment projects.[192] Given that IT principles help to reduce the time and effort required to discover the common ground between IT and business managers and to speed up effective IT decision making, IT investment projects that are consistent with the enterprise's IT principles should have shorter time to market or a higher conversion effectiveness than those that are not.

How Will the Results of Enterprise IT Architecture, Standards, and Infrastructure Decisions Be Measured?

An enterprise can measure the outcome of enterprise IT architecture decisions by confirming the existence of a one-page enterprise IT architecture blueprint (also called enterprise architecture core diagram).[193] An enterprise can also decide to measure the number of strategic enterprise application choices that challenge the enterprise's IT architecture or technical standards, as it is an indication that the enterprise's IT architecture or portfolio of technology standards ought to be refreshed or reviewed.[194]

Enterprises can also choose to measure the number of clearly defined IT standards, keeping in mind that the more standards there are, the more predictable or integrated the IT platform will be. Enterprises can also ascertain the number of new standards added per year to the existing repository of enterprise IT standards in order to measure the refresh rate of enterprise IT standards. The number of enterprise applications proposed by IT vendors that were rejected as a result of being off-standard might also be of significance to enterprises because a high number of rejected enterprise applications might be a sign that enterprise IT standards are obsolete and need an upgrade.

How Will the Results of IT Funding Governance Decisions Be Measured?

Enterprises can measure their IT funding governance decisions by comparing the percentage of their capital spending/revenues/gross domestic product that was allocated to IT investment projects with that of their peers who are successfully managing and leveraging their investments in IT to achieve their strategic and operational objectives.[195,196] The board of directors of enterprises can choose to be alerted whenever this percentage falls below a threshold in comparison to the enterprises being benchmarked.

How Will the Results of IT Sourcing Governance Decisions Be Measured?

Enterprises can measure the results of IT governance sourcing decisions by ascertaining the availability of enterprise-wide, business-aligned IT sourcing principles as well as ascertaining the existence of an IT sourcing strategy for every major IT investment project. Enterprises can further measure the results of this decision by comparing the cost of running the IT function by itself (in-sourced) against the cost of outsourcing it or compare the cost of developing new IT services in-house (in-sourced) against the cost of outsourcing it, given the same level of service (quality and availability), security, and privacy.[197,198]

Following this comparative analysis, enterprises can decide whether to outsource the IT function or IT services development or not. This comparative analysis can also help enterprises to ascertain the business value or measure the outcome of IT outsourcing decisions, as the decrease of the total cost of ownership (TCO) of IT services is one of the major arguments in favour of the decision to outsource the IT function or services development.[199]

Enterprises can also compare the time to market for new IT services (or new enterprise application software) when the entire IT function was insourced to when it was outsourced; that is, the time it takes to develop new IT capabilities or services and get them operational.[200,201] The ability of external IT service providers to provide—design, deliver, and operationalize—new IT services faster than enterprises are capable of (i.e., shortening time to market for new IT services) is also one of the major arguments in favour of the decision to outsource IT services provisioning.[202]

The same measurement and comparison approach can be applied to all other IT sourcing-related decisions (i.e., the comparison of cost of service provisioning given the same service level and security and the comparison of time to market for new applications or services). Decision makers can choose to carry out these comparisons continuously in order to determine when a particular decision is no longer effective.

Enterprises can also choose to measure the percentage of IT budget spent for applications software developed in-house, package applications purchased in a box, and those bought as a service in the cloud. IT sourcing decisions can also be measured by ascertaining the availability of preferred enterprise application software (either in a box or in the cloud) vendors or IT services providers and the existence of processes for selecting the right enterprise application software vendor or IT services provider from the list of preferred vendors or service providers. Afterward, enterprises can choose to measure the number of enterprise application software or IT services that were selected from vendors within the preferred list and those selected outside the list.

How Will the Results of IT Solutioning Governance Decisions Be Measured?

The results of IT solutioning governance decisions can be measured first by ensuring the existence of a well-formulated, business-aligned IT strategy (i.e., the specification of strategic IT objectives and the identification of right strategic IT initiatives to achieve the objectives). Second, enterprises can measure the result of IT solutioning governance decisions by ensuring the existence of technical solutions architecture (i.e., the contextual, conceptual, logical, and physical descriptions) for every strategic IT investment initiatives-cum-solutions.

To quantify the business impact of IT strategies, enterprises can then assess the degree to which their investments in IT initiatives or investment projects contribute directly to the achievement of their strategic business objectives or to the execution of their business strategies.[203]

Following the existence of solution architecture for strategic IT investment initiatives-cum-solutions, enterprises can assess their impact by measuring the number of *first-time-right* strategic IT application development projects; these projects, in other words, had the required functionalities on the first attempt.[204] Enterprises can also choose to quantify the number of strategic IT initiatives that were identified and found to be technically, financially, and business feasible in a given financial year (called the strategic IT initiatives pipeline), as this can help to measure an enterprise's innovativeness. A team of business executives and US academicians described the strategic analysis of enterprises to identify opportunities for the use of IT in improving enterprise performance (also referred to as enterprise applications needs identification in earlier sections of this book) as value innovation.[205]

How Will the Results of IT Execution Governance Decisions Be Measured?

IT execution governance consists of three main decisions, the outcomes of which should be measured and communicated: the IT portfolio management decisions, IT investment programme management decisions, and IT investment project management decisions.

Quantifying the percentage mix or distribution of IT investment project spending across multiple management objectives for investing in IT, such as strategic, informational, transactional, and infrastructural, provides a comprehensive view of an enterprise's IT investment profile or asset classes that support the achievement of its business strategy. In addition, classifying IT investment project spending into categories or classes of IT investments will help the enterprise to compare its size or mix of its IT investment portfolio with industry benchmarks, which can help to align future investments and ascertain areas of under- or over-investment.

In addition, enterprises can quantify the number of IT investment projects approved according to a particular mix of financial and non-financial evaluation criteria (e.g., strategic alignment, ROI, IRR, NPV, payback, architecture and standards compliance, and so forth) and how well they have fared compared to the projects evaluated using different criteria.

Following the assessment of IT portfolio management decisions, enterprises can measure the results of (pre) IT investment project management and delivery (development or implementation) decisions. The results of IT project management decisions can be measured by ascertaining the existence of standardised methodologies for managing the life cycle of IT investment projects. The results of IT project delivery can also be assessed by finding out if the enterprise has chosen standardised methodologies for developing new custom software applications (called software development life cycle methodologies [SDLC]) or for implementing new commercial package software.

Now, enterprises can assess the outcome of (post) IT investment project management decisions by examining the following:

- Percentage of IT investment projects that were completed on time and the average schedule variance[206]
- Percentage of projects completed on budget and the average budget variance
- Number of projects cancelled before delivery[207]
- Number of IT investment projects on hold
- Percentage of IT investment projects executed using the project management methodologies standardised by the enterprise
- Percentage of IT investment projects executed using the enterprise standardised application development methodology or SDLC

- Percentage of IT investment projects in queue (calculated by taking the number of approved projects and dividing that by the number of approved projects plus active projects)

Last, the enterprises should confirm the availability of an enterprise change management plan.

How Will the Results of IT Operationalization Decisions Be Measured?

Enterprises can measure the results of their IT operationalization decisions by confirming the existence of a service level agreement (SLA) for all the IT services available in their IT services portfolio, which is a consolidated repository of IT services. Enterprises can also choose to maintain up-to-date, relevant, and accurate information about the individual services in their IT services portfolio and make it accessible to authorised stakeholders who need this information to monitor and assess the performance of the IT services.

Enterprises can maintain the following information about IT services: cost of service delivery, cost of service operation (maintenance and support), estimated cost of upgrading/replacing IT services, number of active users, user satisfaction, business services supported, infrastructure/applications that provide the services, service contact, service hours, hosting location, owner, life span, uptime, number of outages (planned/unplanned), and response time.[208]

Because of the availability of the aforementioned information, enterprises can now calculate the average resolution time for service requests. This information can also be used to evaluate the quality of IT support services provided. The mean time to respond and mean time to resolve problems, for example, can be ascertained. Enterprises can also use the consolidated store of information to support the making of outsourcing, replacement, upgrade, and change and retirement decisions.

Enterprises can also measure the results of IT operationalization decisions by ascertaining the existence of a business continuity plan for critical enterprise IT services, or a plan of how the enterprise intends to meet the business resilience and continuity requirements.

How Will the Results of IT Benefiting and Retirement Be Measured?

The results of IT benefiting decisions can be measured by first ascertaining the existence of a business case for every major IT investment project, except for IT investment projects that are mandatory. Enterprises can also ascertain the existence of the benefit realisation plan for every project, which can also be followed by the quantification of the value contributed by the individual IT services (i.e., the benefits realised). Enterprises can also compare the actual benefits realised or value generated from each IT investment project to their expected benefits that the investment projects promise to deliver, as stated in their business cases.

Enterprises can also maintain accurate and updated information about the life span/retirement schedule of IT services and the probability of on-going operational IT services meeting their value contribution target, with the name of the stakeholders who are responsible for realising the benefits.

How Will the Results of These Decisions Be Monitored and Communicated?

The results of IT governance decisions can be monitored through the automation of the IT investment management (ITIM) processes or IT investment decision processes (i.e., the automation of *how* IT governance decisions are made). Enterprises can choose to develop custom applications to automate these processes, or they can choose to buy COTS applications packages to automate IT investment management processes, which include the following low-level processes: principles management, EA management, standard management, strategic planning management, IT finance management, requirement management, IT portfolio management, IT programme/project management, and IT services management. The benefit of this automation is that mundane and repetitive processes that are prone to errors can be automated together with the business policies that control them. Automation will also allow many common and complex IT investment governance activities, such as notification alerts, periodic reviews, and policy checks, to be simplified.

The automation of IT investment management processes makes it easy to communicate the results of these decisions and other information to relevant stakeholders in the enterprise using an enterprise intranet/portal (i.e., internal computer network). Enterprises can also choose to buy COTS web portal application software, such as Microsoft Exchange and SharePoint, Oracle Portal/WebCenter Suite, or they can develop their own custom web portal application to further improve their ability to make IT investment management decisions and to communicate available information to relevant stakeholders wherever they may be located across the enterprise.

Summary

Enterprises need to develop the ability to design and implement an effective IT governance architecture or system—that is, to select the right people, organisational structure, processes, and communication mechanisms— to make IT alignment and investment decisions that will help to generate maximum value from their investments in IT at an acceptable level of risk. This capability will help to ensure that enterprises have the formal means of ensuring that they are making the right IT alignment and investment decisions most of the time, which, consequently, helps to ensure that they are embarking on the right strategic IT investment initiatives that can help them achieve their strategic business objectives.

Case Study 2.0

Kredietbank ABB Insurance CERA (KBC) Bank is one of the major financial services organisations in Belgium, while KBC Group NV, the parent company, is reputed to be the third largest bancassurer in Belgium and the eighteenth largest bank in Europe (by market capitalisation). KBC is also a major financial player in Central and Eastern Europe, with 2,026 branches in Belgium, Central, and Eastern Europe, employing some 51,000 staff worldwide and serving 11 million customers worldwide.[209]

The bank started as Volksbank van Leuven in 1889 and merged with Algemeene Bankvereeniging in 1935, after which the two banks adopted the name Kredietbank. Sixty-three years later in 1998, Kredietbank merged with two Belgian banks, ABB Insurance and CERA Bank, to create the current KBC Bank.[210] And in 2005 the bank merged with its parent company, Almanij, an Insurance Holding Company to create a single entity called KBC Group NV with two major underlying companies: KBC Bank and KBC Insurance.[211]

KBC Group Organisation Structure

KBC Group NV has three major activity or product domains:[212]

1. KBC Bank NV
    - Personal (Savings & Investing, Borrowing, Payments, and Mortgages)
    - Corporate Banking, Treasury, and Capital Markets
2. KBC Insurance NV
3. KBL European Private Bankers (EPB) SA

KBC Group NV's major activity domains (banking, insurance, and EPM) are delivered by its strategic business units (SBUs) in Belgium, Central, and Eastern Europe and are supported by its shared services and operations business unit and group functions.

KBC Group uses the following three (3) structures to guide the management of its business domains:

- ***Strategic Business Units (SBUs)***
    - Belgium
    - Central & Eastern Europe (CEE)
    - Merchant Banking

- **Shared Services & Operations (SSO) Business Unit**
    - Operations: ICT Create and Maintain, ICT Infrastructure & Technology, Group Organisation & Support
    - GWPP: Group Payments, Leasing, Asset Management, Consumer Finance
- **Group Functions (GFs)**
    - Finance, Legal, Tax, Treasury, HR, Strategy & Corporate Development, Communication, Audit, Compliance, Risk Management, Public Policy, Investors Relations, and PMO

KBC Group Corporate/Enterprise Governance Structure

Each strategic business unit (SBU) of the Group is managed by its own management committee, which operates under the Group Executive Committee and oversees both the banking and the insurance activities. The Shared Services & Operations (SSO) Business Unit includes group-wide product factories and departments providing support to the strategic business units. A chief executive officer (CEO) chairs the management committees of the Belgium, CEE, and merchant banking SBUs, while the chief operations officer (Group COO) chairs the management committee of the Group Functions and Shared Services & Operations Business Unit.

The Group's Executive Committee consists of the following:[213]

- Group Chief Executive Officer (Group CEO)
- Chief Executive Officers of Strategic Business Units
- Group Chief Operations Officer (Group COO)—to whom the CIO reports
- Group Chief Financial Officer (Group CFO)
- Group Chief Risk Officer (Group CRO)

KBC Group's Board of Directors is responsible and accountable for determining the general strategy of the entire group and supervising management, or Group Executive Committee, while Belgian company law and the articles of association of KBC Group regulate the activities of the

Board of Directors. The Group Executive Committee consists of seven members chaired by the Group CEO, all of whom are appointed by the Board of Directors. The Group Executive Committee is responsible for managing the group in line with the strategic directions set by the Board of Directors. The members of this committee reach resolutions by consensus and divide duties up among its members.

KBC Group IT Exploitation Archetype or the Role of IT in the Group

KBC Group's Executive Committee specified their business goal for IT as achieving economies of scale in its IT departments, bearing in mind that increased usage volume can reduce the unit cost of fixed IT investments, which is one of the reasons why the bank merged with ABB Insurance and CERA Bank in 1998.[214] KBC Group's second business goal for IT is to provide business units with the IT capability that is required to enable or support the business capability for attracting and retaining new clients and for improving operational excellence or to increase process efficiency.[215]

Achieving economies of scale within the IT unit means to reduce the unit cost per IT service delivered, to leverage IT to attract and retain customers, and to achieve operational excellence; are all typical example of the combination of solid utility and the trusted supplier IT exploitation archetype discussed in previous sections of this book. According to Forrester Research, enterprises with *solid utility and the trusted supplier* IT exploitation archetype usually have their CIOs report to either the CFO or COO.[216] This is not far from the truth, as this was exactly the case in KBC Bank; the bank's CIO reports to the Group COO (Head of Shared Services & Operations).

In order to achieve KBC Bank's business goal for IT and to provide the capabilities they require to achieve their objectives, the bank's Executive Committee initiated an *IT governance architecture or framework* development project to provide the following capabilities:[217]

1. Develop flexible IT infrastructure to enable business agility and provide high quality IT services to the business units[218]
2. Develop the capability to allocate enterprise resources, including IT resources, effectively:[219]

- Develop the IT investment management capability of business units to enable the business units to manage IT in a well-thought out manner,
- Provide business units with the mechanisms for making effective IT-related decisions or choices and the means to hold them accountable for the consequences of their choices
- The IT unit needs to create the right environment for the business units in making effective IT governance decisions
- The ICT unit needs to develop a solid understanding of the needs of business units and set clear expectations for the successful delivery of IT investment projects and for the expected benefits of those projects

3. Develop the ability to achieve economies of scale and specialisation through centralisation of IT competence

KBC Group IT governance framework

The rational IT governance capability model developed in the previous sections of this chapter will be used to analyse KBC Group's IT governance framework (see Figure 2.0 above).

Who is Accountable or Responsible for IT Governance?

KBC Group's Board of Directors held the Executive Committee *accountable* for the outcome of the IT governance capability or system development. The Executive Committee initiated the governance projects in 2000 and made the CIO *responsible* for the development of the IT governance model.[220]

KBC Bank's Key IT Governance Decisions

- Use business cases to prioritise IT investment projects
- Sourcing decisions
- Define IT service level agreements (SLAs)
- Use of external IT benchmarking to achieve market conformity
- Consolidate all standard services into a service catalogue/repository
- Determine criteria for evaluating IT investment projects
- Use maturity models as an IT governance mechanism

KBC Bank's Decision-Making Structures/People

KBC Bank set up the following structure to make effective IT governance decisions:[221]

- *IT strategy committee*: Focuses on establishing and reviewing IT strategies

- *One IT/business steering committee (IBSC)*: Per activity domain; can set up one or more

- *Domain consultative body (DCB)*: For specific functional business domains such as borrowing or investing; both IBSC and DCB play an important role in preparing and making IT investment decisions

- *Project management steering group (PMSG)*: Responsible for delivering IT investment projects upon their approval

- *Management operational systems committee (MOSC)*: Following the operationalization of IT systems, MOSC decides and delivers maintenance projects for the new systems

KBC Bank's People and Processes for Making IT Governance Decisions

KBC Group's IT investment decision processes consist of the following steps together with the responsible process owners:[222]

- *Request pre-study*: The owner is the business architect; usually assigned to the business staff, he or she collects and manages the information required for developing the investment business case documents

- *Validate ideas*: The owner is the DCB, which consists of the director of the domain, business architect, process owner, IT architect, and business analyst

- *Prioritise projects*: The owner is the IBSC

- *Consolidation of investment projects and ICT basic budgets*: Owned enterprise wide

- *Funding*: The owner is the Executive Committee
- *Development*: The owner is the PMSG, which consists of a project sponsor, business and IT directors, and programme manager
- *Maintenance*: The owner is the MOSC, which consists of the director of the business domain, process manager, application manager, business analyst, and systems manager

KBC Bank's IT Governance Decision Communication Mechanisms

The following mechanisms enabled KBC Bank's business and IT unit to understand each other and work together effectively:[223]

- Created an internal magazine to communicate IT governance decisions and other related information
- Conducted training sessions for IT on business activities
- Supported senior IT personnel to move into key positions in the business and vice versa, (job rotation)
- Established a business-IT governance site on their web portal or intranet site to disseminate information about the bank's IT governance framework (structure, processes, people and their roles, responsibilities, and so forth) and IT governance decisions

Alignment of KBC Corporate Governance & IT Governance

Although the CIO is not a member of the Executive Committee, he reports to the Group COO, who is a member of the committee. Also, the CIO is occasionally invited to Executive Committee meetings. The near direct to business reporting structure of the bank and the occasional invitation of the CIO to Executive Committee meetings helped to align business IT and the business at the highest level of the bank.

NOTES

1. Weill, P., & Ross, J. (2005). A Matrix Approach to Designing IT Governance. *MITSloan Management Review, 46*(2), 26-34, p. 26.
2. Weill, P., & Woodham, R. (2002, April). Dont Just Lead, Govern: Implementing Effective IT Governance. *CISRWP No. 326*. Cambridge, US: MIT Sloan School of Management.
3. Collins, J. (2001). *Good to Great: why some companies make the leap and others don't*. London: Random House Business Books, p. 13.
4. Bossidy, L., Charan, R., & Burck, C. (2002). *Execution: The Discipline of Getting Things Done*. London: Random House Business Books, p. 109.
5. U. S. General Accounting Office. (2004). *Information Technology Investment Management: A Framework for Assessing and Improving Process Maturity*. Washington, D. C.: U. S. General Accounting Office, p. 16.
6. Broadbent, M., & Kitzis, E. (2005). *The New CIO Leader: Setting the Agenda and Delivering Results*. US: Harvard Business School Press, p. 106.
7. Weill, P., & Ross, J. W. (2004). *IT Governance: How Top Performers Manage IT Decision Rights for Superior Results*. US: Harvard Business Press, p. 8.
8. IT Governance Institute. (2007). *COBIT 4.1*. US: IT Governance Institute, p. 5.
9. Ibid.
10. Deloitte Touche Tohmatsu Limited. (2010). *Unlocking the value of IT Governance*. Belgium: Deloitte Consulting, p. 5.
11. Symons, C., Cecere, M., Young, G. O., & Lambert, N. (2005). *IT Governance Framework: Structures, Processes, And Communication*. US: Forrester Research Inc., p. 2.
12. Peterson, R. (2004). Crafting Information Technology Governance. *Information Systems Management*, 7-22.
13. Nolan, R., & McFarlan, F. W. (2005). Information Technology and the Board of Directors. *Harvard Business Review*, 1-11.
14. Marks, N. (2010). The Pulse of IT Governance. *Internal Auditor*, 33-37.
15. The Standish Group International. (2009). *CHAOS Summary 2009*. US: The Standish Group.

16 Carr, N. G. (2004). *Does IT Matter? : Information Technology and the Corrosion of Competitive Advantage*. US: Harvard Business School Press, p. 110.
17 Kumar, M. (2006). CRM Implementation Failure at Cigna Corporation. *ICMR Center for Management Research*. UK: ECCH.
18 Weill & Ross, *IT Governance*, p. 3.
19 Ibid., p. 4
20 Nolan & McFarlan, Information Technology and the Board of Directors, p. 1.
21 Ibid., p. 1
22 Ibid.
23 Ibid., p. 2
24 Andriole, S. J. (2009). Boards of Directors and Technology Governance: The Surprising State of the Practice. *Communications of the Association for Information Systems, 24*(1), 374-394, p. 378.
25 Nolan & McFarlan, *Information Technology and the Board of Directors*. p. 1
26 Ibid.,
27 Symons, et al, *IT Governance Framework*, p. 2.
28 Peterson, *Crafting Information Technology Governance*, p. 13.
29 Weill & Ross, *IT Governance*, p. 85.
30 Weill & Woodham, *Dont Just Lead, Govern*, p. 6.
31 Weill & Ross, *A Matrix Approach to Designing IT Governance*.
32 De Haes, S., & Van Grembergen, W. (2004). IT Governance and its Mechanisms. *Information Systems Control Journal*, 1-7, p. 1.
33 Weill & Ross, *IT Governance*, p. 58.
34 Broadbent, & Kitzis, *The New CIO Leader*, p. 113.
35 Weill & Ross, *A Matrix Approach to Designing IT Governance*.
36 Davenport, T. H., & Prusak, L. (1997). *Information Ecology: Mastering the Information and Knowledge Environment*. US: Oxford University Press, p. 69.
37 Weill & Ross, *A Matrix Approach to Designing IT Governance*.
38 Weill & Woodham, *Dont Just Lead, Govern*.
39 Weill, P., & Ross, J. W. (2004, November). IT Governance on One Page. *CISR WP No. 349 and Sloan WP No. 4516-04*. Cambridge, US: MIT Sloan School of Management, p. 7.

40 Ibid.
41 Weill, P., & Aral, S. (2005, May). IT Savvy Pays Off: How Top Performers Match IT Portfolios and Organizational Practices. *CISRWP No. 353 and SloanWP No. 4560-05*. Cambridge, US: MIT Sloan School of Management, p. 7.
42 Symons, C., Orlov, L. M., Bright, S., & Brown, K. (2005). *IT Governance Structures: Organizing for Success*. US: Forrester Research Inc., p. 1.
43 Broadbent, & Kitzis, *The New CIO Leader*, p. 113.
44 Weill & Ross, IT Governance on One Page, p.7
45 IT Governance Institute, *COBIT 4.1*. p. 42.
46 Maizlish, B., & Handler, R. (2005). *IT Portfolio Management Step-by-Step: Unlocking the Business Value of Technology*. US: John Wiley & Sons Inc, Loc. 1931.
47 Weill & Ross, *A Matrix Approach to Designing IT Governance*, p. 28.
48 Weill & Ross, *IT Governance on One Page*, p.7
49 Ibid.
50 Weill & Ross, *IT Governance*, p. 227.
51 IT Governance Institute, *COBIT 4.1*. p. 5.
52 Weill & Ross, *IT Governance*, p. 227.
53 Symons et al, *IT Governance Structures*, p. 2.
54 Weill & Ross, *A Matrix Approach to Designing IT Governance*, p. 28.
55 Ibid.
56 Weill & Ross, *IT Governance*, p. 4
57 Weill, P. (2004, March). Don't Just Lead, Govern: How Top-Performing Firms Govern IT. *CISRWP No. 341 and SloanWP No. 4493-04*, 1-21. Cambridge, US: MIT Sloan School of Management.
58 Weill & Ross, *IT Governance*, p. 85.
59 Ibid., p. 10
60 Symons, et al, *IT Governance Framework*, p. 2
61 Weill & Ross, *IT Governance*, p. 10.
62 Ibid.
63 Ataya, G., & Thorp, J. (2007). Portfolio Management: Unlocking the Value of IT Investments. *Information Systems Control Journal, 4*, 1-2, p. 1.

64 Sambamurthy, V., & Zmud, R. W. (1999). Arrangements for Information Technology Governance: A Theory of Multiple Contingencies. *MIS Quarterly, 23*(2), 261-290, p. 262.

65 Verzuh, E. (2008). *The Fast Forward MBA in Project Management.* US: John Wiley & Sons, Inc., p. 360.

66 Smith, S. G. (2006). *Straight to the Top: Becoming a World-Class CIO.* US: John Wiley & Sons Inc, p. 56.

67 Sambamurthy & Zmud, *Arrangements for Information Technology Governance*, p. 262.

68 Ward, J., & Elvin, R. (1999). A New Framework for Managing IT-enabled Business Change. *Information Systems Journal*, 197-221, p. 198.

69 Cullen, A., Symons, C., Scott, J., & An, M. (2010). *Using Business Capability Maps To Guide IT Investment Governance.* US: Forrester Research Inc, p. 4.

70 Leganza, G. (2009, October 19). *Good Order-taking Is Not Good Enough.* Retrieved August 31, 2011, from Mostly Enterprise Architecture : http://geneleganza.wordpress.com/tag/it-archetypes/

71 Weill & Ross, *IT Governance*, p. 127

72 Mata, F. J., Fuerst, W. L., & Barney, J. B. (1995, December). Information Technology and Sustained Competitive Advantage: A Resource Based Analysis. *MIS Quarterly, 19*(4), 487-505.

73 Clemons, E. K., & Weber, B. E. (1990). Strategic Information Technology Investments: Guidelines for Decision Making. *Journal of Management Information System, 7*(2), 9-28, p.15.

74 Weill & Woodham, *Dont Just Lead, Govern*, p. 9.

75 Ibid.

76 Davenport, T. H., Hammer, M., & Metsisto, T. J. (1989, April). How Executives Can Shape Their Company's Information Systems. *Harvard Business Review*, 130-134, p. 131.

77 The Open Group. (2009). *TOGAF Version 9.* Netherlands: Van Haren Publishing, p. 265.

78 Davenport et al, *How Executives Can Shape Their Company's Information Systems*, p. 130.

79 Ibid., p. 131.
80 Weill & Woodham, *Dont Just Lead, Govern*, p. 2.
81 Ibid., p. 134.
82 Ibid., p. 133.
83 Rockart, J. F., Earl, M. J., & Ross, J. W. (1996). Eight Imperatives for the New IT Organization . *Sloan Management Review*, 43-55, p. 49.
84 Feeny, D. F., & Willcocks, L. P. (1998). Core IS Capabilities for Exploiting Information Technology. *Sloan Management Review*, 9-21, p. 13.
85 Weill, P., & Broadbent, M. (1998). *Leveraging the New Infrastructure: How Market Leaders Capitalize on Information Technology*. US: Harvard Business School Press, p. 14.
86 Ibid., p. 15.
87 Ross, J. W. (2003, April). Creating a Strategic IT Architecture Competency: Learning in Stages. *CISR WP No. 335 and Sloan WP No. 4314-03*, 1-15. Cambridge, US: MIT Sloan School of Management, p. 2.
88 Britton, C., & Bye, P. (2004). *IT Architectures and Middleware: Strategies for Building Large, Integrated Systems*. US: Addison-Wesley, p. 1.
89 McKeen, J. D., & Smith, H. A. (2003). *Making IT Happen: Critical Issues in IT Management*. England: John Wiley & Sons Ltd, p. 234.
90 Ibid.
91 Ross, *Creating a Strategic IT Architecture Competency*, p. 2.
92 Britton & Bye, *IT Architectures and Middleware,* p. 1.
93 Microsoft Inc.,. (2011). *Microsoft Application Platform Middleware for SOA*. Retrieved November 14, 2011, from Microsoft Corporation Web Site: http://www.microsoft.com/applicationplatform/en/us/Key-Technologies/Middleware.aspx
94 Oracle Corporation Inc.,. (n.d.). *Java EE at a Glance*. Retrieved November 14, 2011, from Oracle Corporation Web Site: http://www.oracle.com/technetwork/java/javaee/overview/index.html
95 Microsoft Inc., *Microsoft Application Platform*.
96 Britton & Bye, *IT Architectures and Middleware*, p. 87.

97 Microsoft Inc.,. (n.d.). *Application Infrastructure Technologies*. Retrieved August 29, 2011, from Microsoft Corporation: http://www.microsoft.com/en-us/appfabric/default.aspx

98 eWeek. (2008, 10 29). *How to Better Manage Your Application Infrastructure*. Retrieved August 29, 2011, from eWeek.com: http://www.eweek.com/c/a/Enterprise-Applications/How-to-Better-Manage-Your-Application-Infrastructure/

99 The Open Group, *TOGAF Version 9*, p. 563.

100 Ross, *Creating a Strategic IT Architecture Competency*, p. 6.

101 Boh, W. F., & Yellin, D. (2006). Using Enterprise Architecture Standards in Managing Information Technology. *Journal of Management Information Systems, 23*(3), 163-207.

102 Rockart et al, *Eight Imperatives for the New IT Organization*, p. 49.

103 Smith, *Straight to the Top*, p. 145.

104 Weill & Broadbent, *Leveraging the New Infrastructure*, p. 26.

105 Ibid.

106 Weill & Woodham, *Dont Just Lead, Govern*, p. 3.

107 Weill, P., Subramani, M., & Broadbent, M. (2002). Building IT Infrastructure for Strategic Agility. *MIT Sloan Management Review*, pp. 57-65., p. 58.

108 Symons, C., Cullen, A., Orlov, L., & Belanger, B. (2007). *Making The Right Investment Decisions: Best Practices for IT Steering Committees*. US: Forrester Research Inc., p. 1.

109 Xue, Y., Liang, H., & Boulton, W. (2008, March). Information Technology Governance in Information Technology Investment Decision Processes: Impact of Investment Characteristics, External Environment, and Internal Context. (B. Tan, C. Soh, R. Chandrasekaran, & A. Boonstra, Eds.) *MIS Quarterly, 32*(1), 67-96, p. 68.

110 Xue et al, *Information Technology Governance in Information Technology Investment Decision Processes*, p. 68.

111 Weill & Ross, *IT Governance*, p. 40.

112 Ford, J. (1996). Evaluating Investments in Information Technology. *Computer Audit Update*, 7-14, p. 10.

113 Xue et al, *Information Technology Governance in Information Technology Investment Decision Processes*, p. 69.
114 Ross, J.W., & Johnson, E. (2009, March). Prioritising IT Investments. *Research Briefing*. MIT Center for Information Systems Research.
115 Weill, P., & Ross, J.W. (2009). *IT Savvy:What Top Executives Must Know to Go from Pain to Gain*. US: Havard Business Press, p. 45.
116 Ibid., p. 46.
117 Mechling, J., & Sweeney, V. (1997, November 30). *Findind and Funding IT Projects: Government Technology Website*. Retrieved October 19, 2011, from http://www.govtech.com/magazines/gt/Finding-and-Funding-IT-Projects.html?page=1
118 Weill, P., & Olson, M. H. (1989, March). Managing Investments in Information Technology: Mini Case Examples and Implications. *MIS Quarterly, 13*(1), 3-17, p. 11.
119 Ibid.,
120 Kaplan, R. S., & Norton, D. P. (2008). *The Execution Premium: Linking Strategy to Operations for Competitive Advantage* . US: Harvard Business Press, p. 115.
121 Broadbent, & Kitzis, *The New CIO Leader*, p. 143.
122 Micallef, M. (1996, April). Maximizing Return on Technology Investments (3). *Computer Audit Update*, 8-21, p. 14.
123 IT Governance Institute. (2008). *Enterprise Value: Governance of IT Investments,The Val IT Framework 2.0*. US:The IT Governance Institute, p. 17.
124 Cohen, L., & Young, A. (2006). *Multisourcing: moving beyond outsourcing to achieve growth and agility* . US: Harvard Business School Press, p. 113.
125 Michell, V. (2011). A Focused Approach to Business Capability. *First International Symposium on Business Modeling and Software Design*, (pp. 105-113), p. 105.
126 McKeen & Smith, *Making IT Happen*, p. 222.
127 Ross, J. W., & Weill, P. (2002, November). Six IT Decisions Your IT People Shouldn't Make. *Harvard Business Review*, 1-10, p. 5.

128 Ross, J. W., Weill, P., & Robertson, D. C. (2006). *Enterprise Architecture as Strategy : Creating a Foundation for Business Execution*. Boston: Harvard Business School Press, p.144.
129 Cohen & Young, *Multisourcing*, p. 3.
130 McKeen & Smith, *Making IT Happen*, p. 227.
131 Broadbent, & Kitzis, *The New CIO Leader*, p. 186.
132 Cohen & Young, *Multisourcing*, p. 119.
133 Smith, *Straight to the Top*, p. 155.
134 Microsoft Corporation. (2009). *Microsoft Application Architecture Guide*. US: Microsoft Press, p. 379.
135 Lacity, M. (2002, Augusut). Lessons in Global Information Technology Sourcing. *IEEE*, 26-33, p. 27.
136 Ibid., p. 28.
137 McKeen & Smith, *Making IT Happen*, p. 227.
138 Cohen & Young, *Multisourcing*, p. 35.
139 Ross, J. W., & Westerman, G. (2003, October). Architecting New Outsourcing Solutions: The Promise of Utility Computing. *CISR WP No. 337 and MIT Sloan WP No. 4458-03*. Cambridge: MIT Sloan School of Management, p.9.
140 Ibid.
141 Cohen & Young, *Multisourcing*, p. 40.
142 Ibid., p. 64.
143 Robertson, B. (2008). *Enterprise Solution Architecture: An Overview*. US: Gartner Inc., p. 6.
144 Paul, D., Yeates, D., & Cadle, J. (2010). *Business Anlaysis*. UK: British Informatics Society Limited, p. 228.
145 Weill & Ross, *IT Savvy*, p. 50.
146 Hunter, R., & Westerman, G. (2009). *The Real Business of IT: How CIOs Create and Communicate Value*. US: Harvard Business Press, p. 119.
147 Milis, K. and R. Mercken. "Success Factors Regarding the Implementation of ICT investment projects." *International Journal of Production Economics* (2002): 106-114, p. 111.
148 De Reyck, B., Grushka-Cockayne, Y., Lockett, M., Calderrini, S. R., Moura, M., & Sloper, A. (2005). The Impact of Project Portfolio

Management on Information Technology Projects. *International Journal of Project Management*, 524-537, p. 524.
149 Ataya & Thorp, *Portfolio Management*, p. 1.
150 Broadbent, & Kitzis, *The New CIO Leader*, p. 136.
151 Ibid.
152 OGC. (2009). *Managing Successful Projects with PRINCE2*. UK: The Stationery Office, p. 21.
153 Fitzpatrick, E. W. (2005). *Planning and Implementing IT Portfolio Management: Maximizing the Return on IT Investments*. US: IT Economics Corporation, p. 6.
154 Weill & Olson, *Managing Investments in Information Technology*, p. 10.
155 Weill & Broadbent, *Leveraging the New Infrastructure*, p. 211.
156 Ford, *Evaluating Investments in Information Technology*, p. 14.
157 Hunter & Westerman, *The Real Business of IT*, p. 121.
158 Weill & Ross, *IT Savvy*, p. 58.
159 Hunter & Westerman, *The Real Business of IT*, p. 120.
160 Ataya & Thorp, *Portfolio Management*, p. 1.
161 IT Governance Institute. (2005). Optimising Value Creation From IT Investments. *IT Governance Domain Practices and Competencies*. US: IT Governance Institute, p. 12.
162 Weill & Broadbent, *Leveraging the New Infrastructure*, p. 25.
163 Weill & Olson, *Managing Investments in Information Technology*, p. 7.
164 Gliedman, C., & Brown, A. (2004). *Defining IT Portfolio Management: Holistic IT Investment Planning*. US: Forrester Research Inc, p. 2.
165 Micallef, *Maximizing Return on Technology Investments*, 8-21, p. 18.
166 Norfolk, D. (2005). *IT Governance: Managing Information Technology for Business*. London: Thorogood Publishing Ltd, p. 64.
167 Schwalbe, K. *Information Technology Project Management*. US: Course Technology, Cengage Learning, 2010, p. 56.
168 Shields, M. G. (2001). *E-Business and ERP: Rapid Implementation and Project Planning*. Canada: John Wiley & Sons, Inc, p. 179.
169 The UK Chapter of the itSMF. (2007). *An Introductory Overview of ITIL V3 Version 1.0*. UK: itSMF Ltd, p. 5.
170 Norfolk, *IT Governance*, p. 63.

171 IT Governance Institute, *Enterprise Value: Governance of IT Investments, The Val IT Framework 2.0*, p. 9.
172 Weill & Broadbent, *Leveraging the New Infrastructure*, p. 250.
173 Hunter & Westerman, *The Real Business of IT*, p.
174 Weill & Woodham, *Dont Just Lead, Govern*, p. 13.
175 Ibid.
176 Weill, *Don't Just Lead, Govern*, p. 8.
177 Ibid., p. 9
178 Ibid.
179 Weill & Ross, *IT Savvy*, p. 46.
180 Ross & Weill, *Six IT Decisions Your IT People Shouldn't Make*, p. 5
181 Ibid.
182 Weill, *Don't Just Lead, Govern*, p. 9.
183 Weill, *Don't Just Lead, Govern*, p. 9.
184 Ross & Weill, *Six IT Decisions Your IT People Shouldn't Make*, p. 8.
185 IT Governance Institute. (2005). Measuring and Demonstrating the Value of IT. *IT Governance Domain Practices and Competencies* . USA: IT Governance Institute, p. 17.
186 Hunter & Westerman, *The Real Business of IT*, p. 160.
187 Weill & Woodham, *Dont Just Lead, Govern*, p. 8.
188 Hunter & Westerman, *The Real Business of IT*, p. 43.
189 Rouse, W. B. (2006). *Enterprise Transformation: Understanding and Enabling Fundamental Change*. US: John Wiley & Sons Inc., p. 4.
190 Gordon, S. (1994, November). Benchmarking The Information Systems Function. *Center for Information Management Studies (CIMS) Working Paper Series 94-08*. Massachusetts, US: Babson College.
191 Hunter & Westerman, *The Real Business of IT*, p. 54.
192 Davenport, T. H., Hammer, M., & Metsisto, T. J. (1989, April). How Executives Can Shape Their Company's Information Systems. *Harvard Business Review*, 130-134, p. 134.
193 Ross et al, *Enterprise Architecture as Strategy*, p.53.
194 Ibid.
195 itmWEB Media Corp. (2006). *Information Technology Budgeting Scoreboard*. Retrieved November 30, 2011, from The itmWEB Site: http://www.itmweb.com/blbenchbgt.htm

196 itmWEB Media Corp. (2006). *Information Technology Capital Spending Scoreboard*. Retrieved November 30, 2011, from The itmWEB Site: http://www.itmweb.com/blbenchcap.htm
197 Swaminathan, K. S. (2008, June 12). Computing In The Cloud. *U. S. Business Review*, pp. 12-13.
198 Cohen & Young, *Multisourcing*, p. 9.
199 Beulen, E., Ribbers, P., & Roos, J. (2011). *Managing IT Outsourcing*. New York: Routledge.
200 Swaminathan, *Computing In The Cloud*
201 McKeen & Smith, *Making IT Happen*, p. 215.
202 Beulen et al, *Managing IT Outsourcing*.
203 Broadbent, & Kitzis, *The New CIO Leader*, p. 137.
204 Hunter & Westerman, *The Real Business of IT*, p. 52.
205 Hogue, F., Sambamurthy, V., Zmud, R., Trainer, T., & Wilson, C. (2006). *Winning the 3-Legged Race: When Business and Technology Run Together*. US: Prentice Hall, p. 103.
206 Hunter & Westerman, *The Real Business of IT*, p. 65
207 Ford, *Evaluating Investments in Information Technology*, p. 10
208 Ibid.
209 BC Group. (n.d.). *Group Profile: Corporate History*. Retrieved March 28, 2012, from KCB Group Web Site: https://www.kbc.com/MISC/D9e01/~E/~KBCCOM/~BZJ07U3/-BZIZTPN/BZJ07TR/BZJ07W4.
210 Ibid.
211 KBC Group. (n.d.). *Group Profile: Organisational structure*. Retrieved March 28, 2012, from KCB Group Web Site: https://www.kbc.com/MISC/D9e01/~E/~KBCCOM/~BZJ07X6/-BZIZTPN/BZJ07TR/BZJ07VH.
212 Ibid.
213 Ibid.
214 De Haes, S., & Van Grembergen, W. (2005). IT Governance Structures, Processes and Relational Mechanisms: Achieving IT/Business Alignment in a Major Belgian Financial Group. *Proceedings of the 38th Hawaii International Conference on System Sciences*, 1-7, p. 4.

215 Ibid., p. 3.
216 Leganza, *Good Order-taking Is Not Good Enough.*
217 De Haes & Van Grembergen, *IT Governance Structures, Processes and Relational Mechanisms*, p. 4.
218 Ibdi., p. 3.
219 Ibid., p. 4.
220 Ibid.
221 Ibid., p. 5.
222 Ibid., p. 6.
223 Ibid., p. 9.

CHAPTER 3

THE SECOND RATIONAL STEP: IT SOLUTIONING
HOW-TO FORMULATE IT STRATEGY AND DESIGN SOLUTION ARCHITECTURES

IT SOLUTIONING

*Not all problems have a technological answer,
but when they do, that is the more lasting solution.*

—Andrew Grove[1]

Following the IT governance step or the development of the ability to make effective IT alignment and investment decisions, enterprises must develop *IT solutioning capability*: the second of the five rational IT investment management (ITIM) steps/capabilities that must be developed by enterprises to manage their IT investments successfully and generate maximum business value.

IT solutioning capability is the ability of enterprises to formulate an IT strategy that is aligned to their business strategy—that is, the ability of enterprises to specify strategic IT objectives (*the what*) and identify the right strategic IT initiatives (*the how*) that should be executed to develop the capabilities that are needed to achieve their strategic IT objectives.

The definition of IT solutioning given above strongly emphasises the significance of formulating an IT strategy that is aligned with the business strategy for one major reason: the generation of maximum value from IT investments. According to Forrester Research, 'You can't deliver sustained business value if the IT strategy and business strategy are not aligned and tightly linked.'[2] Aligning IT strategy to business strategy has long been globally accepted as a critical success factor for generating maximum value from IT investments and has consequently become a major goal of enterprise CIOs globally.

In July 2009, looking back at the top priorities of CIOs a couple of years earlier, Forrester Research reported that 'Business and IT alignment remains a top priority for CIOs and other business leaders.'[3] Two years later, CIO-Insight of 2011 also reported that IT and business alignment is the number one IT management concern.[4] Although CIOs and other business managers have identified the significance of IT and business alignment in generating value from IT, achieving this alignment has proved to be a difficult task.

In order to align IT with the business, organisations might need to adopt a capability orientation or model that describes the enterprise as a whole (i.e., the first of the twelve rational IT investment management principles discussed in chapter one) and follow two major steps. According to Forrester Research, 'Capabilities close the gap between business interests and IT concerns by providing the right level of detail and consistency to facilitate an on-going dialogue between business and IT leaders.'[5] If enterprises were to base this discussion on processes, it would be too detailed and would not capture the interest of business executives; alternatively, if enterprises were to base their discussion on applications, it would be too complex for business executives to comprehend. Finally, if it were to be based on projects, it would be too tactical.[6]

Therefore, in order to align IT with the business, the first critical step is to identify business capabilities that are required to achieve strategic business objectives or to execute business strategies.[7] The second critical step is to specify strategic IT objectives. A strategic IT objective, for example, might be to *deliver up-to-date customer information* to support or enable the development of the required business capabilities.

Organisations can align their IT strategy to their business strategy by specifying strategic IT objectives, or by setting specific, measurable, and time-bound IT goals that must be achieved in order to enable or support the development of the business capabilities needed to achieve strategic business objectives or to execute business strategies. A group of top US chief information officers (CIOs) and academicians expressed a similar view: 'A business-driven IT strategy begins by articulating capabilities necessary to achieve the business strategy, and then the technology needed to enable those capabilities.'[8] Further supporting the view expressed earlier, the IT Governance Institute declared that in order

> to respond to the business requirements for IT, the enterprise needs to invest in the resources required to create an adequate technical capability (e.g., an enterprise resource planning [ERP] system) to support a business capability (e.g., implementing a supply chain) resulting in the desired outcome (e.g., increased sales and financial benefits).[9]

IT solutioning capability also includes the ability to translate the outcome of IT strategy formulation (i.e., strategic IT initiatives) into the architecture of technically feasible IT solutions needed to develop the IT capabilities required to deliver IT services; in other words, IT solutioning also involves designing the architecture of enterprise solutions or enterprise solution architecture (ESA).

Enterprise solution architecture helps to ensure that enterprise IT capabilities, such as *the ability to digitally manage customer information* that support the development of business capabilities, such as *customer account/service management,* needed to deliver *business services,* such as *handling customer inquiries, transferring/receiving funds, or paying customers* are developed in the right way. It is good to note that business capabilities are *enabled* by IT capabilities—those capabilities that are provided by fully automated systems, such as an employee self-service portal, and cannot exist without the use of IT.[10] Business capabilities can also be *supported* by IT capabilities—those capabilities that are produced through the collaboration between people and automated processes and can exist without IT.[11]

At the lowest level, IT solutioning can be defined as the identification and design of the right IT services, which are simply information systems (IS) services that are enabled by IT, while an IT *service* can be defined as a unit of IT capability and a thing that IT does to support or enable the delivery of business services.[12,13] Therefore, if the main goal of IT service is to support or enable the delivery of business service, what then is a business service?

A business service can be defined as a unit of business capability and a thing that a business does to meet the needs of customers, or to deliver value.[14] Enterprises can use a manual processes or fully automated systems to fulfil business services.

In addition, an organisation may choose to fulfil a business service by itself internally or outsource the fulfilment of a business service to external service providers.[15] Because IT/business services are units of IT/business capabilities, the portfolio of resources (people, processes, and information, and IT) that constitute IT/business capabilities are required to deliver both business and IT services.[16]

Why Should Enterprises Develop Excellent IT Solutioning Capability?

Enterprises need to develop an excellent IT solutioning capability because of the large numbers of strategic IT investment project failures that have occurred in the last couple of decades. IT systems that result from the investment of enterprise capital on strategic IT projects often lack the required functionalities; they don't perform according to required standards; they are underutilised or rejected by users; their cost outweighs their benefits; they don't deliver the value they promised; and sometimes these projects are simply abandoned or written off.[17] Therefore, enterprises must develop IT solutioning capability in order to stem the tide of strategic IT investment project failures.

Although enterprises invest their scarce resources mainly on two major categories of IT investments, strategic and tactical/operational, the focus of this book will be on strategic IT investment projects because they have the most profound impact on the competitiveness or survival of enterprises. In *IT Savvy*, Peter Weill and Jeanne W. Ross proposed that the ideal situation for enterprises would be to focus on key strategic IT investment initiatives.[18] Despite the focus on strategic IT investment initiatives, they stress the fact that enterprises will always need to respond to tactical IT investment demands that arise from either external changes to the enterprise (e.g., IT initiatives required to comply with regulations) or internal changes to the enterprise (e.g., IT initiatives required to run and maintain the enterprise).

Given the significance of strategic IT initiatives outlined in the previous paragraph, enterprises should therefore develop an excellent IT solutioning capability that will counter the failure of strategic IT investment projects. This recommendation is based on the discovery that the failures of strategic IT investment projects is mostly due to ineffective IT solutioning capability, or the lack of ability to formulate business-aligned IT strategies—that is, to specify IT objectives, identify the right IT initiatives, and design the technical architecture for translating those initiatives into implementable strategic IT solutions. According to William R. King, professor at Katz Graduate School of Business of the University of Pittsburgh, one possible explanation for most strategic IT investment project failures is that they have been conceived and designed from the same bottom-up (tactical) approach that was used in the development of electronic data processing (EDP) systems in the mainframe computer era.[19] King further stated that bottom-up design approaches focus mainly on achieving operational efficiency, such as saving costs, rather than focusing on achieving organisational effectiveness.

In *Billion Dollar Lessons*, Paul B. Carroll and Chunka Mui sustained this point by carrying out extensive research to find the reasons why major investments fail. Most of the very large investment failures are due to bad strategies.[20] This discovery refutes the popular reason given by most business literatures that attribute the cause of investment failure solely to poor execution.

However, besides the challenges of ineffective conception, such as bad strategies, strategic IT investment projects also fail because most enterprises lack effective *IT execution capability* (i.e., the ability to execute their strategies effectively). In other words, they are not able to select and deliver the best IT investment projects on time, within budget, and with the required functionalities. According to Peter Weill and Richard Woodham:

> In recent years there have been spectacular failures of large information technology (IT) investments—major enterprise resource planning (ERP) systems initiatives that were never completed, e-business initiatives that were *ill-conceived* or *poorly executed* and new systems developed that *were never used effectively*.[21]

Another factor that is responsible for the infectiveness of enterprises' IT execution capability is the inability of most enterprises to design the technical solution architecture of strategic IT initiatives effectively (the second aspect of IT solutioning). In other words, this meant that most enterprises lack the ability to *do things the right way*, to translate the strategic IT initiatives that will enable the achievement of their strategic IT objectives into technically feasible strategic IT solutions (i.e., implementable strategic IT solutions).

This is justifiably so because it is at the IT solutioning step that specific end users/stakeholders of the proposed strategic IT initiatives-cum-solutions are identified and mobilised in order to gather, analyse, and specify the requirements that will be used to design the architecture of the initiative-cum-solution: a critical factor to getting IT investment projects *done the right way*. It is also at this stage that an enterprise seeks to gain the users' or executives' support and buy-in for the proposed IT solution.

According to the Standish Group study, three major factors were found to constitute the bulk of the reasons why IT investment projects succeed:[22]

- User involvement in the design of IT solutions (15.9 percent) to business problems

- Executive management support and/or buy-in (13.9 percent)

- The availability of unambiguous functional and non-functional requirements specification (13.0 percent) to guide the development/implementation of IT solutions

The Standish Group carried out a second study on the same survey participants to discover the factors working against IT investment projects; they found the lack of user input (12.8 percent), incomplete or changing requirement specifications (24.1 percent), and lack of executive support (7.5 percent) to be the factors militating against the success of IT investment projects.[23] These factors give birth to a particular category of strategic IT project risk called functionality risk, in which the enterprises deliver strategic IT systems on time, within budget, and according to the defined specifications or the specified functional requirements, but the investment still fails because it does not deliver the expected benefits.[24] This type of situation happens for two reasons: first, the user requirements or needs were not accurately gathered, analysed, and specified, thereby leading to the design of the wrong IT system; second, the requirements or the needs of users for the system have changed, which makes the system's design inappropriate.[25]

Simon More, in *Strategic Project Portfolio Management*, provided a perfect summary of the evidence stressing the importance of both IT solutioning and execution capability in the successful management of IT investments and to the generation of value from IT. More said, 'Organisations that outperform do so because of a combination of strong execution and great strategy.'[26] He further stressed that the lack of either strong execution or great strategy is the reason why enterprise investments fail. Two notable authorities on enterprise architecture, Dana Bredemeyer and Ruth Malan, also shared More's view by stating that they 'know there are no "silver bullets" in IT and that successful implementation and employment of a technology is as crucial as the selection of that technology.'[27]

The ability to identify the right strategic IT investment initiatives required to achieve the strategic IT objectives of an enterprise and to design their solutions architecture thereof is the next critical step in managing how enterprises invest in IT and generate maximum value from IT investments, second only to the development of IT governance capability.

The aforementioned supposition clearly indicates that without first getting the right people (the *who*) into the right seat to figure out the *what*[28] or to *identify* a problem to be solved or an opportunity to be exploited that requires the use of IT, there will be no need to invest in IT or to design effective IT solutions architecture. This explains why this book refers to this chapter as *IT solutioning*, which the Urban Dictionary defined as 'the process of finding a solution to a problem.'[29]

John A. Zachman, an authority in the field of Strategic Information Systems Planning (SISP), confirmed that the first step in the process of creating a technology-based solutions to an enterprise problem is the requirement to *select* information systems or technology (IS/IT) resource investment opportunities with the *best* potential to deliver maximum value to the whole enterprise relative to others.[30] Zachman further stressed that prior to the *selection* of the best IS/IT investment opportunities among other opportunities, enterprises must first *identify* all the probable opportunities for using IT to solve enterprise problems (i.e., to identify all the right IT investment opportunities across the whole enterprise) in order to build the context for assessing the relative worth of each opportunity. Zachman made a clear distinction between the identification of the right portfolio of strategic IT investment opportunities and the selection of the best strategic IT investment opportunities, or the investment opportunities with the greatest potential value relative to other investment opportunities in the portfolio.

Richard Hunter and George Westerman in *The Real Business of IT* corroborated Zachman's affirmation by pointing out that, finding the opportunities to improve organisation performance (or needs identification) is the first of a number of key IT investment activities, after IT oversight task, because it is the glue that holds everything else together.[31]

Research reveals that the identification of the right portfolio of strategic IT investment opportunities falls within the domain of strategic IS/IT planning, the domain where business needs for strategic IT applications are identified, while the selection of the best IT investment opportunities falls within the domain of IT portfolio management, the domain where enterprise-wide IT investment decisions are made.[32,33,34]

In previous paragraphs, this book established that investing in the right strategic IT investment opportunities or initiatives is necessary for the growth and transformation of enterprises and, consequently, to their survival. Based on this realisation, it is rational to conclude that the ability to identify the right strategic IT investment initiatives or opportunities and to design the solution architecture (i.e., IT solutioning capability) is equally critical to enterprise survival. If this is true, what does this capability entail? And how can enterprises develop this capability?

What Is IT Solutioning Capability?

Let start by first examining the meaning of capability, Dana Bredemeyer and Ruth Malan defined capability as the critical building blocks of an enterprise that are created by the combination of enterprise resources, such as people, process, information, and systems, through the support of other enterprise resources such as infrastructure or facilities and capital.[35] Forrester Research corroborated this definition by stating that 'capabilities are the fundamental elements that make up a business; they are the building blocks of business execution.'[36] From these definitions, it is evident that IT systems or enterprise applications represent just one component or building block of an enterprise's capability.

Capability can also be defined from a business perspective, which is then called business capability. Dr. Vaughan Michell in his paper titled 'A Focused Approach to Business Capability' defined business capability as 'the collective capability or a group of resources with potential to deliver a specific business value output to an external customer.'[37] Forrester Research, on the other hand, defined business capability as 'the organization's capacity to successfully perform a unique business activity to achieve a specific outcome.'[38]

Now, we move from the previous high-level definition of IT solutioning capability to a more detailed definition and leverage the previous definitions of capability and business capability. IT solutioning capability is the availability of the right combination and type of enterprise resources: the right organisational structure filled with competent people (i.e., IT solutioning governance architecture/framework), processes, information, systems, and tools/technology that are necessary and sufficient for formulating business-aligned IT strategies.

IT solutioning capability is also required to design the solution architecture of the strategic IT investment initiatives that result from the IT strategy formulation process, as solution architecture helps to describe the detailed functionalities of the proposed IT investment initiatives-cum-solutions, which then helps to guide their successful delivery (implementation/development).[39] Having dealt with the people or structural aspect of IT solutioning capability or the design of effective IT solutioning governance architecture in the first chapter of this book, we now turn to the remaining three relevant components of IT solutioning capability, which are IT solutioning process, information, and systems.

The IT solutioning process—which is a complete and interdependent sequence of steps for formulating business-aligned IT strategy—steps for specifying strategic IT objectives, identifying the right strategic IT investment initiatives or opportunities that enterprises should invest in and for designing the solution architecture of the identified strategic IT investment opportunities—has two major goals. The first goal is to ensure that enterprises are *doing the right things*, which means investing in the strategic IT initiatives-cum-solutions or strategic IT applications that will help to achieve their strategic IT objectives. According to Mark Morgan, Raymond Levitt, and William Malek in *Executing Your Strategy*, 'Effective strategy consists of choosing to do the right things.'[40] The second goal is to ensure that the strategic IT investment solutions-cum-projects are *done the right way* through the design of solutions architecture that contributes to the execution of the projects.

In summary, the availability of IT solutioning governance architecture or framework, process, information, and tools constitute IT solutioning capability. The diagrammatic representation or description of the relationship and integration between these four (4) critical components and the environment—called the IT solutioning capability model—will be the focus of subsequent sections of this book.

The Evolution of the IT Solutioning Capability Model

The IT solutioning capability evolved from two major enterprise planning efforts, which are strategic IS planning and strategic IT planning. Strategic IS planning is the process of identifying the most desirable strategic IS investment initiatives in which an enterprise should invest or identifying enterprise demand for strategic IT applications that will provide the information required to achieve its strategic objectives.[41] This implies that strategic IS planning addresses *what* information and systems are required to achieve the enterprise's strategic objectives.

Strategic IT planning, on the other hand, is the process of translating the identified IS investment initiatives into technically and financially feasible strategic IT solutions that can meet IS demand,[42] which implies that strategic IT planning addresses *how* IT will be used to fulfil enterprise's information requirements within the limits of its financial and human resources and risk appetite.

For the sake simplicity and readability, this book has integrated both strategic IS and IT planning and refers to them simply as *strategic IT planning*. In addition, this book further recommends that strategic IT planning should change to *IT solutioning* because all enterprise planning efforts, including strategic IT planning, boils down to one thing: finding the right solutions to enterprise problems, which is best described by the single term *solutioning*—'the process of finding a solution to a problem.'[43] Although the word *solutioning* is not yet a Standard English word, there is high hope that it will not remain so for too long.

The evolution of IT planning can be traced to the classical concept of enterprise or organisational planning, and the difference between the two is based on the broadness of their focus. Enterprise planning focuses on developing plans for the allocation of resources (including IT resources) to achieve the objectives of the enterprise as a whole.[44,45] Strategic IT planning, on the other hand, focuses on how IT as an individual resource can *contribute* to the attainment of enterprise goals or the execution of enterprise strategies.[46]

Overview of Common IT Planning Approaches

Dr. William J. Doll, Professor of E-Business Strategy at the University of Toledo, studied thirty-three (33) organisations to find out the ways in which their IT function is managed and how management practices influence the overall success of IT investment projects throughout their life cycle.[47] He found that firms that delivered projects that meet their objectives on time and within budget (i.e., successful firms) were almost three times as likely (60.0 percent vs. 23.1 percent) to have a comprehensively documented plan for IT development. He also pointed out that the most successful enterprises considered the development of a plan as a precondition for managing IT investment efforts effectively, as it helps top management to understand the *as-as* and the *to-be* situation of development activities and the estimated cost of getting from the current to the target state. In this situation, the planning efforts of successful enterprises are concerned with ensuring that the IT function is executing the right investment projects, doing the right things, and less concerned with IT investment projects being done the right way. He also discovered that in less successful firms, if a written plan existed at all, it was perceived more as a budget document or technical plan. If indeed IT plans existed as a budget document, Doll found that less successful enterprises dedicated such plans to elucidating resource requirements rather than providing the means to determine whether the organisation is executing the right IT investment projects, or doing the right things. In situations where the plan existed as a technical plan, enterprises used the plan mainly for presenting the technical context of current and proposed IT systems rather than their business context.

In organisations without a comprehensively documented IT plan that links strategic to tactical and operational plans, planning activities usually originates from IT leaders who use management consultants and IT portfolio managers to gather yearly business requirements at the edges of the organisation in a bottom-up approach.[48] In this approach, IT leaders collect the list of tactical IT investment projects to be considered for the next financial year from the line-of-business managers and translate them into an enterprise-wide list of projects; the result of this approach is a set of IT investment projects that are 300 percent to 500 percent more than the available IT investment capital.[49,50]

To avoid this ordeal—coupled with the need for enterprises to leverage IT for growth and transformation and driven by emerging technologies, such as the Internet, mobile computing, and so forth—IT leaders must adopt a comprehensive, structured, and strategic planning approach to identify the right strategic IT investment projects.[51]

Overview of Existing Structured IT Planning Approaches

Like enterprise planning, IT planning has three (3) main planning approaches:[52]

1. Strategic IT planning: A systematic approach for clarifying and understanding enterprise objectives and capabilities in order to identify the right strategic IT initiatives or strategic IT applications in which the enterprise should invest, which will help to develop the IT capabilities or provide the information required to enable the achievement of its strategic objectives or the execution of its strategies.[53,54]

Strategic IT planning also involves translating the identified initiatives into implementable solutions through the design of effective solution architecture and policies.[55] The time horizon for this planning effort is usually long-range, which can be between three (3) to five (5) years or more, and it is the primary responsibility of senior management, the CIO, and the chief enterprise architect (CEA).

2. Tactical IT planning: From an IT solutioning perspective, strategic IT planning is concerned with *identifying* the right strategic IT investment initiatives that can help to grow or transform an enterprise or to execute an enterprise's strategies; tactical IT planning, on the other hand, is concerned with *identifying* tactical IT investment initiatives that can help to run or maintain the enterprise.[56,57] The time horizon for this type of IT planning is usually between one and two years, and it is usually the responsibility of middle or functional managers.

From an IT execution (i.e., the third rational step for ITIM) perspective, tactical IT planning is mainly concerned with the execution of IT strategy (i.e., *selecting* the best strategic IT solutions-cum-programmes and developing road maps),[58,59,60] and it encompasses activities such as the management of IT investment portfolio and programmes, activities that are usually assigned to independent management offices and not functional business units.[61] According to Mark Morgan, Raymond Levitt, and William Malek in *Executing Your Strategy*, 'There is simply no path to executing strategy other than the one that runs through project portfolio management.'[62]

3. *Operational IT planning:* From an IT execution perspective, operational IT planning is concerned mainly with the allocation of work packages or tasks that are required to achieve the operational objectives of the enterprise's tactical IT plan to functional business units.[63] The time horizon for this planning stage is usually between one month to twelve years; the key activities at this stage are the management of IT investment projects (meeting time, budget targets, and delivering the required functionalities), and it is usually the responsibility of the IT project manager, IS professionals, line managers, and partners. However, from an IT solutioning perspective, operational IT planning is concerned with identifying operational IT investment initiatives that can help to address the needs of specific business processes or to run or maintain a particular unit of an enterprise. This type of IT planning is usually the responsibility of business process managers or a line manager, with the time horizon between one and thirty days.

Strategic IT Planning

The concept of strategic IT planning, often referred to as strategic information systems planning (SISP) or IT strategic planning, evolved in the late 1970s as 'the process of identifying a portfolio of computer-based applications that will assist an organization in executing its business plans and consequently realizing its business goals.'[64] This definition was later extended to include the design of solution architecture (i.e., a technical plan that contains the detailed description of the computer-based applications capabilities or functionalities, together with requisite databases, storage, hardware servers, networks, and other systems infrastructure) required to support or enable the development or implementation and operation of computer-based applications.[65] This definition assumes that enterprises have set their goals and developed their plans and strategies for achieving their goals, all of which are known by IT planners. This obvious assumption error led to the second extension of the definition to include the search for high-impact application software or those with capabilities to create a competitive advantage for enterprises, especially for those enterprises that did not have clearly documented goals, plans, and strategies.[66]

Enterprises generally engaged in the development of strategic IT planning for a number of important reasons, including the following:[67,68]

a) To align IT investments with business strategies or needs
b) To identify the right strategic IT investment initiatives-cum-solutions or strategic IT applications for enterprises to invest in
c) To generate maximum business value from IT investments
d) To develop enterprise solutions architecture (ESA) for strategic IT initiatives
e) To carry out long-range IT planning that will enable accurate forecasting of IT resource requirements
f) To create sustainable competitive advantage
g) To develop an IT budget or allocate IT resources effectively and efficiently

Given the definitions of strategic IT planning outlined in the preceding paragraphs, it is clear that the strategic IT planning process has the following five (5) major outputs:

1. Business-aligned IT strategy
2. Solution architecture of strategic IT initiatives
3. Road map of strategic IT solutions
4. Sourcing strategy
5. Funding strategy

The first output of strategic IT planning is business-aligned IT strategy, which consists mainly of the following:[69]

- Strategic IT objectives that are linked to strategic business objectives

- Strategic IT capabilities assessment report that lists the capabilities that are *missing* between the current strategic IT capabilities of the enterprise and those required to achieve its *strategic IT objectives*

- Strategic IT initiatives for developing the *missing* capabilities

A business-aligned IT strategy consists of two main critical components. The first is strategic IT objectives, which are the instrument for aligning the strategic IT capabilities of an organisation to the achievement of its strategic business objectives, or to the execution of business strategies. The second critical component is strategic IT initiatives, which is the portfolio of interdependent projects (programmes) that must be executed by the enterprise in order to build the capabilities required to achieve its strategic IT objectives. In *The Execution Premium*, Robert S. Kaplan and David P. Norton defined strategic initiatives as 'the collections of finite-duration discretionary projects and programs, outside the organisation's day-to-day operational activities, that are designed to help the organisation achieve its targeted performance.'[70]

The second output of an enterprise's strategic IT planning process is the solution architecture of strategic IT initiatives. Solution architecture is the combination of the identified packaged application software or envisioned solution concept (custom application software), architectural description (i.e., the specification of functionalities and databases together with the security and other technology infrastructure), the people, and other components that are essential for implementing the application software or for constructing and deploying the solution.[71] Put another way, enterprise solution architecture (ESA) can be defined as the high-level (i.e., conceptual, logical, and physical) description of the structural composition of application software and the data elements, networks, and other technology systems it uses, their inter-relationships to each other, and the principles governing their design and evolution.[72,73]

The third output of an enterprise strategic IT planning process is the road map of strategic IT solutions or IT investment opportunities, which is the time-phased and technically interdependent set of strategic IT initiatives-cum-solutions that will help the enterprise to develop the IT capabilities it needs to achieve its objectives.[74] Road mapping is a technique that allows enterprises to visualize their business-aligned IT strategy on one page through the continuous linking of the key components of their time-phased IT strategies—that is, the continuous linking of strategic IT solutions to their strategic IT objectives.[75]

The last two major outputs of the strategic IT planning process are sourcing and funding strategies for the strategic IT solutions-cum-projects. The sourcing strategy specifies how the strategic IT solutions will be sourced in line with the existing enterprise IT sourcing policies (see chapter two on IT sourcing governance decisions). The funding strategy specifies how the strategic IT solutions will be funded in line with the existing enterprise IT funding policies (see chapter two on IT funding governance decisions).

Typical Examples of Strategic IT Planning Methodologies

In earlier years, enterprises generally used a number of varying structured methodologies to support the performance of strategic IT planning or to formulate business-aligned IT strategies. Examples of commonly cited, applied, and popular strategic IT planning (also called strategic information systems planning [SISP]) methodologies are as follows:[76,77]

- *Business Systems Planning (BSP) & Business Information Control Study (BICS) Methodology:* Two strategic IT planning study methodologies that use enterprise analysis techniques to model and analyse enterprise data to identify enterprise improvement and transformation opportunities that require the use of IT. At the beginning of their application, both methodologies leverage the critical success factors (CSFs) methodology to identify management priorities for investing in IT assets.[78,79]

- *Enterprise Modelling (EM) Methodology:* Developing a holistic model of an enterprise to visualise, analyse, and understand the enterprise in order to identify possible areas of improvement and transformation.[80]

- *Critical Success Factors (CSFs) Methodology:* Focuses mainly on identifying top management's critical areas of concern in which the enterprise must excel in order to be successful; these critical areas of concern also help the enterprise to prioritise its investments in IT.[81]

BSP/BICS Methodology

The first commercially available and seemingly popular strategic IT planning study methodology is the IBM Business Systems Planning (BSP) methodology, which was developed in 1970 by the IBM Corporate Information Systems Architecture group for use as a market support program.[82] In order to reduce the time to market for the deliverables (i.e., the results of analysis) of the BSP methodology, as well as to reduce the number of people required to carry out the analysis, the IBM Laboratory in Santa Teresa developed yet another IS/IT planning study methodology called Business Information Control Study (BICS) in the mid-1970s. IBM based the development of the BICS methodology on the theoretical constructs of the Business Information Analysis and Integration Technique (BIAIT) and upon its earlier developed BSP study methodology. However, it is important to note that the major similarities between the two strategic IS/IT planning study methodologies is that they both focus mainly on the use of data-oriented enterprise analysis as the key technique of their study, with the joint objectives of supporting the strategic IS/IT planning effort of enterprises.

Both methodologies provide detailed processes for identifying potential IT investment opportunities that will have the highest impact on enterprise performance.[82] Furthermore, both methodologies gather data by interviewing an enterprise's top management to elicit their priorities for IT investment initiatives. Their differences are worth noting as well.

The BSP interview technique, for example, is centred on eliciting business objectives or business problems from an individual management executive in order to determine the relative priority of IT investment opportunities.[84] The BICS methodology, on the other hand, advocates the interviewing of a group of management executives to achieve the same end result while using the CSF's methodology. For example, during the interview sessions, the BSP methodology asks, "What are your objectives?" or "What are your problems?" while the BICS methodology asks, "What are your critical success factors?"

The two methodologies also adopt different approaches in carrying out their analysis. That is, BSP commences its analysis by defining the products or services of the business unit, followed by identifying the resources required to provide these products or services. Consequently, the enterprise identifies the business processes that must be carried out to manage the products or resources throughout their life span.[85] Finally, enterprises elicit the data requirements for the identified business processes. As a result of this requirement elicitation, the architecture or functional/data specification (i.e., a documentation of the relationship between the enterprise data and business processes) of the information product required to support the functional business unit is developed. The BICS methodology, on the other hand, centres its analysis on the orders that the enterprise receives, rather than on the products or services that the enterprise offers.

Both methodologies have three major limitations. First, the results of the analyses of the two methodologies do not yield design specifications,[86] which means that their outputs do not immediately translate into an implementable technical solution—infrastructure and application—architecture (i.e., low-level hardware and software design specifications); consequently, further analysis is required to achieve the required level of detail. John Zachman recommended that enterprises revert to classic application development techniques such as the Structured Analysis and Design Technique (SADT)[87] or other Software Development Life Cycle (SDLC) methodologies to compensate for this limitation.[88]

Second, the BSP documentation does not provide clear guidance in classifying, defining, relating, analysing, and concluding the strategic IT planning effort.[89] The BSP methodology left these planning activities to the manual manipulations of the study team, which implies that the quality of the study results will depend on the team's capability.

Third, since both methodologies are data-oriented,[90] they focus mainly on analysing enterprise data as the sole means of identifying prospective IT investment opportunities with the greatest potential rather than offering multiple orientation capabilities such as process, information, or service orientation, and so forth.

Finally, the development of both the BSP and BICS methodologies are not rigorously grounded in theory. According to John Zachman, 'The structures and classifications are based on empirical evidence rather than theoretical foundation.'[91] It is a tired secret that theory is the foundation of every scientific endeavour. It is defined as the cumulative collection of studies or findings about a particular subject matter that help researchers and other interested parties discover what other researchers know, to determine what they need to discover, or to determine new areas to study.[92] However, 'a theory is needed to enable researchers to study strategic information systems planning and present their findings in an organized, comprehensive and parsimonious, and meaningful manner'[93] and to 'prevent researchers from being exposed to criticism that their work lacks scientific rigor.'[94]

Enterprise Modelling

Enterprise Modelling (EM) is yet another popular methodology for carrying out strategic IT planning activities. EM helps to develop detailed documentation of enterprise strategies and capabilities to enable analyses that will help to uncover the gap between current enterprise—business and technology—capabilities and the capabilities that are required to execute enterprise strategies.

The simple philosophy that underpins the EM methodologies is that large organisations are too complex for one person to retain in his/her memory all the information that is required to support the process of making decisions about the ways the organisation can be improved or transformed. This type of decision making usually requires information about the constituents' parts of the organisation (i.e., structure, people, processes, systems, infrastructures, standards, and so forth), their interactions and relationships, and the principles guiding their evolution, which can run into thousands of megabytes. This fundamental philosophy led to the evolution of EM as a methodology that provides the tools for developing a model (i.e., the documentation about the organisation's structure, processes, systems, infrastructures, standards, and so forth) of the organisation that helps to facilitate effective analysis that will support the planning, improvement, and transformation of large and geographically distributed complex entities or enterprises.[95] Dr. Leon F. McGinnis, Professor of Manufacturing Systems at Georgia Institute of Technology, offered the following definition of EM:

> A loosely defined, emerging discipline focused on developing formal models of the enterprise as tools to use in decision making, and especially in designing and implementing software systems that support enterprise operations.[96]

Mark S. Fox and Michael Gruninger of the University of Toronto gave another explicit definition and explanation of the essence of enterprise modelling:

> An enterprise model is a computational representation of the structure, activities, processes, information, resources, people, behavior, goals, and constraints of a business, government, or other enterprise. It can be both descriptive and definitional – spanning what is and should be. The role of an enterprise model is to achieve model-driven enterprise design, analysis, and operation.[97]

Enterprise modelling (a methodology for IT strategic planning) has evolved into what is now called Enterprise Architecture (EA). EA is a well-developed framework or method that has comprehensive documentation and automated tools. In addition, EA is rigorously grounded in theory. Due to this transformation and its inherent strengths, enterprise modelling (now enterprise architecture) has become the de facto method for carrying out strategic IT planning in enterprises today.

One of the objectives of this section is to establish the relationship between strategic IT planning (called IT solutioning in this book) and enterprise architecture. Thus, this book will first provide a common and acceptable definition for EA from the solution-oriented and documentation-oriented perspectives.

Two definitions of EA will be presented from a solution-oriented perspective. The first definition is provided by the Institute of Electrical and Electronics Engineers (IEEE), who defined EA as 'the fundamental organization of a system embodied in its components, their relationships to each other and to the environment and the principles guiding its design and evolution.'[98]

The second solution-oriented definition of EA comes from Jeanne W. Ross, Peter Weill, and David C. Robertson in *Enterprise Architecture as Strategy*. They defined EA as 'the organising logic for business processes and IT infrastructure, reflecting the integration and standardisation requirements of the company's operating model.'[99] They also added that EA enables an enterprise to develop a long-term view of its capabilities—processes, systems, and technologies—so that they can embark on projects that build strategic capabilities instead of just fulfilling tactical needs.[100]

From a documentation-oriented perspective, Scott Bernard, assistant professor at Syracuse University, gave the only definition considered in this perspective, defining EA as 'the analysis and documentation of an enterprise in its current and future states from an integrated strategy, business, and technology perspective.'[101] He further stated that getting the most value from key enterprise resources, such as people, process, and technology, requires a shift in the way enterprises think about solving their problems, a shift from adopting a project-centric or tactical approach to adopting an holistic or enterprise-wide solutions approach, which corroborates the conclusion drawn by Ross, Weill, and Robertson above.

From the definitions above, it is evident that EA's main objective is to facilitate, support, and enable enterprise analysis or strategic IT planning so that enterprises are able to identify and design IT-enabled solutions that will help to achieve their enterprise-wide goals.

Following these definitions, the stage is now set for establishing the relationship between IT strategic planning and enterprise architecture (EA). EA is related to IT strategic planning because they both share a similar intent; both are high-level approaches concerned with capturing the current state of the enterprise architecture, defining the future state, and providing a road map for getting there.[102,103] Both approaches also generate similar deliverables such as business-aligned IT strategies, solution or information architecture, and so forth.[104]

Betsy Burton, vice president and distinguished analyst at Gartner Inc., concurred with EA's relation to strategic IT planning by pointing out that EA is not the same as strategic IT planning; rather, EA must support, facilitate, and enable IT strategic planning.[105] In addition to these statements, Capgemini, a top tier IT consulting firm and early pioneer of EA, confirmed both statements by pointing out that architecture helps to improve IT planning and the management of IT road maps (i.e., the sequencing of IT initiatives) and portfolios.[106]

Although IT strategic planning and enterprise architecture (EA) have a similar scope and objectives (high-level intent), there is a fundamental difference between the two approaches. This difference mainly concerns their scope and deliverables. While the scope of EA covers the whole enterprise, including the business and IT aspects of the enterprise, the scope of IT strategic planning covers only the IT aspect of the enterprise. The two disciplines also differ in their deliverables; the key outputs of the IT strategic planning process includes business-aligned IT strategy, enterprise solutions architecture, and an IT investment road map that informs enterprise programmes and budgets. On the other hand, the key outputs of EA consists of the current and future architectural descriptions of business (including business strategies), information, IT (including business-aligned IT strategies), and enterprise solutions architecture, including their individual road maps and technical standards.[107]

Based on these findings, it is now obvious that IT strategic planning and enterprise architecture complement each other, and there is great benefit in combining the elements of both to produce a new and revolutionary IT planning and management approach.[108] In short, EA is an enterprise analysis tool that can be used to support the IT strategic planning process by providing the information required for analysing the enterprise, helping to design the architecture of IT solutions identified during the IT strategic planning process, and helping to specify the technical standards that will guide the evolution of the solution. In support of the conclusion drawn above, Meta Group (now Gartner) stated that: 'A flexible enterprise architecture can provide a consistent framework for strategic decisions about the information technology used to support business initiatives.'[109]

Here are just a few of the frameworks or methodologies that exist today for developing the architecture of the enterprise:

- The Zachman Framework for Enterprise Architecture: focused on solution design

- The Open Group Architecture Framework (TOGAF): focused on achieving strategic alignment, identifying business and technology initiatives, and designing the solution architecture of the identified initiatives

- Capgemini Integrated Architecture Framework (IAF): focused on designing service-oriented solutions to enterprise problems

- Department of Defense Architecture Framework (DoDAF): an architecture framework for the United States Department of Defense

- Federal Enterprise Architecture (FEA): the enterprise architecture of the US Federal Government

Apart from helping enterprises govern their IT resources and enable, support or improve IT solutioning, EA also delivers the following benefits to enterprises:

1. EA helps enterprises to generate maximum value from their strategic IT investments by reducing IT investment and operation

costs, increasing IT investment project delivery success, and increasing IT responsiveness, enabling them to meet strategic business goals.

2. EA helps to reduce IT solutions development or implementation, operations, and maintenance costs[110,111] first by solving the integration and coordination problems across strategic business units (SBUs) through the use of EA/IT standards to guide IT investment decisions, or by managing IT resources throughout the enterprise, and second, by facilitating the sharing or reuse of IT resources across business units.[112,113]

3. EA helps to improve IT project delivery success[114] by facilitating the identification of the right strategic IT initiatives in order to do the right things and ensuring that the right things are done the right way through the design of effective solutions architecture for the identified strategic IT initiatives, which, in turn, helps to lower the risk of IT investment project failure.[115]

4. EA helps IT to become agile or responsive to business change[116,117] by increasing the ability of IT units to change quickly and easily to meet changing business requirements, which, in turn, helps the enterprises to become flexible; as a result, enterprises are now able to adapt quickly to new or emerging conditions.[118]

In order to simplify the meaning of enterprise architecture (EA) and to state explicitly the value it delivers to the enterprise based on previous research, EA is now defined as a tool that helps to develop, optimise, and transform an enterprise through the following means:[119,120]

- *Develop Enterprise*
    - Facilitate business and IT strategy development and execution
        - Facilitate strategic enterprise analysis and synthesis
        - Enable the development of business & IT investment road maps

- o Enable business & technology *innovation* and *change* management
  - ▪ Provide a blueprint for developing business and IT capabilities
- o Enable IT value maximization (doing more with less)
- *Optimise Enterprise*
  - o Improve IT effectiveness
    - ▪ Improve alignment between business & IT
    - ▪ Improve IT governance
    - ▪ Support effective IT-enabled business solutions design
    - ▪ Shorten the time required to implement enterprise applications (ERP, CRM, BPM, SOA, and so forth)
  - o Improve IT efficiency (reduce IT costs)
    - ▪ Identify and eliminate duplicate IT assets
    - ▪ Enable the standardisation of IT infrastructure
    - ▪ Enable enterprise application interoperability
    - ▪ Improve IT sourcing or procurement
  - o Improve operational efficiency (reduce business costs)
    - ▪ Enable business process improvement
    - ▪ Enable the standardisation of business processes
    - ▪ Improve risk management (reduce enterprise complexity)
- *Transform Enterprise*
  - o Increase IT flexibility (enable business agility or accommodate dynamic business requirements)
  - o Improve IT responsiveness (reduce time-to-market for new solutions)
  - o Increase business agility (accelerate new mergers & acquisitions (M&As), develop new business capabilities, and market new products and services)

o Support business process re-engineering initiatives
   o Support business innovations that create new products or services, new value propositions, and new markets

What was initially considered the key strength or advantage (i.e., the availability of comprehensive documentation) of popular enterprise architecture methodologies, such as TOGAF, over other methodologies that support strategic IT planning has now grown to such an extent that it has become its Achilles' heel—the source of its weakness—instead of serving as a source of strength. As the documentation of the current release of the Open Group Architecture Framework (TOGAF) version 9 is now 744 pages long, it will take a die-hard enterprise architect to make sense of the entire framework, let alone apply it to strategic IT planning in a meaningful way. The complexity that arises from the overly detailed and constantly changing TOGAF documentation might be a reason why most enterprises choose to develop their own variants of the framework/methodology.

Critical Success Factors (CSFs) Method

The last strategic IT planning methodology reviewed in this book is the Critical Success Factors (CSFs), a methodology based upon the concept of "success factors" conceived by D. Ronald Daniel, former managing director of McKinsey & Company, to identify the information needs of chief executive officers.[121] John F. Rockart, Senior Lecturer Emeritus at the MIT Sloan School of Management, refined and renamed the concept "critical success factors" and pioneered its use as an information systems planning methodology that can help enterprises to direct their computer-based information systems development efforts toward the areas of critical concern to top management.[122]

From an enterprise perspective, the philosophical underpinning of the CSFs is that every enterprise has a limited number of key areas where the achievements of superior outcomes will help to ensure the successful execution of the enterprise strategy, or the achievement of enterprise goals.[123] Moreover, CSFs can be defined from the line manager's viewpoint as the few key result areas where the achievement of superior results will ensure the successful achievement of the line manager's goals.[124] Consequently, these numbers of key areas or few key activities denote those areas where the enterprise or its managers must give special consideration to in order to generate maximum value and to ensure enterprise's survival.

Organisations can use CSFs in a wide variety of ways. First, the enterprise can use the CSF's methodology to direct or support their strategic business planning efforts, or to identify the courses of actions or initiatives that are perfectly aligned to their objectives.[125,126] Second, the CSF's methodology can be used to identify the critical areas of concern or the major issues facing an enterprise that require the use of IT, or where IT can best be applied to deliver maximum impact,[127] thereby ensuring that IT resources are directed to areas important to enterprise success. It is obvious from the two aforementioned areas where enterprises can use the CSF method and that the method is an enterprise-wide strategic planning method, supporting both strategic business planning and strategic IT planning.

In order to apply the CSF's method effectively, the CSF method must be directed by a skilled analyst[128] who should be required to carry out the following sequence of activities:

1. Identify and seek clarifications with senior managers on key result areas (KRAs)—those areas where superior results are absolutely necessary for the organisation to achieve its vision or goals.[129,130] For example, based on its vision, an enterprise's KRAs might be customer loyalty, human capital, and quality service.

2. Determine how to measure success in the KRAs and then set objectives for those measures. This can be done by interviewing senior managers or going through existing business plan documents. During the interview with managers, agree on the strategic business objectives (SBOs) necessary to reach an organisation's goals. For example, the objective for the customer loyalty KRA

might be to increase the customer satisfaction rating from two (2) to four (4) in the next four years, where five (5) is the highest rating. Moreover, the objective for the human capital KRA might be to reduce employee turnover from 30 percent to 10 percent in two financial years.[131]

3. Identify the essential building blocks of the enterprise, or the *required* strategic business capabilities (SBCs). Examples include attracting, retaining, and developing the right customers (customer management) or hiring and retaining the right people (human resource management) *required* for achieving superior results in those key result areas.[132,133] Business capabilities are typically made up of a group of resources, such as people (their competencies or expertise), processes, information, systems (IT systems, reward systems, and so forth), and supporting infrastructure (buildings or power) and financial resources required to deliver business value or achieve positive results.[134,135]

4. Identify the current SBCs and analyse the gap between the current and the required SBCs, and then produce a report of this analysis, called the strategic business capabilities (SBCs) gap assessment report.

5. Based on the strategic business capabilities assessment report, identify the strategic business initiatives (SBIs) or action programmes (e.g., recruiting a competent human resources manager, training the customer service reps on how to interact with customers, re-engineering customer service, or gathering and distributing customer information) that should be carried out to close the gap between the *current* and *required* SBCs, or develop the business capabilities required to achieve strategic business objectives or to execute business strategy.[136]

6. Identify the business process automation and information needs or requirements critical to the development of the SBCs required to implement the business strategy or to achieve strategic business

objectives. Use this to devise strategic IT objectives (SITOs) or to identify IT goals that must be achieved in order to develop strategy business capabilities. For example, an enterprise's strategic IT objectives might be to provide up-to-date information about customer profitability and satisfaction, provide up-to-date information about employee retention percentages, and so forth.[137]

7. Identify the strategic IT capabilities (SITCs) required to achieve specific strategic IT objectives. Examples of these types of SITCs might be customer information management, employee information management, and so forth.

8. Identify the current SITCs and analyse the gap between the required and current SITCs, and then produce a report of this analysis: the strategic IT capabilities gap assessment report.

9. Based on the strategic IT capabilities gap assessment report, identity the strategic IT initiatives (SITIs) or applications software (e.g., human resources management system [HRMS] or customer relationship management [CRM] system) that should be implemented to deliver the IT capabilities, that, in turn, will help to achieve the strategic IT objectives.[138,139]

Based on the argument of Bredemeyer and Malan, identifying and documenting the current business and technology capabilities of an enterprise as well as the enterprise capabilities—business and technology required to execute business strategies—should be the responsibility of an enterprise architect.[140] Consequently, this book recommends that a team of skilled CSF analysts and an enterprise architect should carry out the sequence of steps outlined above.

The CSF methodology has three major advantages over other strategic IT planning methodologies. First, the CSF methodology is easier to understand and use by senior managers compared to other methodologies.[141] Second, the method's flexibility makes it easy to tailor it. Third, the method does not require rigorous analyses during its usage.[142] Because of all these advantages, senior managers in most enterprises favour this method when identifying their critical areas of concern.

The CSF method also has two major drawbacks. The first drawback is that the obvious strength of the CSF method—that is, its flexibility—may cause enterprises to neglect the application of the methodology; they might adopt an overly casual approach in their application of the method.[143] The second drawback is that the success or quality of the CSF effort depends largely on the skill of the CSF analysts or the individual directing the CSF exercise, which, in turn, is dependent on the quality of the dialogue between the analysts and the manager. The quality of this dialogue can be improved if the CSF analysts develop an in-depth knowledge of the industry and organisation of the enterprise under consideration.

Problems with Existing Strategic IT Planning Methodologies

According to Michael J. Earl, Professor of Information Management at the University of Oxford, the majority of strategic IT planning methodologies that exist today, including those mentioned in this book, suffer from three (3) major categories of issues: method, process, and implementation.[144] Method-oriented issues are the problems emanating from underlying principles upon which the methodologies were developed and from the techniques, approaches, and processes adopted by the methodologies, which are reflected in the output. Process-oriented issues are the problems that arise from the insufficient support (i.e., participation) given to the methodology process by the users and line managers (e.g., poor top management support, poor user involvement, and so forth). Finally, implementation-oriented issues are the problems arising from the ineffective integration of people, process, and resources required to perform strategic IT planning (e.g., technological constraints and incomplete implementation).

Because the process and implementation issues categorised by Earl cannot easily be resolved through the development of a new method, this book will focus mainly on the detailed discovery and analysis of method-oriented issues, with the intent of justifying the need for a new strategic IT planning method that will help to solve identified issues. During an extensive research of existing literature in the subject area, the following method-oriented issues that inhibit the success of strategic IT planning methodologies were discovered (this list is not meant to be exhaustive and can be expressed in other terms):

1. They are unable to cope with situations where business strategy does not exist or with the changing nature of business strategies[145] because most of the methodologies assume that enterprises are involved in some sort of business planning that enables them to have business strategies in place; as a result, the lack of business strategies poses a big threat to these strategic IT planning methodologies.[146]

2. They lack well-defined and documented methodologies that show how the output from one phase translates into the input for the next phase (i.e., that depicts the input/output relationship between their phases).[147]

3. The development of the methodologies is not based on a rigorous theoretical framework.[148]

4. The successful implementation of the methodologies or the quality of the methodologies output is dependent on the team leader rather than on the specificity (i.e., the description of the steps to follow in applying the methodologies) and robustness of the methodologies.[149]

5. The application of the methodologies takes too much time and effort, or requires a large team, to complete.[150]

6. The methodologies are not sufficient in themselves, as their output still requires further analysis.[151]

7. The methodologies did not make provisions for assessing whether current and planned IT capabilities are capable of supporting the execution of business strategies.

8. The methodologies were developed in isolation; as a result, they do not integrate well with other methodologies (e.g., governance,

enterprise project management, IT services, and so forth) that are essential to the realisation of value from strategic IT investments. Because the methodologies were developed without consideration of other activities or methodologies that are essential to generating value from IT, they are not able to help enterprises answer questions about what comes before and after strategic IT planning.

In conclusion, the strategic IT planning process and the IT solutioning process are one and the same, and this book has adjudged IT solutioning to be the best term that perfectly expresses the purpose of IT strategic planning without much mental effort. It is interesting to note that all of the key inhibitors of the strategic IT planning methodologies identified above are the inverse of the factors that are critical to the success of the strategic IT planning effort (now called IT solutioning) in enterprises.

Tactical IT Planning (from an Integrated Perspective)

Tactical planning, the second stage in the IT planning process, receives input from two major sources. First, it takes the output of the IT solutioning or strategic IT planning process; that is, it takes the strategic IT initiatives-cum-solutions as its input. Second, it accepts input from functional business units in the form of request to invest in tactical IT initiatives-cum-solutions that provide information or automate business transactions that will help to run and maintain the enterprise or to achieve functional or operational objectives. Both the strategic and tactical IT investment solutions-cum-projects are then evaluated based on their business cases, after which they are either approved or disapproved with justifiable reasons. Consequently, the approved solutions (now called IT investment projects) are then allocated the requisite funds or resources needed for their delivery, while the rejected solutions are either reviewed or abandoned. This process is now commonly referred to as project portfolio management (PPM), or simply IT portfolio management.

According to Peter Weill and Margrethe H. Olson, an enterprise gets the opportunity to invest in IT-enabled enterprise solutions from three major sources.[152] The first opportunity usually originates from the CEO in a top-down approach, especially in organisations where the enterprise strategy also includes the objective to exploit IT. The second impetus for IT investment comes from the enterprise's functional business units in a bottom-up approach, especially in situations where lower-level managers could not complete their day-to-day transactions using existing IT capabilities. The third opportunity for investing in IT can also originate from business divisions or strategic business units (SBUs) in a middle-down approach, especially for large and multidivisional enterprises, where most times IT investment decisions are left to the SBUs.

Michael John Earl affirmed the top-down and bottom-up approach for IT investment opportunities identification, and related them to the concepts of strategic and tactical IT planning discussed earlier in this book.[153] Nevertheless, he went further to suggest another approach, which is the inside-out innovation approach. He argued that the objective of the inside-out approach is to identify opportunities afforded by IT, which can yield competitive advantage or create new strategic options.

Bryan Maizlish and Robert Handler, in *IT Project Portfolio Management Step-by-Step*, supported the arguments presented above to a large degree when they suggested that IT investment opportunities should be identified using two main approaches.[154] The first approach they recommended was the strategic, also referred to as the top-down approach, where strategic IT initiatives usually originate from the CEO. The second approach was the tactical, also referred to as the bottom-up approach, where IT investment opportunities emerge from the lower levels of the organisation. This approach leverages existing and planned IT assets and investment projects in the pipeline to define the architecture of new tactical IT investment initiatives-cum-solutions that will help the organisation to achieve its tactical (run and maintain) objectives or to lay the foundation for the achievement of strategic (grow and transform) objectives.

Although enterprises' invest in both strategic and tactical IT investment initiatives, be they mandated by regulations or discretional, the focus of this book is solely on discretional strategic IT investment initiatives.

In summary, the portfolio of IT initiatives that are identified by the IT solutioning team belong to the portfolio of strategic IT initiatives, while those identified by line-of-business managers belong to the portfolio of tactical IT initiatives. This book, then, will regard the combination of these two portfolios as the portfolio of enterprise IT initiatives.[155] However, it is good to note that strategic IT investment initiatives and tactical (i.e., informational and transactional) IT investment initiatives differ in the way they are evaluated.[156]

The strategic IT initiatives in this portfolio are checked for their business viability or feasibility, which means they are checked for alignment with business strategy and EA/IT standards. And both strategic and tactical IT initiatives are checked for technical feasibility or achievability; and finally, both categories of initiatives are checked for their financial feasibility or desirability, which means they are checked for their cost/benefit/risk profile.[157,158] Assessing the business, technical, and financial feasibility of both strategic and tactical IT initiatives should be the major function of the enterprise solutions architecture development team, and the end result of this process should be the architecture of feasible (business, technically, or financially) strategic and tactical IT solutions (see chapter six for more details). Because tactical IT investment projects are not the focus of this book, further references to tactical IT investment projects will be discontinued from this point going forward.

Each of the feasible strategic IT solutions in the strategic IT solutions portfolio—that is, portfolio of potential strategic IT projects—are then evaluated based on the content of their business cases and as a portfolio of investment opportunities. And if they are approved, they now become the strategic IT programmes or projects in which the enterprise will invest. In order to deliver and manage the entire life cycle of their portfolio of strategic IT projects, enterprises might need to set up a database or repository to maintain up-to-date, accurate, and easily accessible information about all the approved, on-going, and delivered strategic IT investment projects.

The evaluation of strategic IT investment initiatives-cum-solutions has two major outcomes. The first outcome of this evaluation is a consolidated list or portfolio of approved IT projects that have been re-prioritised or sequenced according to the prevalent business objectives/goals, conditions, and risk appetite, without losing sight of the technical dependencies between the solutions in the portfolio,[159] (see chapter four for more details). The second outcome is the list of strategic IT investment initiatives-cum-solutions whose business cases have failed to meet the enterprise's strategic IT investment evaluation criteria, and, as a result, they have been recommended for re-work or expulsion from the portfolio of IT solutions.

Operational IT Planning and Execution

Operational IT planning and execution is the third and final stage in the IT planning process that accepts the output of the tactical IT planning process—the approved IT project portfolios, their solution architecture, and project implementation plans. Consequently, the deliverables of the tactical IT plan are executed based on their specific sourcing and funding distribution or strategy, and the pre-selected project management and software development or package application implementation methodology to deliver the IT programmes and projects contained in the IT project portfolio (i.e., to translate IT programme and projects into IT systems). Accordingly, the delivered IT systems are then also translated into IT services at the IT operationalization step of the IT investment management life cycle, which now becomes a member of the enterprise's IT services portfolio (see chapter five for more details).

Rational Steps for IT Solutioning

In an earlier section of this book, the development of IT solutioning capability was identified as one of five critical success factors for managing IT investments successfully and generating maximum business/organisational value.

Subsequently, in earlier sections of this book, it was discovered that the availability and application of the right methodologies to support or enable the development of IT solutioning capabilities are critical to the successful performance of IT solutioning. In short, IT solutioning methodologies are comparable to having a blueprint for developing the ability of enterprises to perform IT solutioning—that is, to use IT to solve enterprise problems.

Although many IT solutioning methodologies exist today to help enterprises develop IT solutioning capabilities and perform IT solutioning, almost all of these methodologies have inherent limitations.

Due to the problems that are associated with the available IT solutioning or strategic IT planning methodologies, this book has developed a new methodology that will help enterprises to overcome the eight (8) IT solutioning methodologies challenges identified above. This new method will simply be referred to as the rational IT solutioning system or capability model.

The rational IT solutioning system is the prescription for developing excellent IT solutioning capability and for performing IT solutioning. This prescription consists of best practice IT solutioning processes, their input and output (i.e., informational raw materials and products), the people responsible or accountable for their performance, and the systems and tools required to support them. Two notable academicians—Albert L. Lederer, a professor at the University of Kentucky, and Hannu Salmela, a professor at the Turku School of Economics—corroborated the fact that strategic IS/IT planning accepts input in the form of business strategies (strategic business objectives and key action programmes) and business resources, processes these inputs, and generates output.[160]

Rational IT Solutioning Capability Model or Method

The rational IT solutioning method or capability model is a model that consists of four (4) major steps: clarify business strategy, formulate IT strategy, architect strategic IT-enabled enterprise solutions (or architect strategic IT solutions), and manage strategic IT solutions portfolio (see Figure 3.0). Each of the steps is an entity in itself, with each having its own goal, requiring specific input and producing their own unique benefits and outputs/deliverables. In addition, each step requires people with specific skills, tools, and procedures for performing its tasks. Going forward, IT-enabled enterprise solutions will now be called IT solutions for the sake of simplicity and space.

Critical Input for the Rational IT Solutioning Method or Capability Model

Business strategies and the outcome of the analysis of the gap between the business capability required to achieve business strategies and the existing business capability are the main internal inputs, aside from other external input, such as IT trends, available external IT capabilities, and so forth, into the IT solutioning process.

Business Strategy

Despite the significance of business strategy to provide focus and direction to organisations to accomplish their mission and fulfil their vision, the domain of business strategies has suffered so many tragedies, mainly from the lack of clarity in its meaning. According to John McGee et al., strategy receives a lot of attention, recognition, and acknowledgement, and yet no single and mutually acceptable definition of strategy exists.[161]

In order to avoid this confusion, this book will seek to find common patterns among the numerous definitions of strategy and use these patterns as the basis for understanding strategy. Alfred D. Chandler, renowned Harvard Business School Professor, propounded the first definition of strategy in 1963: he defined strategy as 'the determination of the basic long-term goals and objectives of an enterprise and the adoption of the courses of action and the allocation of resources necessary for carrying out these goals.'[162] His definition is the most common and, to some degree, the most acceptable definition of strategy, often referred to as the classical view of strategy simply because it is rational in analysis and follows militarist ideologies.[163]

The second definition of strategy considered in this book was propounded in 1977 by George A. Steiner, Professor Emeritus at UCLA Anderson School of Management, and John B. Miner, a former professor at the University of Oregon. They defined strategy as

> the formulation of basic organisational missions, purposes, and objectives; policies and program strategies to achieve them; and the methods needed to ensure that strategies are implemented to achieve organisational ends.[164]

In 1980, William F. Glueck, Professor of Management at the University of Missouri-Columbia, propounded the third definition of strategy considered in this book. He defined strategy as 'a unified, comprehensive, and integrated plan designed to ensure that the basic objectives of the enterprise are achieved.'[165]

From the three definitions of strategy presented above, three common key elements have emerged:

1. The determination of business objectives, or *the end*

2. The identification of courses of action, or *the means* to achieve *the end* (business objectives)

3. The allocation of resources for executing the courses of action

Results of Business Capability Assessment

In order to identify what must be done (i.e., the strategic business initiatives) to achieve their strategic business objectives successfully; enterprises must assess the gap that exists between the business capabilities (i.e., the human, organisation, information, and financial capital) that are required to achieve their strategic business objectives or execute their business strategies and their current business capabilities. According to Larry Bossidy, Charles Burck, and Ram Charan in *Execution*, 'An astonishing number of strategies fail because leaders don't make a realistic assessment of whether the organization can execute the plan.'[166] Furthermore, they argued, enterprises should assess if they have the right people, processes, and systems to execute their strategic plan successfully.

Packaging the Input of the IT Solutions Method or Capability Model

A team of business leaders usually performs the strategic business planning process or formulates business strategies.[167] They do this by selecting business goals, specifying the business objectives that must be met to achieve the goals, identifying the business capabilities required to achieve the objectives, assessing current business capabilities, analysing the gap between the required and the current business capabilities. Next, business and IT leaders identify the business or technology initiatives that will help to develop the missing business or IT capabilities and close the gap.

Following the development of the enterprises' strategies, the CIO/CEA should at the same time develop the IT strategy (i.e., objectives and initiatives), and tactical plan required to enable the achievement of the business objectives.[168] This implies that, following the formulation of the business strategy, the IT solutioning process should be initiated to formulate an appropriate IT strategy using the business strategy as its input and leveraging the enterprise's IT solutioning governance decisions and the governance architecture that has been designed. According to William R. King, 'The process of MIS strategic planning is one of transforming the Organizational Strategy Set into an appropriate, relevant, and consistent MIS Strategy Set.'[169]

The components of business strategy that serve as input for the IT solutioning process are as follows:

1. Strategic Business Objectives (SBOs)
2. Strategic Business Capability (SBC) Gap Assessment Report
3. Strategic Business Initiatives (SBIs)
4. Business Sourcing Policy
5. Business Funding Policy (BFP)

From the above list of strategic business planning output, only the strategic business capability gap assessment report, the business funding policy (BFP), and the business sourcing policy will actually serve as input for the IT solutioning process; the remaining output is needed to facilitate communication about business strategy with the IT unit.

According to the Open Group, 'A business capability assessment is used to define what capabilities an organisation will need to fulfil its business goals and business drivers.'[170] The Open Group also pointed out that once the current and desired business capabilities are understood, their likely implications for the organisation's technology capability can be assessed, creating an initial picture of new IT capability that will be required to support the Target Architecture Vision.[171]

THE SECOND RATIONAL STEP: IT SOLUTIONING

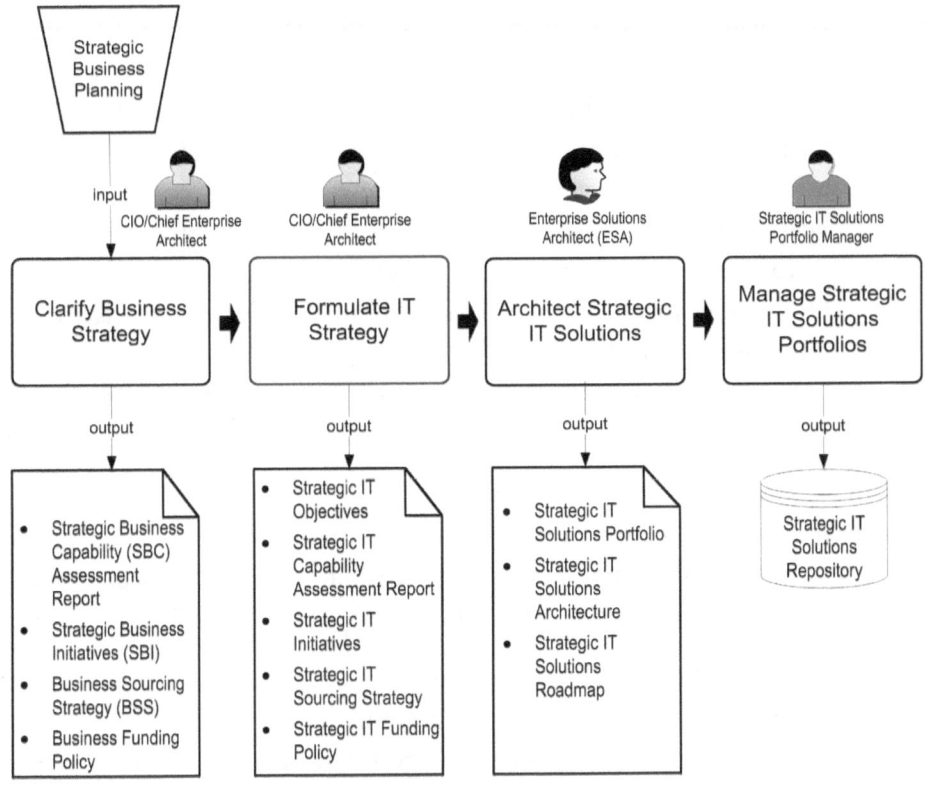

Figure 3.0 Rational IT Solutioning Capability Model

Rational IT Solutioning Capability Model or Method Steps

1. *Clarify Business Strategy:* The goal of this step is to understand the business strategies that set the direction of the business. This process requires the understanding of strategic business objectives and the current business capabilities, assessing the gap between the business capabilities required to achieve the objectives and the current business capabilities. This process also requires the identification of the business initiatives that will help to develop the missing components of the business capabilities (e.g., competent people, formal processes, information, and IT systems) required to close that gap (see the critical success factor section above for a detailed analysis).

2. *Formulate IT Strategy:* The main goal of this step is to formulate an IT strategy that is aligned with the business strategy. This step involves specifying strategic IT objectives and identifying strategic IT-enabled business initiatives required to develop the strategic IT-enabled business capabilities that will provide the missing components of the business capabilities required to achieve strategic business objectives or execute business strategy. It is, however, important to note that IT strategy formulation occurs in a constantly changing environment; as a result, formulating IT strategy is not an event, but a continuous and dynamic process that is constantly being refreshed and modified to reflect a dynamic environment.[172]

3. *Architect Strategic IT Solutions:* The main goal of this step is to translate the strategic IT initiatives identified at the IT strategy formulation step into a portfolio of technically feasible strategic IT-enabled business solutions (simply referred to as strategic IT solutions).

4. *Manage IT Solutions Portfolio:* The main goal of this step is to gather all the artefacts (i.e., the documentation) produced during the entire IT solutioning process, store them in the strategic IT solutions repository, and manage the currency of the repository.

Clarify Business Strategy

Eliciting, understanding, and agreeing on business strategy is a critical first step in the IT solutioning process (also called strategic IS/IT planning)[173,174] because without a clear understanding of the business strategy, it is almost impossible to create an IT strategy that is aligned with or derived from business strategies. According to Richard Hunter and George Westerman in *The Real Business of IT*, 'When the strategy is clear, it will also be clear how an IT organisation that delivers value for money can deliver improved business performance.'[175] Consequently, without aligning IT to business strategy, organisations runs the risk of delivering IT systems or projects that may be unrelated to the overall objectives of the organisation; as a result, the chances of generating maximum value from the completed IT investment project might be limited, or the completed project may be of limited value to the organisation.[176] Peter Weill and Jeanne W. Ross also agreed that enterprises must clarify business strategy prior to formulating IT strategy.[177] They asserted that one of the ways in which top performing organisations generate up to a 40 percent return on their IT investments is by clarifying their business strategies and identifying the role of IT in achieving them.

Although clarifying business strategy is the critical first step in the IT solutioning process, it is also one of the most difficult steps to perform due to the reasons given by Albert L. Lederer and Aubrey L. Mendelow:[178]

1. *Lack of formal business strategy*: Most organisations lack a formal strategic business planning process, which means that a documented—corporate, competitive, and functional—strategy may not even exist.

2. *Dynamic nature of business strategy*: A business strategy may exist, but it changes too frequently.

3. *Lack IT involvement in business strategy formulation*: In most organisations, IT managers are usually not involved in business strategy formulation efforts, or they are not part of the group of people who formulate business strategies.

4. *Poor communication of business strategy*: Top management in most organisations doesn't communicate the business strategies to IT management because of the fear of losing control, the need to maintain confidentiality, or the inability of top management to communicate the business strategies in a way that IT personnel can understand.

Gartner conducted research on 179 EA practitioners as respondents in order to ascertain how well they understood their firm's business strategy and found the following:[179]

- Ten (10) percent don't know the state of their business strategy, and 1 percent stated that they don't have a business strategy.

- Sixteen (16) percent stated that they hear different ideas from senior management, but the strategy is not clearly communicated.

- Forty-four (44) percent stated that they have a business strategy, but it is not broadly understood or supported.

- Thirty-three (33) percent stated that their business strategy is well understood.

The chief information officer (CIO) should be accountable for clarifying business strategy, though he or she can also choose to be responsible for this activity at the same time, or he or she can choose to delegate this responsibility to the chief enterprise architect (CEA). The person responsible for this activity should endeavour to perform the business strategy pre-clarification screening in accordance with the steps depicted in Figure 3.1 before clarifying, eliciting, understanding, and seeking concurrence on the business strategies that will serve as input for the IT strategy formulation.

Enterprises need to pre-clarify business strategies because of the availability of business strategy, the unavailability of business strategy, the stable or dynamic nature of business strategy, and the different types of business strategies call for different types of clarification approaches and techniques.

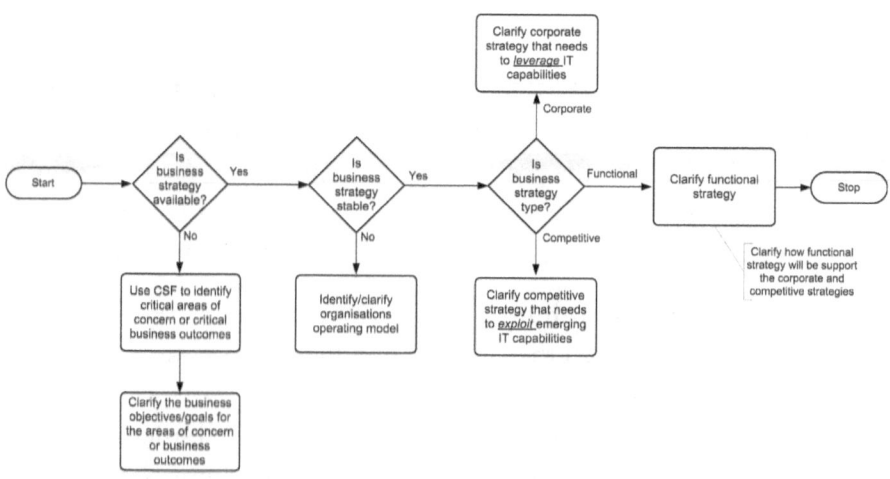

Figure 3.1 Business Strategy Pre-clarification Screening Flowchart

Screening 1: Business Strategy is Unavailable. If an enterprise does not have a formal business strategy, the IT manager (CIO or CEA) should use the Critical Success Factors (CSFs) methodology to identify a manageable number of top management's critical areas of concerns, those areas where the achievement of favourable results will help to ensure managerial or organisational success.[180,181]

Consequently, the IT manager can proceed to ascertain the strategic goals that top management seeks to achieve in those critical areas, after which the manager identifies the business capabilities requiring IT support (i.e., strategic IT-enabled business capabilities) necessary to achieve those goals. Next, the manager moves on to assess IT's ability to support the required business capability or need and to identify the gap between the IT capabilities that are needed and those currently in place.[182]

Furthermore, IT managers also need to identify the information measures that reflect the achievement of top management objectives in those critical areas—that is, to identify key outcomes or performance indicators. Finally, IT managers develop the list of strategic IT investment initiatives, or portfolios of strategic IT projects needed to develop the capabilities required to achieve success in the critical areas of concern or to improve the outcomes.

Screening 2: Business Strategy is Available and Unstable. If business strategies exist but are not stable enough to base the formulation of IT strategy upon or to guide IT investment decisions, the IT manager should identify and clarify the operating model of the organisation instead. Jeanne W. Ross, Peter Weill, and David C. Robertson, in *Enterprise Architecture as Strategy,* defined an operating model as 'the necessary level of business process integration and standardization for delivering goods and services to customers.'[183]

According to Ross et al., business strategies have many different aspects to consider, from making decisions about which market segment to compete in to deciding on how the company should be positioned in each of the choosing market segments, and, most often times, it extends to deciding which capabilities the business enterprise should build and exploit. Furthermore, strategic priorities can change as business enterprises try to counter the effects of competitors' initiatives or to seize new and emerging opportunities. Hence, business strategy seldom provides a stable direction for the development of business and technology capabilities.

Therefore, in order for businesses to support strategies effectively, Ross et al. recommended that they define the model of how they will operate (i.e., an operating model). In their final analysis, they argued that focusing on the operating model rather than on individual strategies provides businesses a better and more stable guiding beacon for directing the formulation of IT strategies or the development of IT capabilities and by implication for investing in IT.[184]

Screening 3: Business Strategy is Available and Stable. If business strategies exists and are stable, the IT manager should seek clarification on the choice of business strategy or a combination of business strategies—corporate, strategic business unit (SBU), or functional—the organisation wants to focus on. Based on the choice of the organisation, the IT manager can seek further clarification on the strategies.

If the organisation's focus is on the execution of its corporate strategy, then the IT manager should seek clarification on the corporate strategy and the organisation's vision for leveraging IT to execute the strategy, or the IT manager should seek to clarify the role IT should play in the execution of the corporate strategy.

Furthermore, if the organisation's focus is on competitive strategy, the IT manager should elicit, understand, and agree on the competitive strategy of the organisation, as well as understand the organisation's vision for leveraging existing IT capabilities and for *exploiting* emerging IT capabilities to support the execution of its competitive strategy.

Finally, if the organisation's focus is on functional strategies, the IT manager should focus on eliciting, understanding, and gaining consensus on the functional strategy (i.e., the line of business/functional business unit manager's goals and tactical initiatives) and, if possible, establish the alignment between the functional strategy and competitive strategy.

The clarify business strategy processes consists of two major deliverables that serve as input into the next stage of the IT solutioning process—that is, the IT strategy formulation stage. The first of these deliverables is the strategic business capability (SBC) gap assessment report, the report of the gap that exists between the current strategic business capability (c.SBC) and the strategic business capability required (r.SBC) to achieve the strategic business objectives or execute an organisation's strategies. The second deliverable is the list of strategic business initiatives (SBIs) that will be executed to develop the capabilities required to close the gaps identified in the strategic business capability assessment report.

Formulate IT Strategy

IT strategy formulation is a dynamic and continuous process; as a result, enterprises and their IT managers must actively manage this process for it to be effective.[185] The process should never be mistaken for a static or one-time event or exercise, as the process takes its major input from all the strategies of an enterprise, which in turn is dependent on the dynamisms of its surrounding environment.

Therefore, as soon as IT managers (CIO or CEA) have elicited, understood, and concurred on the business strategies on which to focus and the organisation's vision for exploiting, leveraging, or using IT to support the execution of enterprise strategy, the CEA can now formulate the IT strategy using the framework depicted in Figure 3.2.

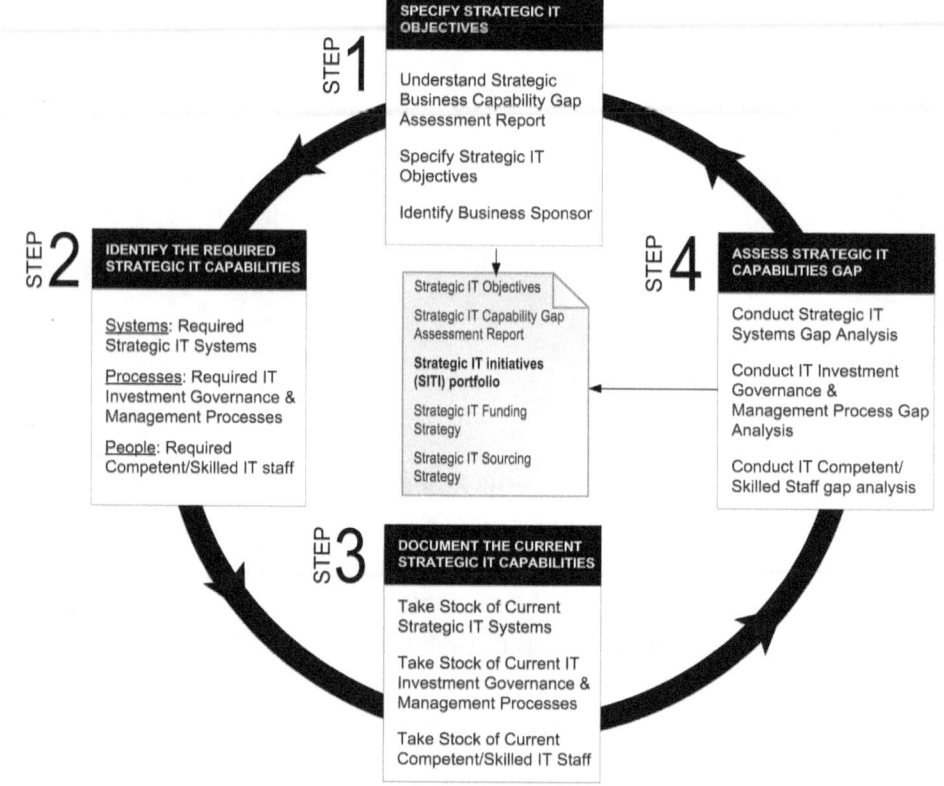

Figure 3.2 IT Strategy Formulation Framework

Enterprise Architecture (EA) documentation or an EA program office that maintains the repository of information about business strategies, current strategic business and technology capabilities, and assets portfolios will help to speed up the strategy formulation process tremendously—up to 50 percent.

This is one of the reasons why setting up an EA program office or maintaining a living EA document is recognised as a critical factor in the success of strategic IT planning efforts. According to Forrester Research, 'A well-defined business architecture creates a common view of business capabilities, processes, and strategic needs for business and IT leaders.'[186]

Architect Strategic IT Solutions

Following the identification of the strategic IT initiatives needed to develop the IT capabilities required to achieve IT objectives, the enterprise solution architect (ESA) works collaboratively with other architects (infrastructure, security, technology, vertical, and enterprise architects), and solutions owner to translate the strategic IT initiatives into a technically feasible portfolio of strategic IT solutions (see Figure 3.3 below).[187]

For example, the ESA might need an infrastructure architect (IA) to manage the architecture of the strategic IT solution's hardware and network configuration so that the solution meets the specified quality of service and business and IT requirements. The IA might also be needed to design an optimum way to deploy the solution into the target production environments.[188] In addition, the ESA might enlist the help of a "specialist" or domain architect, such as a security architect, technology architect (that specialises in specific products), or a vertical architect (that specialises in particular industries vertical), depending on the complexity of the business requirements or the target production environment.[189]

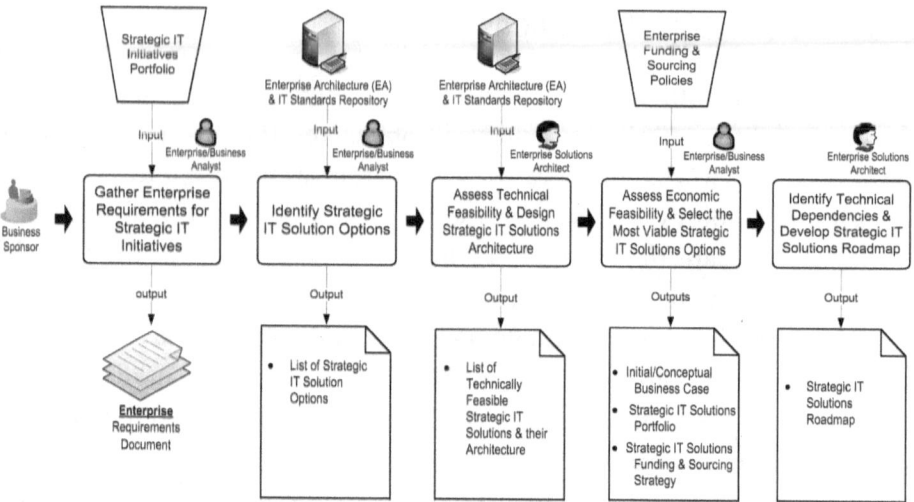

Figure 3.3 Architect Strategic IT Solutions

Manage Strategic IT Solutions Portfolio

Following the completion of the IT solutioning process, the IT solutions portfolio manager gathers all the output of the process or the artefacts generated by the activities of the IT solutioning process, stores them in the strategic IT solutioning repository, and manages the processes for keeping them up-to-date.

THE SECOND RATIONAL STEP: IT SOLUTIONING

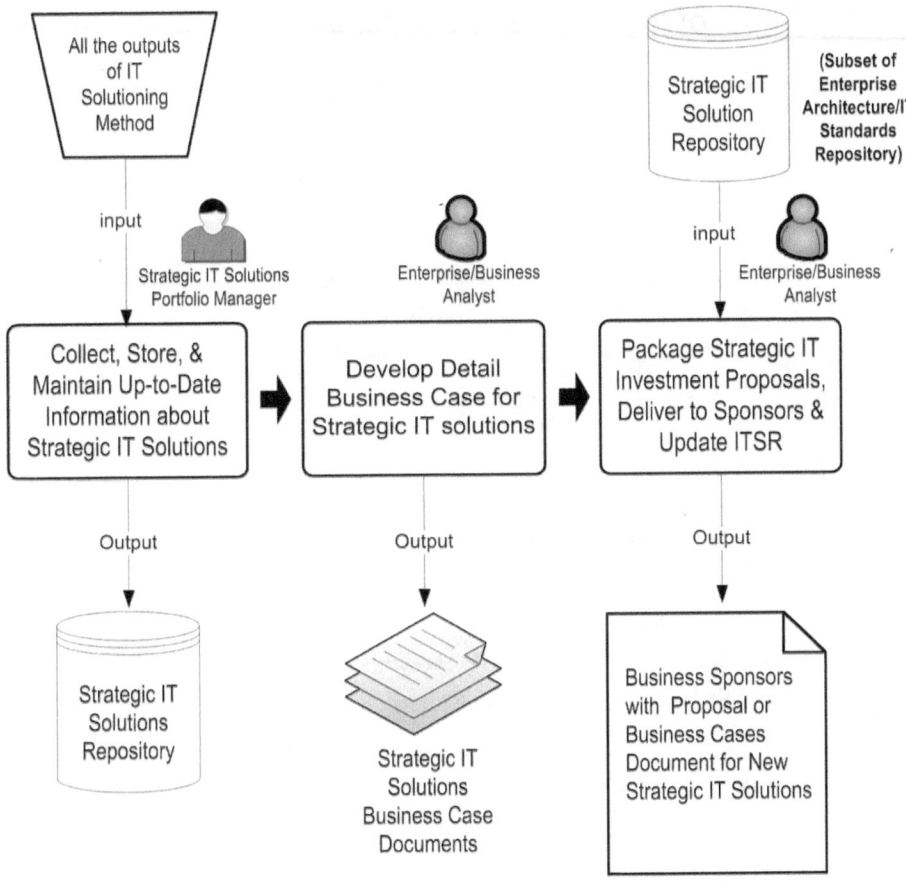

Figure 3.4 Manage IT Solutions Portfolio

Critical Output of the Rational IT Solutioning Method

The critical output or artefacts of the IT solutioning process according to the individual's activities are as follows:

- Clarify Business Strategy
    - Strategic Business Capability (SBC) Assessment Report
    - Strategic Business Initiatives (SBIs)
    - Business Sourcing Strategy (BSS)
    - Business Funding Policy

- Formulate IT Strategy
    - Strategic IT Objectives
    - Strategic IT Capability Assessment Report
    - Strategic IT Initiatives
    - Strategic IT Sourcing Strategy
    - Strategic IT Funding Policy

- Architect Strategic IT Solutions
    - Strategic IT Solutions Portfolio
    - Strategic IT Solutions Architecture
    - Strategic IT Solutions Road Map

- Manage Strategic IT Solutions Portfolio
    - Strategic IT Solutions Repository

Summary

Enterprises need to develop the ability to formulate IT strategy that is aligned to their business strategies in order to manage their investments in IT successfully and generate maximum value. This ability will help to ensure that enterprises are *doing the right things*: that is, enterprises are investing in strategic IT investment initiatives that will help to achieve their strategic business objectives. IT solutioning will also help to ensure that enterprises are investing in strategic IT initiatives that are technically, financially, and business feasible so that the selected strategic IT investment initiatives-cum-solutions *are done the right way*.

Case Study 3.0

Hess Corporation, founded in 1919 as an integrated oil company based in New York City, is engaged in oil exploration, production, transport and refines crude oil and natural gas. The IT unit of Hess Corp. has eighty application developers with fifty employees supporting its infrastructure, with a total budget of $45 million.

Following the appointment of Jeff Steinhorn as the new CIO to head the IT organisation of its marketing and refining division, the division discovered six (6) major challenges with the way in which they invest in IT.[190] The division's current IT investment is based on a short-term approach to project planning, an approach that is focused on the individual investment needs of each business division. As a result of the adoption of this approach, Jeff Steinhorn found that the IT unit now faces the following six (major) challenges:

1. The IT group could not determine the IT systems, equipment, or resources required to support its near-term initiatives.

2. IT investment projects to deliver new systems or enhance existing ones take a long time to deliver.

3. The IT system in each of the divisions do not share common customer and market information with each other—that is, they are not integrated.

4. The IT group could not evaluate IT investment projects based on how each project might affect the overall IT infrastructure.

5. It was not clear how Hess Corp.'s IT investment projects support the achievement of its long-term or strategic business objectives, or how IT projects align with its long-term objectives.

6. The IT organisation of Hess Corp.'s marketing and refining division was perceived as a low-cost provider. The IT organisation was also perceived to be conversant with investing only in small-scale IT investment initiatives.

To solve the problems with the IT unit of Hess Corp., the new CIO, Jeff Steinhorn, decided to embark on the following initiatives:

1. Develop an IT strategy that will allow Hess Corp. to figure out how IT will support or enable the achievement of strategic business objectives or the execution of business strategies over the next five years.

2. Get executive buy-in into strategic IT investment projects by getting them to quantify the anticipated benefits.

3. Establish an integration framework to connect the common systems used by various business units within the division—that is, the Hess marketing and refining group.

4. Adopt standardised application development, project management, and IT governance methodologies.

Following the change from a project-centric or bottom-up (tactical) approach to investing in IT to a top-down (strategic) approach and the adoption of standardised methodologies, Hess Corp. recorded the following benefits:

- Improved alignment of Hess IT group's investment projects with its business strategy

- Hess IT group now possesses the platform and the environment to grow with the business and become more agile

- Improved economies of scale due to the standardisation of hardware and software across Hess marketing and refining group's multiple business units

- Within the first nine months of Hess IT group's strategic planning efforts, the IT group has completed seven of the seventeen IT investment projects they kicked, which include a major SAP upgrade and a retail energy system reconfiguration

- IT-enabled business investment projects (i.e., business-related projects) are expected to deliver tens of millions of dollars in business benefits once they've been completed

- Business perceptions of IT have changed; there is now equal partnership between IT and the rest of the business; IT group now goes to the business and they partner on ideas

Case Study 3.1

The Commonwealth of Virginia, a US state on the Atlantic Coast of the Southern United States, was founded in 1607 in Jamestown. Since its early beginnings, Virginia has grown and prospered into a thriving state, rich with diversity from culture to climate.

> The Commonwealth of Virginia is continually striving to improve its competitive position in the national and global marketplace and to provide the best environment for economic development and quality of life for citizens. Virginia's investment in information technologies plays a critical supporting role in reaching the state's business goals as well as in maintaining Virginia's position as best-managed state in the nation.[191]

In 2007, Virginia Information Technologies (IT) Agency decided to develop a five-year strategic IT plan (2007–2011) to offer technology direction and guidance for the rest of the state agencies and institutions, and to provide a solid foundation upon which to base the IT investment decisions that support the state's business direction.

Strategic IT Plan Development Process

Approach

VITA set up a strategic planning workgroup team to be responsible for the development of the strategic plan. In order to develop the plan, the workgroup gathered a fair number of external and internal stakeholders across Virginia that would be affected by or who would affect the outcome of the plan. The stakeholders were drawn from the following:[192]

1. Virginia citizen and business representatives
2. Virginia government and IT leaders
3. Council on Technology Services (COTS) members
4. Higher education representatives
5. Legislators and legislative staff

The workgroup conducted numerous workshops and one-on-one sessions with these stakeholders totalling 150 people in order to elicit their IT needs (or enterprise requirements) be it strategic, informational, transactional, or both, that arose from their IT-related problems, challenges, issues, and trends.

Following the elicitation of Virginia's enterprise requirements for IT, the strategic IT planning workgroup conducted another set of workshops with IT vendors in order to elicit their perspective on leading-edge technologies that can help the state to actualise its enterprise requirements. During this workshop, all the vendors presented their latest solution offerings to the workgroup. In concluding the technical perspective elicitation, the workgroup reviewed research reports from IT research firms such as Gartner.

Following the elicitation of the State's enterprise IT requirements and the elicitation of technical perspectives, the workgroup clarified the state's existing planning cycle and strategic objectives in order to ensure that the strategic IT plan aligns with it—that is, to ensure that the plan will support the achievement of the strategic objectives of the state. The workgroup partnered with the Department of Planning and Budget and the executive director of the Council on Virginia's Future throughout the project to achieve this.

After the clarification of the planning cycles and the strategic objectives of the state, the workgroup developed the initial draft of the strategic IT plan and scheduled a two-day retreat with the representatives of following stakeholders (IT governance stakeholders):[193]

1. The Council on Virginia's Future
2. The Department of Planning and Budget
3. The Secretary of Technology
4. The Chief Information Officer of the Commonwealth
5. Members of the Information Technology Investment Board (ITIB) (the approving body)

The Outcome of the Approach

One of the critical success factors of Virginia's strategic IT planning approach was the adherence of the strategic IT plan workgroup to the strategic planning taxonomy used by the Department of Planning and Budget and that of the Council on Virginia's Future. These strategic planning taxonomies are as follows:[194]

- *Strategic Mission*: States the reasons why Virginia exists.
- *Strategic Vision*: Describes where Virginia intends to be in the future.
- *Strategic Goals*: States the results that must be achieved by the state in the long-term that will enable the accomplishment of its mission and the achievement of its vision.
  - *Objectives for each goal*: States measurable results that must be achieved to move the state toward the achievement of its goals.
    - *Measurements for each objective*: A value that signifies the magnitude of a thing and a tool used to ascertain the effects of the initiatives on the accomplishment of goals and objectives.
    - *Initiatives for each objective*: The short-term courses of action or things such as programmes or projects to help achieve the objectives, goals, and vision of Virginia.

The strategic IT plan specifies the following:

- The strategic Mission and Vision for IT in the Commonwealth
- Five strategic IT goals aligned to one or more of the Council on Virginia's Future's eight long-term strategic objectives
- Strategic IT objectives, measurements, and initiatives

Strategic IT Plan Maintenance

In order to keep the plan current and abreast of the dynamics of government environments, the strategic IT planning workgroup updates the plan every year.

NOTES

1. Woopidoo Quotations. (n.d.). *Business Solutions Quotes*. Retrieved Frebruary, 2012, from Woopidoo Web site: http://www.woopidoo.com/business_quotes/business-solutions.htm
2. Symons, C., Peters, A., Cullen, A., & Worthington, B. (2008). *The Five Essential Metrics for Managing IT*. US: Forrester Research Inc, p. 2.
3. Scott, J., Cullen, A., & An, M. (2009). *Business Capabilities Provide The Rosetta Stone for Business-IT Alignment: Capability Maps Are a Foundation for Business Architecture*. US: Forrester Reseach, Inc, p. 1.
4. CIO Insight. *IT Management Slideshow: Business, IT alignment a Top Priority for CIOs*. 6 October 2011. 24 January 2011. <http://www.cioinsight.com/c/a/IT-Management/Business-IT-Alignment-a-Top-Priority-for-CIOs-547064/>
5. Scott et al, *Business Capabilities Provide The Rosetta Stone for Business-IT Alignment*, Inc, p. 2.
6. Ibid., p. 2.
7. Bossidy, L., Charan, R., & Burck, C. (2002). *Execution: The Discipline of Getting Things Done*. London: Random House Business Books, p.179.
8. Hogue, F., et al. *Winning the 3-Legged Race: When Business and Technology Run Together*. US: Prentice Hall, 2006, p. 54.
9. IT Governance Institute. (2007). *COBIT 4.1*. US: IT Governance Institute, p. 12.
10. Bredemeyer, D., Malan, R., Krishnan, R., & Lafrenz, A. (2003). *Enterprise Architecture as Business Capabilities Architecture*. *Presentation*. Bredemeyer Consulting.
11. Ibid.,
12. Peppard, J. (2003). Managing IT as a Portfolio of Services. *European Management Journal, 21*(4), 467-483, p. 467.
13. The Open Group. (2009). *TOGAF Version 9*. Netherlands: Van Haren Publishing, p. 251.
14. Ibid., p. 254.

15   Ibid., p. 251.
16   Ibid.
17   Yeo, K. T. (2002). Critical Failure Factors in Information Systems Projects. *International Journal of Project Management*, 241-246.
18   Weill, P., & Ross, J. W. (2009). *IT Savvy: What Top Executives Must Know to Go from Pain to Gain*. US: Havard Business Press, p. 51.
19   King, W. R. (1978). Strategic Planning for Management Information Systems. *MIS Quarterly, 2*(1), 2-37, p. 2.
20   Carroll, P. B., & Mui, C. (2008). *Billion-Dollar Lessons: What you Can Learn from the Most Inexcusable Business Failures of the Last 25 Years*. New York: Penguin Group Inc., p. 2.
21   Weill, P., & Woodham, R. (2002, April). Dont Just Lead, Govern: Implementing Effective IT Governance. *MIT Sloan School of Management Working Paper*. Massachusetts Institute of Technology, p. 1.
22   The Standish Group International, Incorporated. (1995). *The Standish Group Report*. Boston: The Standish Group International, Incorporated, p. 4.
23   Ibid.,
24   Clemons, E. K., & Weber, B. E. (1990). Strategic Information Technology Investments: Guidelines for Decision Making. *Journal of Management Information System, 7*(2), 9-28, p. 21.
25   Ibid.,
26   Moore, S. (2010). *Strategic Project Portfolio Management: Enabling a Productive Organisation*. US: John Wiley & Sons, Inc.,
27   Bredemeyer, D., & Malan, R. (2004). *What it Takes to Be a Great Enterprise Architect*. US: Cutter Consortium.
28   Collins, J. (2001). *Good to Great: why some companies make the leap and others don't*. London: Random House Business Books, p. 41.
29   Urban Dictionary. (n.d.). *Urban Dictionary: Solutioning*. Retrieved December 18, 2011, from Urban Dictionary Website: http://www.urbandictionary.com/define.php?term=solutioning

30 Zachman, J. A. (1982). Business Systems Planning and Business Information Control Study: A Comparison. *IBM Systems Journal, 21*(1), 31-53, p. 31.

31 Hunter, R., & Westerman, G. (2009). *The Real Business of IT: How CIOs Create and Communicate Value.* US: Harvard Business Press, p. 81.

32 Weill, P., & Ross, J. W. (2004). *IT Governance: How Top Performers Manage IT Decision Rights for Superior Results.* US: Harvard Business Press, p. 40.

33 Broadbent, M., & Kitzis, E. (2005). *The New CIO Leader: Setting the Agenda and Delivering Results.* US: Harvard Business School Press, p. 135.

34 Lutchen, M. D. (2004). *Managing IT as a Business: a survival Guide for CEOs.* US: John Wiley & Sons, Inc, p. 48.

35 Bredemeyer & Malan, *What it Takes to Be a Great Enterprise Architect.* p. 6.

36 Scott et al, *Business Capabilities Provide The Rosetta Stone for Business-IT Alignment*, Inc, p. 2.

37 Michell, V. (2011). A Focused Approach to Business Capability. *First International Symposium on Business Modeling and Software Design*, (pp. 105-113), p. 111.

38 Scott et al, *Business Capabilities Provide The Rosetta Stone for Business-IT Alignment*, Inc, p. 3.

39 Robertson, B. (2008). *Enterprise Solution Architecture: An Overview.* US: Gartner Inc., p. 6.

40 Morgan, M., Levitt, R. E., & Malek, W. (2007). *Executing Your Strategy: How to Break it Down and Get it Done.* US: Harvard Business School Press, p. 4.

41 Ward, J., & Peppard, J. (2002). *Strategic Planning for Information Systems.* UK: John Wiley and Sons Ltd, p. 40.

42 Ibid.

43 Urban Dictionary. (n.d.). *Urban Dictionary: Solutioning.*

44 Daft, R. L. (2003). *Management.* Mason: Thomson Learning - South Western.

45 Whalen, P. J. (2007). Strategic and Technology Planning on a Roadmapping Foundation. *Industrial Research Institiute* , 40-51, p. 41.
46 Lederer, A. L., & Salmela, H. (1996). Toward a theory of strategic information systems planning. *Journal of Information Systems*, 237-253, p. 237.
47 Doll, W. J. (1985, March). Avenues for Top Management Involvement in Successful MIS Development. *MIS Quarterly*, 17-35, p. 21.
48 Curran, C. (2009, December 7). *CIO*. Retrieved 7 6, 2011, from How to Improve Your IT Planning in 2010: http://www.cio.com/article/510114/How_to_Improve_Your_IT_Planning_in_2010
49 Ibib.,
50 Bradway, B. (2011, January 24). *Strategic vs. Tactical IT: Both Add Value -- Timing Is Important*. Retrieved December 05, 2011, from Bank Systems and Technology Website: http://www.banktech.com/management-strategies/229100087.
51 Smith, S. G. (2006). *Straight to the Top: Becoming a World-Class CIO*. US: John Wiley & Sons Inc, p. 7.
52 Daft, *Management*.
53 Ward, J., & Peppard, J. (2002). *Strategic Planning for Information Systems*. UK: John Wiley and Sons Ltd, p. 64.
54 Lederer, A. L., & Sethi, V. (1996). Key Prescriptions for Strategic Information Systems Planning. *Journal of Management Information Systems, 13*(1), 35-62.
55 Ibid.,
56 Bradway, *Strategic vs. Tactical IT: Both Add Value -- Timing Is Important*.
57 Weill & Ross, *IT Savvy*, p. 150.
58 Lutchen, *Managing IT as a Business*, p. 7.
59 IT Governance Institute, *COBIT 4.1*, p. 30.
60 Steffensen, R. E. (1991). *Information Systems Planning Methodologies: A Framework for Comparison and Selection*. Master's Thesis, US Naval Postgraduate School, California. Available at: http://www.dtic.mil/cgi-bin/GetTRDoc?Location=U2&doc=GetTRDoc.pdf&AD=ADA246527 (Accessed: 11 July 2011), p. 7.

61 Maizlish, B., & Handler, R. (2005). *IT Portfolio Management Step-by-Step: Unlocking the Business Value of Technology*. US: John Wiley & Sons Inc.
62 Morgan et al, *Executing Your Strategy*, p. 5.
63 Steffensen, *Information Systems Planning Methodologies*, p. 7.
64 Lederer, A. L., & Sethi, V. (1988). Implementation of Strategic Information Systems Planning Methodologies. *MIS Quarterly, 12*(3), 445-461, p. 446.
65 Ibid., p. 447.
66 Ibid. p. 446.
67 Lederer & Sethi, *Key Prescriptions for Strategic Information Systems Planning*, p. 38.
68 Earl, M. J. (1993, March). Experiences in Strategic Information Systems Planning. *MIS Quarterly, 17*(1), 1-24, p. 3.
69 Lutchen, *Managing IT as a Business*, p. 41.
70 Kaplan, R. S., & Norton, D. P. (2008). *The Execution Premium: Linking Strategy to Operations for Competitive Advantage* . US: Harvard Business Press, p. 103.
71 Robertson, *Enterprise Solution Architecture*, p. 3.
72 Lederer & Sethi, *Key Prescriptions for Strategic Information Systems Planning*, p. 37.
73 The Open Group, *TOGAF Version 9*.
74 Lederer & Sethi, *Key Prescriptions for Strategic Information Systems Planning*, p. 37.
75 Whalen, *Strategic and Technology Planning on a Roadmapping Foundation*, p. 40.
76 Lederer & Sethi, *Implementation of Strategic Information Systems Planning Methodologies*, p. 446.
77 Steffensen, *Information Systems Planning Methodologies*, p. 14.
78 Zachman, *Business Systems Planning and Business Information Control Study*, p. 35.
79 Basahel, A., & Irani, Z. (2009). Evaluation of Strategic Information Systems Planning (SISP) Techniques: Drivers and Perspective. *European and Mediterranean Conference on Information Systems* , 1-15, p. 4.

80 Delen, D., Dalal, P. N., & Benjamin, P. C. (2005). Integrated Modeling: The Key to Holistic Understanding of the Enterprise. *Communications of the ACM, 48*(4), 107-112.
81 Boynton, A. C., & Zmud, R. W. (1984). An Assessment of Critical Success Factors. *Sloan Management Review*, 17-27, p. 17.
82 Zachman, *Business Systems Planning and Business Information Control Study*, p. 8
83 Ibid.,
84 Ibid., p. 35.
85 Ibid., p. 36.
86 ibid., p. 33.
87 ibid., p. 32.
88 ibid., p. 48.
89 ibid., p. 48.
90 ibid., p. 9.
91 Ibid, p. 49.
92 Lederer & Salmela, *Toward a theory of strategic information systems planning*, p. 239
93 Ibid.,
94 Ibid.,
95 McGinnis, L. F. (2007). Enterprise Modeling and Enterprise Transformation. *Information Knowledge Systems Management*, 123-143, p. 123.
96 ibid., p. 123.
97 Fox, M. S., & Grüninger, M. (1998). Enterprise Modeling. *American Association of Artificial Intelligence*, 109-122, p. 109.
98 IEEE Computer Society. (2000). *IEEE Recommended Practice for Architectural Description of Software-Intensive Systems*. US: The Institute of Electrical and Electronics Engineers, Inc, p. 3.
99 Ross, J. W., Weill, P., & Robertson, D. C. (2006). *Enterprise Architecture as Strategy : Creating a Foundation for Business Execution*. Boston: Harvard Business School Press, p. 9.
100 Ibid.

101 Bernard, S. A. (2005). *An Introduction to Enterprise Architecture.* Bloomington: Author House, p. 31.
102 Lakhdissi, M., & Bounabat, B. (2011). Toward a Novel Methodology for IT Strategic Planning. *Proceedings of the European Conference on Information Management & Evaluation* (pp. 263-273). Academic Conference Ltd, p. 263.
103 Wilton, D. (2004, October). The Relationship Between IS Strategic Planning and Enterprise Architecture Practice. *Proceedings of the First Postgraduate Conference of the Institute of Information and Mathematical Sciences*, 100-107, p. 102
104 Ibid., p. 103.
105 Burton, B. (2009). *EA Best and Worst Practices.* US: Gartner Inc.
106 Capgemini. (2007). *Enterprise, Business and IT Architecture and the Integrated Architecture Framework.* France: Capgemini, p. 9.
107 Lakhdissi, M., & Bounabat, B. (2011). Toward a Novel Methodology for IT Strategic Planning. *Proceedings of the European Conference on Information Management & Evaluation* (pp. 263-273). Academic Conference Ltd, p. 266.
108 Wilton, *The Relationship Between IS Strategic Planning and Enterprise Architecture Practice*, p. 100.
109 Meta Group. (2002). Enterprise Architecture Fact Sheet. *CIO Insight*, 77.
110 The Open Group, *TOGAF Version 9*, p. 6.
111 Ross et al, *Enterprise Architecture as Strategy*, p. 93.
112 Boh, W. F., & Yellin, D. (2006). Using Enterprise Architecture Standards in Managing Information Technology. *Journal of Management Information Systems*, 23(3), 163-207, p. 164.
113 Spewak, S. H., & Hill, S. C. (1993). *Enterprise Architecture Planning.* New York: John Wiley & Sons, p. 7.
114 Capgemini. (2006). *Architecture and the Integrated Architecture Framework.* France: Capgemini, p. 6.
115 The Open Group, *TOGAF Version 9*, p. 6.
116 Ross et al, *Enterprise Architecture as Strategy*, p. 93.
117 Spewak & Hill, *Enterprise Architecture Planning*, p. 7.
118 Capgemini, *Architecture and the Integrated Architecture Framework.*

119 Boh & Yellin, *Using Enterprise Architecture Standards in Managing Information Technology*, p. 16
120 Bernard, *An Introduction to Enterprise Architecture*, p. 67.
121 Rockart, J. F. (1979). Chief executives define their own data needs. *Harvard Business Review*, 81-93, p. 85.
122 Boynton & Zmud, *An Assessment of Critical Success Factors*, p. 17.
123 Rockart, *Chief executives define their own data needs*, p. 85.
124 Bullen, C. V., & Rockart, J. F. (1981, June). A Primer on Critical Success Factors. *CISR Working Paper, 69*, 1-64, p. 7.
125 Earl, M. J. (1989). *Management Strategies for Information Technology*. UK: Prentice Hall International.
126 Boynton & Zmud, *An Assessment of Critical Success Factors*, p. 18.
127 ibid., p. 25.
128 Ibid., p. 18.
129 Bullen & Rockart, *A Primer on Critical Success Factors*, p. 3.
130 Kaplan, R. S., & Norton, D. P. (1996). *The Balanced Scorecard: Translating Strategy into Action*. US: Harvard Business School Press, p. 37.
131 Grant, K., Hackney, R., & Edgar, D. (2010). *Strategic Information Systems Management*. UK: Cengage Learning.
132 The Open Group, *TOGAF Version 9*, p. 28.
133 Kaplan & Norton, *The Balanced Scorecard*, p. 37.
134 Bredemeyer & Malan, *What it Takes to Be a Great Enterprise Architect*. p. 6.
135 Michell, *A Focused Approach to Business Capability*, p. 111.
136 Hax, A., & Majluf, N. S. (1996). *The Strategy Concept and Process: A Pragmatic Approach*. US: Prentice Hall, Inc, p. 27.
137 Lutchen, *Managing IT as a Business*, p. 41.
138 Hax & Majluf, *The Strategy Concept and Process*, p. 361.
139 Lutchen, *Managing IT as a Business*, p. 41.
140 Bredemeyer & Malan, *What it Takes to Be a Great Enterprise Architect*. p. 6.
141 Boynton & Zmud, *An Assessment of Critical Success Factors*, p. 26.
142 Ibid., p. 25.

143 ibid.,
144 Earl, *Experiences in Strategic Information Systems Planning*, p. 4.
145 Luftman, J. (2000). Assessing Business-IT Alignment Maturity. *Communications of the Association for Information Systems*, 4(14), 1-51, p. 6.
146 Lederer, A. L., & Mendelow, A. L. (1987, September). Information Resource Planning: Overcoming Difficulties in Identifying Top Management's Objective. *MIS Quarterly*, 389-399, p. 392.
147 Lederer, A. L., & Sethi, V. (1992). Root Causes of Strategic Information Systems Planning Implementation Problems. *Journal of Management Information Systems*, 9(1), 25-45, p. 27.
148 Lederer & Sethi, *Implementation of Strategic Information Systems Planning Methodologies*, p. 454
149 Ibid.,
150 Ibid.,
151 Ibid.,
152 Weill, P., & Olson, M. H. (1989, March). Managing Investments in Information Technology: Mini Case Examples and Implications. *MIS Quarterly*, 13(1), 3-17. p. 12.
153 Earl, *Management Strategies for Information Technology*.
154 Maizlish & Handler, *IT Portfolio Management Step-by-Step*, loc. 753.
155 Mintzberg, H. (1994). *The Rise and Fall of Strategic Planning: Reconceiving Roles for Planning, Plans, Planners*. US: The Free Press, p. 71.
156 Broadbent & Kitzis, *The New CIO Leader*, p. 137.
157 Paul, D., Yeates, D., & Cadle, J. (2010). *Business Anlaysis*. UK: British Informatics Society Limited, p. 226.
158 OGC. (2009). *Managing Successful Projects with PRINCE2*. UK: The Stationery Office, p. 21
159 Maizlish & Handler, *IT Portfolio Management Step-by-Step*.
160 Lederer & Salmela, *Toward a theory of strategic information systems planning*, p. 240
161 McGee, J., Thomas, H., & Wilson, D. (2005). *Strategy: Analysis and Practice*. UK: McGraw-Hill Education.
162 ibid., p. 7.
163 ibid.

164 Barney, J. (2002). *Gaining and Sustaining Competitive Advantage*. US: Pearson Education Inc., p. 6.
165 Ibid., p. 6.
166 Bossidy et al, *Execution*, p. 195.
167 Lutchen, *Managing IT as a Business*, p. 38.
168 Ibid.,
169 King, *Strategic Planning for Management Information Systems*, p. 31.
170 The Open Group, *TOGAF Version 9*, p. 87.
171 Ibid., p. 87.
172 Lutchen, *Managing IT as a Business*, p. 39.
173 King, *Strategic Planning for Management Information Systems*, p. 31.
174 Luftman & Brier, *Achieving and Sustaining Business-IT Alignment*. p. 115.
175 Hunter & Westerman, *The Real Business of IT*, p. 84.
176 Lederer & Mendelow, *Coordination of Information Systems Plans with Business Plans*, p. 7.
177 Weill & Ross, *IT Governance*, p. 2.
178 Lederer & Mendelow, *Information Resource Planning*, p. 392.
179 Burton, B., & Allega, P. (2011). *Enterprise Architect - Know Thy Business Strategy*. US: Gartner Inc.
180 Boynton & Zmud, *An Assessment of Critical Success Factors*, p. 17.
181 Forrester. (2006). *Moving From Reactive To Strategic IT*. US: Forrester Research.
182 Symons, C., et al. *The IT Strategic Plan Step-By-Step: Deliver An Actionable Plan In A Reasonable Timeframe*. Analyst Report - CIO Road Map. US: Forrester Research Inc., 2007, p. 4.
183 Ross et al , *Enterprise Architecture as Strategy*, p. 8.
184 Ibid., p. 43.
185 Lutchen, *Managing IT as a Business*, p. 55.
186 Scott, J., Smillie, K., Leganza, G., & An, M. (2008). *Business Architecture's Time Has Come: The Current State of Business Architecture*. US: Forrester Research, Inc, p.7.
187 Forrester Research, Inc.,. (2008). *Leverage Solution Architects to Drive EA Results*. US: Forrester Research.

188 Morgan, G. (2007, September 2). *Enterprise Architect vs Solution Architect.* Retrieved March 19, 2012, from A Microsoft Corporation Web Site: http://blogs.msdn.com/b/gabriel_morgan/archive/2007/09/02/enterprise-architect-vs-solution-architect.aspx.
189 Ibid.
190 Hoffman, T. (2008, April 7). *Hess builds a project pipeline with long-term vision.* Retrieved March 19, 2012, from ComputerWorld: http://www.computerworld.com/s/article/314711/Building_an_IT_Project_Pipeline.
191 Commonwealth of Virginia. (2006, June 4). *COVA Strategic Plan for Information Technology.* Retrieved March 30, 2012, from Common Wealth of Virginia Web Site: http://www.vita.virginia.gov/uploadedfiles/VITA_Main_Public/Library/COVStrategicPlanInformationTechnology07.pdf.
192 Ibid.
193 Ibid.
194 Ibid.

CHAPTER 4

THE THIRD RATIONAL STEP: IT EXECUTION
HOW-TO SELECT, FUND, AND DELIVER IT PROGRAMMES AND PROJECTS

IT EXECUTION

Without strategy, execution is aimless.
Without execution, strategy is useless.

—Morris Chang, CEO of TSMC[1]

This chapter is a continuation of the IT investment management journey that started from the first port (*IT governance* step or capability development), stopping briefly at the second port (*IT solutioning* step or capability development), and continuing the voyage to the third port (*IT execution* step or capability development), where we are now.

IT execution capability is the ability of enterprises to execute the business-aligned IT strategies (strategic IT objectives and investment opportunities) formulated at the IT solutioning step—in other words, it is the ability of enterprises to evaluate, select, fund, and deliver strategic IT investment initiatives-cum-projects that have the best potential to help enterprises achieve their strategic IT objectives. In a few words, IT execution capability is one of the critical capabilities required by an enterprise to convert its IT investment initiatives, programmes, or projects into a thing of immense value.

The challenge facing enterprises today is not the lack of IT investment opportunities, but rather the lack of capability to *select* the strategic IT investment opportunities or projects with the greatest potential to generate value, as well as the lack of capability to deliver the projects efficiently and effectively, so that they deliver their potential value.[2]

In order to overcome this challenge, enterprises must develop excellent IT execution capabilities, *the ability to select the best things from the right things, and get them done well*, with the consequent benefit of helping to curb the increasing failure of brilliantly formulated IT strategies, which then set the stage for generating maximum value from their investments in IT. According to Mark Morgan, Raymond Levitt, and William Malek in *Executing Your Strategy*, 'The global business landscape is littered with expensive, well-intended strategies that failed in the execution phase.'[3] Larry Bossidy and Ram Charan in *Execution* sustained this point by stating that wrong strategy is often not the reason why most companies or their executives fail to deliver on their promise or fail to execute their strategies; instead, strategies most often fail because enterprises or their executives do not have the *capability* for executing their strategies very well.[4]

Three senior executives from Booz & Company, a global management consulting firm, further corroborated the above statement by pointing out that a brilliant strategy can put an enterprise on the competitive map; to remain there requires solid execution capability.[5] Booz & Company executives further stated that enterprises must implement their strategies, which means translate strategic and operational decisions into action. Unfortunately, most enterprises are not good at executing their strategy or delivering their strategic intent, based on their own admissions.

In *The Execution Premium*, Robert Kaplan and David Norton reported that *strategy execution* and *excellence in execution* were found to be the number one priorities of senior executives in the global survey carried out in 2006 by the Monitor Group, and that of the Conference Board in 2007.[6] Ten to eleven years prior to these reports (1996), the duo had conducted a survey to ascertain the state of strategy execution in organisations, and they found that the majority of the organisations surveyed did not have a well-defined process for executing their strategies. They also found that organisations that link their strategies to their budgets were only 40 percent, and employees who understood their organisations strategy were 10 percent or fewer. The duo carried out a follow-up survey in 2006; they found that organisations that have a well-defined process for executing their strategies achieved their goals two to three times more than those without.[7]

Having thoroughly established that IT execution capability (the ability to evaluate, select, fund, and deliver strategic IT investment programmes) is critical to achieving strategic IT objectives and to generating maximum value from IT investments, and ultimately to enterprise success. What then is IT execution? And what does IT execution capability entail? And how can enterprises develop this capability?

A Review of Strategy

In order to define IT execution, it is important to first review the meaning of strategy because strategy is the driver of the need for execution; in the same vein, strategy is the major input of IT execution. In defining strategy, two perspectives were explored in the preceding chapter. In the first perspective, strategy was defined as the process of defining the objectives/goals of an organisation, followed by the identification of the right key action programmes or initiatives required to achieve the defined objectives. In the second perspective, strategy was defined as the collection of an organisation's objectives and the identified courses of actions or initiatives for achieving them, which might also include the allocation of resources to execute the initiatives or to carry out the selected courses of action.

What is Execution?

According to Larry Bossidy and Ram Charan in *Execution*, 'Execution is a systematic process of rigorously discussing hows and whats, questioning, tenaciously following through, and ensuring accountability.'[8] In addition, they added, execution includes assessing the organisation's strategy execution capabilities (i.e., IT execution capabilities), making assumptions about the business environment, aligning the organisation's operations and people to its strategy, and rewarding people based on their performance or the achievement of positive business results. In line with this, they further asserted that an organisation's execution process should be continually synchronised with the organisation's strategic planning or strategy formulation process, while the strategic planning process is also constantly being kept abreast of changing external conditions that informed its execution assumptions.

Following the definitions of strategy and execution the next logical question to ask is 'What are the factors that are critical to executing enterprise strategies?'

In order to identity the rational steps for solving the strategy execution problem, three senior executives from Booz & Company carried out empirical research to identify the factors that were most important in enabling an organisation to execute its strategy.[9] Consequently, they identified three key factors as critical in executing an organisation's strategy.[10] The first critical factor involves the clarification of decision rights and changing the structure of the organisation to reflect its strategy, both of which this book refers to as the *design of effective governance architecture* (see chapter two of this book). The second critical factor includes giving relevant stakeholders access to the metrics and information they need to execute the strategy. Finally, designing the right reward system that will help to align motivations and link rewards to performance is the third critical factor for executing strategy. These three critical factors represent just some of the capabilities that an organisation must develop in order to execute its strategies successfully.

What is IT Execution?

Combining Jim Collins's 'going from good to great' framework,[11] the definition provided by Larry Bossidy and Ram Charan, and Morgan et al., this book defines IT execution as the systematic process for identifying the right *who* (people/structure), selecting the best *what* (strategic IT initiatives-cum-projects), and specifying the *how* (execution process), the *when* (priorities/milestones), and *which* (resources).[12,13]

IT execution also entails ensuring people remain accountable for the performance and outcome of the execution process and ensuring that enterprises or their executives follow through to the end.

What Is IT Execution Capability?

Moving from the previous high-level definition of IT execution to a lower, more detailed definition, this book defines IT execution capability as the availability of the right enterprise resources: the right organisational structure filled with competent people (i.e., IT execution governance architecture), processes, information, systems, and other resources that are necessary for executing IT strategy. It also include the ability to manage the changes provoked by the outcome of the execution.

Recall the governance architecture aspect of IT execution capability, or the design of effective IT execution governance architecture, which was the subject of the first chapter of this book. The remaining three relevant components of IT execution capability—*people, processes,* and *information*—is the focus of this chapter.

The IT execution process is a complete and interdependent sequence of steps for evaluating and selecting the best strategic IT solutions-cum-projects (IT investment opportunities) in which an enterprise can invest, as well as for funding and delivering the selected programmes or projects and for managing the changes that are required to generate maximum value from the investments. The primary goal of the IT execution process is to ensure that enterprises select the *best things from the right things* (strategic IT investment programmes or projects) and are getting them done well—that is, delivered on time, within budget and with the required functionalities, and meeting benefit expectations at minimum risk.

In summary, enterprises use the IT solutioning process to identify the *right* things (strategic IT investment initiatives) and to design the solution architecture of those things to ensure that they are done the right way. Next, enterprises use the IT execution process to evaluate and select the best things from a portfolio of things, fund those things, and get them done well. According to Morgan et al. 'Effective strategy consists of choosing to do the right things,' and 'Effective execution means doing those things right.'[14]

Evolution of the IT Execution Capability Model

The evolution of IT execution will be discussed along the following sub-headings: managing strategic IT project portfolio, managing strategic IT programme, managing strategic IT projects, and managing enterprise change, which are the key building blocks of IT execution. The goal of the discussion is to identify the challenges associated with each of the building blocks and to search for appropriate solutions for overcoming the challenges, in addition to laying the theoretical foundation that is necessary for understanding the IT execution process model developed in a later part of this book.

Just as this book combined project portfolio management, programme management, and project management to conceive a structured and integrated method or framework for executing business-aligned IT strategies—that is, the *rational IT execution model*—so too did Eric Verzuh in *The Fast Forward MBA in Project Management*, where he referred to the trio as enterprise project management (EPM).[15] Verzuh went a step further, defining EPM as 'the conscious integration of processes, technology, organizational structure, and people in order to align strategy with the execution of projects.' Judging from Verzuh's definition, EPM can then be said to be the key capability—people, processes, information, and systems—required to execute business-aligned IT strategies.

Managing Strategic IT Investment Project Portfolio

In enterprises today, it is a common phenomenon to have a plethora of IT investment opportunities begging mercifully for the scarce and difficult to acquire financial and human resources of the enterprise; therefore, it is given that the demand for enterprise resources will always outstrip its supply.[16,17,18] Robert S. Kaplan and David P. Norton emphasised this point in *The Execution Premium*: 'Many companies can justifiably argue that they already have too many initiatives under way and that they don't have the financial or human resources to take on entire portfolios of new ones.'[19]

Selecting the best IT investment project (i.e., investment with the best potential to deliver maximum value) has become a critical factor in generating value from IT, a fact confirmed by Richard Hunter and George Westerman, who stated in *The Real Business of IT* that 'choosing the right project is as important to delivering value as strong execution in project management.'[20]

Although selecting the best strategic IT investment projects in which to invest is critical to generating value from IT, it is not an easy task to undertake as it is very difficult to forecast or to deal with the spectrum of events likely to influence the value that can be realised from an IT system once it is operational.[21,22] Typical examples of these spectra are risk, estimating the cost of maintenance/support, user adoption, estimating expected value, and assessing competitive impact.[23,24]

In addition to the difficulties enterprises face in forecasting the plethora of factors influencing the value of strategic IT investment projects identified above, enterprises also face other challenging factors that make it difficult to evaluate the opportunities to use IT strategically or to select the best strategic IT investment opportunities. These factors include the following:[25,26]

1. *Misapplication of financial model:* The discounted cash flow (DCF) model is applied inappropriately as the intangible benefits are usually ignored because they are difficult to measure; in addition, the focus of the financial model is too narrowly set on cost savings from labour and materials over revenue generation and other benefits.

2. *Long investment project lead-time and payback period:* A typical strategic IT investment project passes through long phases of software development or package implementation life cycles before the final rollout. There is also a long time between the conception of the strategic IT investment initiative and the time when the initiative is actualised and generates business value.

3. *Capital-intensive nature of strategic IT investment projects:* Due to the large capital requirements by most strategic IT investment

projects, their evaluation often faces certain organisational barriers. For instance, they might require board-level justification and approval.

4. *Effect of project interdependencies on value:* The interdependent nature of some strategic IT investment projects (i.e., programmes) makes it difficult to assess the value of individual projects without considering the value it might ignite in another project, as the project by itself might not create much value. Strategic IT investment projects are said to be interdependent when one or more of the other projects require a capability developed for one project.

5. *Difficulty in quantifying intangible benefits of proposed systems:* Because the benefits of strategic IT investment projects are not easily measurable, most enterprises tend to ignore these intangible benefits or set their value to zero.

Following the significance of key activities pertaining to the evaluation, selection, and funding of the best strategic IT investment programmes or projects for an enterprise to execute, coupled with the numerous factors that militate against most enterprises in carrying them out successfully, a management tool called *project portfolio management* has emerged to help enterprises overcome these inherent limitations. According to Morgan et al., 'There is simply no path to executing strategy other than the one that runs through project portfolio management.'[27] Therefore, if project portfolio management is an essential factor for the successful execution of enterprise IT strategies, what is it, and how can enterprises develop this capability?

In order to provide an accurate definition of project portfolio management, it is important to first provide the definitions of its key elements: projects, programmes, and portfolio.

What Is a Project?

The Project Management Institute (PMI) defined a *project* as a temporary venture or unique activity embarked upon in order to create unique deliverables such as products or artefacts, capabilities to perform a service, or some desirable outcome.[28] A project is a temporary venture because it has a definite beginning and a definite end. The Office of Government Commerce (OGC), the publishers and owner of the PRINCE2 methodology, adopted an organisational-centric definition of 'a project as temporary organization that is created for the purpose of delivering one or more business products according to an agreed Business Case.'[29]

What Is a Programme?

A programme is an organised grouping of interdependent or connected projects that are required to achieve the desired outcome sought by enterprises and deliver maximum value.[30] In support of the previous definition, PMI defined a program as 'a group of related projects managed in a coordinated way to obtain benefits and control not available from managing them individually.'[31] From an organisational perspective, OGC defined a programme as a temporary and flexible organisational structure designed to direct, organise, and provide oversight for the planning and delivery of projects and activities that are related to each other in order to realise benefits that will help an organisation to achieve its strategic objectives.[32]

What Is a Portfolio?

OGC defined a portfolio as the totality of enterprise investments in programmes and stand-alone projects or investments in changes that are required to achieve the enterprise's strategic objectives.[33] PMI, on the other hand, defined a portfolio as 'a collection of projects or programs and other work that are grouped together to facilitate effective management of that work to meet strategic business objectives.'[34] The IT Governance Institute (ITGI) defined portfolio from an IT perspective as the categorisation of an enterprise's entire IT assets (systems and services), activities (investment programmes and projects) and resources (human and financial capital) that are required to achieve the enterprise's objectives, which are subsequently managed and monitored in order to optimise their value.[35]

Following the definitions of the three key elements of project portfolio management, PMI now defines project portfolio management as

> the centralized management of one or more *portfolios*, which includes *identifying*, prioritizing, authorizing, managing, and controlling *projects*, *programs*, and other related work, to achieve specific strategic business objectives.[36]

Because this definition does not capture the capability-oriented perspective this book would like its readers to consider with regard to IT project portfolio management, a new definition has been developed that captures the essence of this renewed capability-oriented perspective. Thus, strategic IT project portfolio management is

> the orchestration of enterprise resources—that is, the people, processes, information, systems, facilities, and finances—to centrally evaluate, select, prioritise, and fund the *best* candidate strategic IT investment programmes or projects efficiently and effectively in order to deliver the strategic IT capabilities required to achieve the strategic IT objectives of an enterprise.

This definition is based on the philosophy that high-performing organisations focus their scarce resources on the best strategic IT investment projects, while refusing to do those projects that are good, but not good enough.[37] If we recall, the strategic IT solutions-cum-projects identified at the IT solutioning step already constitute the *right/good* strategic IT investment projects that enterprises should invest in order to generate maximum value.

Strategic IT project portfolio management provides the link between enterprise IT strategies and the specific management activities, such as strategic IT programme/project and the enterprise change management, needed to execute the strategies or to deliver the strategic IT capabilities required to achieve strategic IT objectives.[38] In order to provide this link, strategic IT portfolio management supports the evaluation, selection, funding, delivery, and monitoring of strategic IT investment projects.[39] Corroborating this view are Bryan Maizlish and Robert Handler in *IT Project Portfolio Management Step-by-Step*, who stated that 'IT project portfolio takes input and direction from the corporate strategic plan.'[40] Forrester Research also affirmed that IT portfolio management provides the link between strategic planning functions, or IT solutioning and project arbitration (programme management), project management, and project improvement processes.[41]

The primary objective of strategic IT portfolio management is to ensure that enterprises focus their scarce resources on the best strategic IT investment projects by following a rigorous selection process and using unbiased evaluation criteria to make strategic IT investment solutions-cum-projects selection and funding decisions. The achievement of this objective will help enterprises to maximise the return on their IT investments at an appropriate level of risk. Forrester Research referred to this as 'balancing resources, technology, business needs, and changing situations while simultaneously maximising returns and minimizing risk.'[42]

Marianne Broadbent and Ellen S. Kitzis, in *The New CIO Leader*, provided a succinct summary of IT project portfolio management, concluding that an enterprise follows five steps to select and manage their portfolio of strategic IT investment initiatives effectively.[43]

In the first step, enterprises develop business cases for the right IT investment initiatives using an exhaustive and uniform approach.

In the second step, enterprises categorise the initiatives based on the enterprise's objectives for wanting to invest in them and assess their value using unbiased criteria, such as business strategy alignment, financial impact or ROI, business risk, enterprise IT architecture and standards compliances, and benefits realisation responsibility assignment, varied slightly for each investment category.

In the third step, enterprises score business cases or proposals for each IT investment initiative using the criteria discussed earlier with weights to reflect the relative importance of each criterion in each category, after which the IT investment initiatives are either approved, cancelled, put on hold, or rejected for rework based on their scores. Following the approval of the highest-ranking IT investment initiatives, enterprises further ranked the approved initiatives within each investment category according to their score and balanced them according to their risk and return profile in order to achieve the right investment mix. Finally, the investment initiatives with the best value potential within each category are selected for funding.

In the fourth step, enterprises match the selected IT investment initiatives-cum-projects to available resources in the enterprise (i.e., physical capital, human capital, organisational capital, or financial capital); this step can also include the need to arrange or schedule the IT investment initiatives or projects based on the interdependencies between them, often called strategic road mapping.

In the last step, enterprises actively manage the resulting portfolio of IT investments by re-weighing them annually, or whenever major changes occur. The second step through the fifth step proposed by both Broadbent and Kitzis are the key elements of IT portfolio management.

Critical Input for the Strategic IT Projects Portfolio Management Process

The strategic IT projects portfolio management process requires the following inputs in order to evaluate, select, and fund the best strategic IT investment programmes or projects effectively:

1. Strategic IT execution governance architecture.
   a. Setting up an IT investment review board (ITIRB) or IT execution governance architecture.
   b. Strategic IT execution governance decisions.
2. Enterprise IT portfolios, or a list and descriptions of IT assets and activities that consist of the following:
   a. The portfolio of *proposed* strategic IT solutions-cum-projects, which is an inventory or list of technically, business, and financially feasible solutions from which enterprises can choose (see output of IT solutioning in chapter 3); this is often referred to as setting the solution context for the ITIRB.[44]
   b. The enterprise solution architecture of the proposed strategic IT initiatives-cum-solutions (see output of IT solutioning in chapter 3) used by the ITIRB to verify that enterprises will be executing strategic IT investment

projects the right way. This implies that, in addition to ensuring that strategic IT investment projects are aligned with the business strategy, there is also the need to ensure compliance with enterprise IT architecture and standards.[45]

    c. Portfolio pipeline: inventory of active and on-hold strategic IT investment programmes or projects (see IT governance in chapter 2).

    d. The portfolio of existing strategic enterprise applications or IT systems, also called strategic applications or IT systems portfolio.

    e. The portfolio of existing strategic IT services, which helps to prevent overlaps and to identify possible areas of synergies between the strategic IT services proposed for development in the business case and the ones currently existing in the enterprise.

    f. Portfolio of existing IT unit human resource capability.

Enterprises need to maintain an up-to-date portfolio of their entire IT estate, as it is not easy to select the best IT investment projects from good ones because individual project business cases can be compelling to such an extent that enterprises must look at the entire projects pipeline in order to determine the best course of action.[46]

3. Optionally, the strategic business capability assessment report that will be used to assess how well the proposed strategic IT solutions-cum-projects support the overall business strategy may be included in the business case document (see output of IT solutioning in chapter 3); this is often referred to as depicting the strategic context of the proposed IT investment for the ITIRBs.[47]

4. Transparent process for selecting the best strategic IT investment opportunities (see IT governance in chapter 2).

5. An unbiased and weighted evaluation criterion used within a business case document for determining the potential value of all *proposed* potential strategic IT investments, which implies that, where

possible, all investment opportunities must have a business case (see IT governance in chapter 2).
6. Business cases for each strategic IT solutions, except where it is not possible to quantify the benefits/costs, or in situations where the IT investment solution being proposed is mandatory (see output of IT solutioning in chapter 2).
7. Appointed key stakeholders in the form of a strategic IT project portfolio manager/director and project/business sponsors[48] (see IT governance in chapter 2).
8. Enterprise IT funding and sourcing policies (see IT governance in chapter 2).

Following the identification of the right strategic IT investment initiatives and their translation into technically feasible strategic IT solutions, enterprises evaluate their business cases or investment proposals using a few criteria, after which the *best* strategic IT solutions-cum-programmes are selected and prioritised for funding and inclusion in the portfolio of strategic IT investment programmes. Forrester Research suggested that 'once an IT investment proposal has been reviewed, approved, funded, and sequenced within the portfolio' and 'as investment programs and projects are executed, they must be periodically reviewed to ensure that they are on track to return their projected benefits.'[49]

Strategic IT Project Portfolio Management Process

Enterprises can manage their portfolio of strategic IT investments using the following six (6) major steps:

1. *Initiate* the process by receiving proposals for strategic IT investment opportunities from business sponsors.
2. *Evaluate/Review* the business cases of proposed strategic IT investment projects by scoring each project using weighted criteria. The scores are then added up for each project.[50]

3. ***Rank/Prioritise*** strategic IT investment projects according to their total scores—that is, the projects are ranked in order of their importance.[51]

4. ***Select/Choose/Approve*** the best strategic IT investment projects or the highest-ranking projects.

5. ***Sequence*** the selected strategic IT investment projects according to their rank, availability of funding, and other non-financial resources, while also considering their technical and non-technical interdependencies.[52]

6. ***Fund*** the sequenced strategic IT investment projects and allocate requisite resources by assigning projects managers who possess the required competencies and experience essential for managing the delivery of the project.

Critical Output for Strategic IT Project Portfolio Management

The strategic IT project portfolio management process generates output that will serve as the input of strategic IT project management processes; this output includes the following:

1. The portfolio of approved strategic IT investment programmes or projects with the following:
    a. Appointed strategic IT programme or project manager[53]
    b. Allocated/authorised funds or resources
2. Strategic IT Programmes or projects mandate
3. Business cases of strategic IT programmes or projects

According to Forrester Research,

> the optimal result of investment committee review of investment proposals is a set of projects that address high-priority needs, are aligned with strategic roadmaps, and are sequenced based on priority, dependencies, and resource utilization.[54]

Managing the Strategic IT Programme

Rod Sowden, a leading authority on programme management and author of *Managing Successful Programmes*, defined programme management as the following:

> The actions of carrying out the coordinated organization, direction and implementation of a dossier of projects and transformation activities (i.e. the programme) to achieve outcomes and realize benefits of strategic importance to the business.[55]

This book defines strategic IT programme management as the orchestration of enterprise resources (people, processes, information, systems, facilities and finances) required to effectively govern (direct, coordinate, and oversee) the execution of interdependent sets of strategic IT projects in order to deliver the strategic IT capabilities that are *necessary* and *sufficient* for achieving enterprise strategic IT objectives. From the initial definition of capabilities presented in this book, the strategic IT capabilities delivered through programmes can be said to consist of competent and available technical and business resources (people), business and technical processes, organisational changes/structure, and IT systems required—that is, those that necessary and sufficient to achieve strategic IT objectives. This view is somewhat supported by the IT Governance Institute (ITGI) through the approach adopted by the institute in its definition of programme, which is 'a structured group of interdependent projects that are both necessary and sufficient to achieve the business outcome and deliver value.'[56]

Consider the key conditions that made the strategic IT capabilities delivered by strategic IT programme management to be sufficient for achieving strategic IT objectives. The strategic IT project management life cycle ends when strategic IT systems or products are delivered, deployed, and transited to on-going IT operations or to the strategic IT services operations manager. Strategic IT programme management goes further to manage enterprise (business and technical) changes, which include training, providing documentation, providing support, and reengineering business processes, that are required to effectively operate and use the new strategic IT systems or products. Strategic IT programme management activities further extend to the realisation of the potential value promised by the resulting strategic IT systems.

In summary, managing enterprise change to the new strategic IT systems or products and realising the expected benefits or value of the strategic IT investment programmes are the two main factors that make the strategic IT capabilities delivered by programme management efforts to be sufficient for achieving strategic IT objectives. These two factors also distinguish programme management from project management.

Because of the conditions explicated above, good strategic IT programme management practices advocated the development of a *benefit realisation plan* (BRP) for every strategic IT programme that an enterprise plans to undertake and advocated that a *benefit realisation manager* (BRM) be appointed to implement this plan. In addition, a business and technology (enterprise) *change management plan* should be developed to manage enterprise transition to a new strategic IT system and implemented by the appointed *business change manager* (BCM). According to the OGC, the duty of the business change manager is to act as the bridge between the strategic IT programme and on-going enterprise operations in order to ensure that the strategic IT capabilities delivered by the programme are used effectively by the enterprise to achieve the desired outcome, or to realise the expected benefits.[57]

Due to challenges of resource availability, it is often advised that the roles of the benefit realisation manager and the business change manager be merged; this could also mean that a business change manager should be made to perform the functions of a benefit realisation manager.

In order to consider the selected strategic IT investment initiatives-cum-solutions as a strategic IT investment programme, which consequently introduces another management layer between strategic IT *portfolio management* and strategic IT *project management,* and not as a strategic IT investment project, it must meet certain criteria.[58] First, it must meet a strategic need or achieve strategic objectives; second, it must deliver or enable one or more benefits; third, it must require high-level direction and leadership; and fourth, the realisation of its full value must be dependent upon other similar strategic IT projects.[59]

The main goal of strategic IT programme management is to direct and control the delivery of strategic IT investment solutions-cum-programmes effectively and efficiently and to ensure that the resulting strategic IT systems or capabilities are transited successfully to line-of-business managers or owners, and the potential value of the strategic IT investment programme is fully realised.

Critical Input for Strategic IT Programme Management

The following mandatory input is required to manage strategic IT programmes effectively:

- The output of the strategic IT project portfolio management process
- Strategic business capability assessment report
- Strategic IT capability assessment report

Strategic IT Programme Management Steps

Enterprises can manage their strategic IT investment programmes using the following five (5) steps:

1. Appoint relevant managers
    a. Project Board
        i. Project sponsor or executive
        ii. Senior user
        iii. Senior supplier
    b. Project manager (appointed by executive)
    c. Benefit realisation manager (optional; job role is similar to business change manager)

d. Business change manager
2. Prepare project mandate and brief: corporate directive to carry out a project
3. Review business cases and develop programme benefit realisation strategy and plan
4. Review strategic business and technology capability assessment report and develop business/enterprise change management strategy and plan
5. Transit to new strategic IT systems

Critical Output of Strategic IT Programme Management

Strategic IT programme management generate a set of output that feeds into the strategic IT project management step.

1. Appointed project board members and project manager
2. Project mandate and brief
3. Benefit realisation strategy
4. Benefit realisation plan
5. Enterprise change management plan
6. Transited strategic IT capability or systems

Managing the Strategic IT Project

Strategic IT project management is the orchestration of enterprise resources (people, processes, information, systems, facilities, and finances) required to effectively and efficiently plan and execute strategic IT projects in order to deliver strategic IT systems that will enable or support the development of the strategic IT services required to achieve strategic IT objectives within an agreed timeframe and cost. From this definition, we can deduce that strategic IT projects deliver products/services or components of strategic IT capabilities (e.g., strategic IT systems) that are necessary but not sufficient to achieve strategic IT objectives. This view is somewhat supported by the IT Governance Institute (ITGI) through the approach adopted by the institute in their definition of project:

> A structured set of activities concerned with delivering to the enterprise a defined capability (that is necessary but NOT sufficient to achieve a required business outcome) based on an agreed schedule and budget.[60]

Critical Input for Strategic IT Project Management

The following mandatory input is required to manage strategic IT investment projects effectively and efficiently:

1. All of the output of strategic IT programme management
2. The architecture of strategic IT solutions
3. Enterprise architecture and standards repository
4. IT sourcing strategy
5. Strategic IT procurement plan/acquisition policy
6. Enterprise/business and user requirement document
7. IT funding strategy
8. Allocated funds (full/partial)

Strategic IT Project Management Process

Enterprises can manage their strategic IT investment projects using the following seven (7) steps:

1. Appoint project team manager
2. Select custom software development life cycle (SDLC) method or package application implementation method
3. Select project management system (tools, techniques, and methodologies)
4. Develop strategic IT project plan
5. Procure and engage strategic IT project resources (resourcing)
6. Deliver (develop and/or implement strategic IT projects)
7. Deploy strategic IT systems

Critical Output of Strategic IT Project Management

Strategic IT project management generate the following output (most especially deployed strategic IT system) that feeds into the *IT operationalization step*—the fourth rational step for managing IT investments.

1. Strategic IT project plan (benefit review plan, etc.)
2. Appointed team leader (in PRINCE2 parlance)
3. Functional and non-functional requirement specifications
4. Procured strategic IT project resources
5. Procurement contract
6. Selected SDLC method
7. Deployed strategic IT system (updated strategic IT systems portfolio)

Rational Steps for IT Execution

Although proven processes and methodologies exist for managing strategic IT investment portfolios, programmes, and projects, none of these processes or methodologies utilises or adopts a framework that takes the entire economic life cycle of IT investment projects into consideration, though some claim to have.

Another major limitation for most of the existing processes and methods is that they are designed for all sorts of IT investment projects, from strategic, informational, and transactional to infrastructural IT investment projects, in an attempt to be master of all areas of IT investments. However, these methodologies are not particularly good at any of these IT investment areas.

Because of these limitations, this book has developed an integrated strategic IT execution capability model, leveraging existing methodologies and filling the gaps with informational input and/or output where necessary.

Rational IT Execution Capability Model

The rational strategic IT execution capability model consists of six key capabilities phases (see Figure 4.0 below), each with its own goal, owner, input, activities, supporting systems, and output that contributes to the achievement of the overall goal of strategic IT execution, which is to select and deliver strategic IT systems and transit enterprise users to the newly delivered systems.

THE THIRD RATIONAL STEP: IT EXECUTION

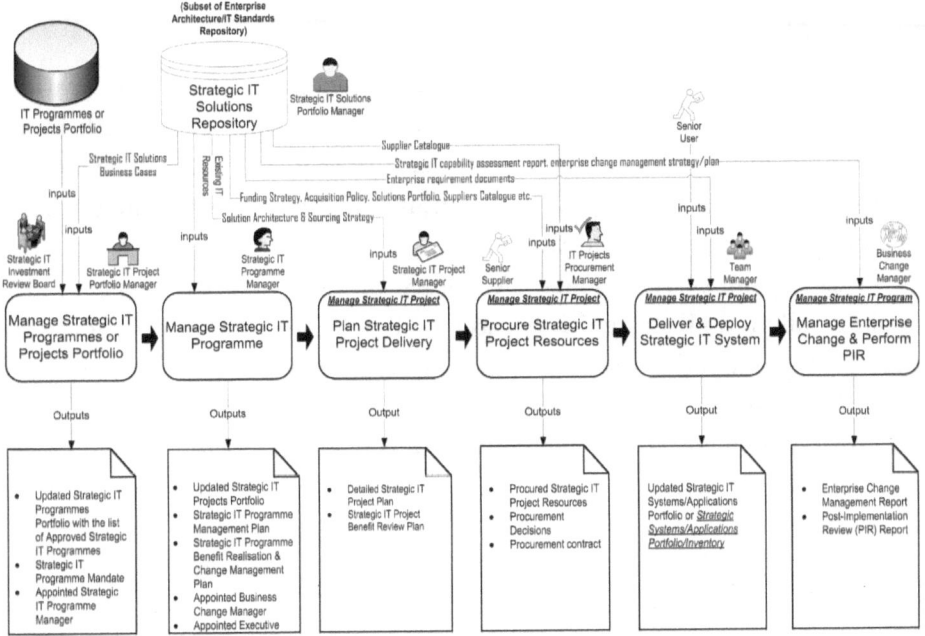

Figure 4.0 Rational IT Execution Capability Model

The goal of the first capability phase, managing the strategic IT investment project portfolio, is to help the enterprises translate their strategic IT initiatives-cum-solutions into a portfolio of approved strategic IT investment programmes or projects, which will now become the enterprise portfolio of new strategic IT investment programme and projects. The goal of the second and the sixth capability phase, managing strategic IT programmes, is to help enterprises direct, coordinate, and oversee the delivery of a group of related strategic IT investment projects that will help enterprises achieve their strategic IT objectives. The goals of capability phases three to five, managing strategic IT projects, is to plan, procure, and deliver the approved strategic IT investment projects contained in the enterprise *strategic IT projects portfolio*.

Summary

IT execution capability is crucial in the management and generation of maximum value from IT investments and for succeeding with IT in general because it helps enterprises to ensure that they are delivering the best IT investment projects; in addition, it helps to ensure that investment projects are being executed well.

This capability represents the ability of enterprises to execute the business-aligned IT strategies (strategic IT objectives and investment initiatives) formulated at the IT solutioning step, or the ability of enterprises to evaluate, select, fund, and deliver strategic IT investment initiatives-cum-projects that have the best potential to help enterprises achieve their strategic IT objectives.

NOTES

1. Brand Autopsy. (n.d.). *Best Quote on Strategy vs. Execution*. Retrieved February 25, 2012, from Brand Autopsy Web Site: http://www.brandautopsy.com/2010/09/best-quote-on-strategy-vs-execution.html
2. Ataya, G., & Thorp, J. (2007). Portfolio Management: Unlocking the Value of IT Investments. *Information Systems Control Journal, 4*, 1-2. p. 1.
3. Morgan, M., Levitt, R. E., & Malek, W. (2007). *Executing Your Strategy: How to Break it Down and Get it Done*. US: Harvard Business School Press, p.1
4. Bossidy, L., Charan, R., & Burck, C. (2002). *Execution: The Discipline of Getting Things Done*. London: Random House Business Books, p. 15.
5. Neilson, G. L., Martin, K. L., & Powers, E. (2008). The Secrets to Successful Strategy Execution. *Harvard Business Review*, 61-70, p. 61
6. Kaplan, R. S., & Norton, D. P. (2008). *The Execution Premium: Linking Strategy to Operations for Competitive Advantage*. US: Harvard Business Press, p. 3.
7. Ibid., p. 5.
8. 10   Bossidy, Charan, & Burck, *Execution*, p.22.
9. Neilson, Martin, & Powers, *The Secrets to Successful Strategy Execution*.
10. Ibid., p. 62.
11. Collins, J. (2001). *Good to Great: why some companies make the leap and others don't*. London: Random House Business Books, p. 42.
12. Bossidy, Charan, & Burck, *Execution*, p.22.
13. Morgan et al, *Executing Your Strategy*, p. 9.
14. Ibid., p. 4.
15. Verzuh, E. (2008). *The Fast Forward MBA in Project Management*. US: John Wiley & Sons, Inc., p. 361.
16. Ataya & Thorp, *Portfolio Management*, p. 1.
17. IT Governance Institute. (2005). Optimising Value Creation From IT Investments. *IT Governance Domain Practices and Competencies*. US: IT Governance Institute, p. 13.

18. Hunter, R., & Westerman, G. (2009). *The Real Business of IT: How CIOs Create and Communicate Value*. US: Harvard Business Press, p. 134.
19. Kaplan & Norton, *The Execution Premium*, p. 106.
20. Ibid., p. 119.
21. Clemons, E. K., & Weber, B. E. (1990). Strategic Information Technology Investments: Guidelines for Decision Making. *Journal of Management Information System, 7*(2), 9-28, p. 10.
22. Davern, M. J., & Kauffman, R. J. (2000). Discovering Potential and Realizing Value from Information Technology Investments. *Journal of Management Information Systems*, 121-143, p. 124.
23. Ataya & Thorp, *Portfolio Management*, p. 1
24. Clemons & Weber, *Strategic Information Technology Investments*, p. 10.
25. Ibid., p. 10
26. Bardhan, I., Bagchi, S., & Sougstad, R. (2004). Prioritising a Portfolio of Information Technology Investment Projects. *Journal of Management Information Systems, 21*(2), 33-60.
27. Morgan et al, *Executing Your Strategy*, p. 5.
28. Project Management Institute . (2004). *Project Management Body of Knowledge* . USA: PMI Publications, p. 5.
29. OGC. (2009). *Managing Successful Projects with PRINCE2*. UK: The Stationery Office, p. 3.
30. Ataya & Thorp, *Portfolio Management*, p. 1
31. Project Management Institute, *Project Management Body of Knowledge*, p. 16.
32. OGC, *Managing Successful Projects with PRINCE2*, p. 153
33. Ibid., p. 308.
34. Project Management Institute, *Project Management Body of Knowledge*, p. 16.
35. IT Governance Institute. (2008). *Enterprise Value: Governance of IT Investments, The Val IT Framework 2.0*. US: The IT Governance Institute, p. 11.
36. Project Management Institute, *Project Management Body of Knowledge*, p. 367.

37. Oltmann, J. (2009). Project Portfolio Management-The Art of Saying No. *PM World Today*, 1-4, p. 1.
38. Ataya & Thorp, *Portfolio Management*, p. 2.
39. Ibid.,
40. Maizlish, B., & Handler, R. (2005). *IT Portfolio Management Step-by-Step: Unlocking the Business Value of Technology*. US: John Wiley & Sons Inc, loc. 785.
41. Gliedman, C., & Brown, A. (2004). *Defining IT Portfolio Management: Holistic IT Investment Planning*. US: Forrester Research Inc, p. 5.
42. Ibid., p. 2.
43. Broadbent, M., & Kitzis, E. (2005). *The New CIO Leader: Setting the Agenda and Delivering Results*. US: Harvard Business School Press, p. 135.
44. Cullen, A., Symons, C., Scott, J., & An, M. (2010). *Using Business Capability Maps To Guide IT Investment Governance*. US: Forrester Research Inc, p. 2.
45. Ibid., p. 3.
46. Enterprise Portfolio Management Council. (2009). *Project Portfolio Management: A View from the Management Trenches*. Hoboken: John Wiley & Sons, Inc, p. 12.
47. Cullen et al, *Using Business Capability Maps To Guide IT Investment Governance*, p. 2.
48. Visitacion, M., Barnett, L., & Schwaber, C. E. (2004, June 14). *The PMO And Value Realization*. US: Forrester Research, Inc, p. 2.
49. Symons, C., L. M. Orlov, and L. Sessions. *Five Best Practices for Portfolio Management*. Best Practices, US: Forrester Research, Inc., 2006, p. 2.
50. Broadbent & Kitzis, *The New CIO Leader*, p. 136.
51. Lutchen, M. D. (2004). *Managing IT as a Business: a survival Guide for CEOs*. US: John Wiley & Sons, Inc., p. 48.
52. Broadbent & Kitzis, *The New CIO Leader*, p. 140.
53. Department for Business Innovation & Skills. *Guidelines for Managing Programmes: Understanding Programmes and Programme Management.*

Report, UK: Department for Business Innovation & Skills, 2010, p. 4.
54. Cullen et al, *Using Business Capability Maps To Guide IT Investment Governance*, p. 2
55. Sowden, R. (2011). Managing Successful Programmes. *Best Management Practice*. UK: The Stationery Office, p. 3.
56. IT Governance Institute. (2006). *Enterprise Value: Governance of IT Investments, The Business Case*. US: The IT Governance Institute, p. 9.
57. OGC, *Managing Successful Projects with PRINCE2*, p. 218.
58. Department for Business Innovation & Skills, *Guidelines for Managing Programmes*, 2010, p. 4.
59. Ibid.
60. IT Governance Institute, *Enterprise Value: Governance of IT Investments, The Business Case*, p. 9.

CHAPTER 5

THE FOURTH RATIONAL STEP: IT OPERATIONALIZATION

HOW-TO SOURCE AND PROVISION HIGH QUALITY IT SERVICES

IT OPERATIONALIZATION

*Firms with more satisfied people using their
systems also get more business value from their
investments in information technology.*
—Peter Weill & Marianne Broadbent.[1]

After executing business-aligned IT strategies to deliver strategic IT systems (IT capabilities), the fourth IT investment management (ITIM) capability that enterprises need to develop in order to manage their IT investments successfully and generate maximum value is IT operationalization capability.

This capability represents the ability of an enterprise to translate the strategic IT systems delivered at the IT execution step into a business-relevant portfolio of strategic IT services or *operational systems* that will be used to support the delivery of business services. This capability also includes the ability of an enterprise to maintain the usability, availability, integrity, and continuity of those IT systems or services throughout their economic life cycle.

Take the quote by Peter F. Drucker, a notable management scholar and author, who said, 'The computer is a moron'[2] and combine it with Vinton Cerf's quote, 'The computer would do anything you programmed it to do,' we would have a new quote that reads 'The computer is a moron that would do anything you programmed it to do.' This statement is true, granted the computer in question is in perfect working condition.

Literatures have identified the relationship between the use of a computer or strategic IT system and the realisation of expected benefits from the system, and that the use of IT systems must precede benefits realisation.[3] Literature, however, failed to stress the relationship that exists between the use of IT systems and the continued availability of systems. There is no doubt that if an IT system is down it is virtually impossible to use it for any meaningful purpose whatsoever, which consequently makes it impossible to realise any form of value from the IT system. According to Forrester Research, an IT system 'technology is providing a capability, but if that capability is not used or not used effectively, it will not produce anything of value.'[4]

From the above argument, it is clear that the operationalization of an IT system is a critical success factor for its effective utilisation and, consequently, for the generation of value from IT investments. This implies that the development of IT operationalization capability (ability to translate/design, source, transit, operate, protect, support, and maintain IT services), or the ability to translate the portfolio of IT systems into business-relevant IT services while ensuring their continued availability and security, is critical for the successful realisation of value from enterprise investments in IT.

Numerous accounts have spelled out the negative consequence of having ineffective IT operationalization capability; for example, Computer Economics & Infocorp Consulting reported that systems downtime in 1996 cost American businesses $4.54 billion due to lost productivity and revenues, and this cost was estimated to rise to $6.6 billion in 1999.'[5]

The IT Operationalization Challenge

Considering the significance of effectively operationalizing IT systems, most enterprises and their managers, academicians, and authors have lost sight of this simple fact. This short sightedness' is evident from the increasing number of IT investment projects that are failing to deliver the value enterprises expect because of the ineffective use or non-use of the services they are delivering. This short sightedness is also evident from the apparent omission of IT operationalization topics and discussion of issues related to it in most IT literature, except for the recent works of organised bodies such as the UK Office of Government Commerce (OGC) and the IT Service Management Forum (itSMF).

The reasons for this obvious mistake is that most enterprises and their managers assume that once strategic IT systems are delivered, deployed, and successfully transited to IT operations for integration into the on-going operations of their enterprise, their work is completed, and they can begin to realise the full benefits of their investments in IT. Richard Hunter and George Westerman in *The Real Business IT* maintained a similar point of view: 'Some CIOs, and many other IT professionals, act as if they believe that their jobs are finished when the technology is installed.'[6] Whereas, business executives in enterprise maintain that IT job is finished only after the benefits that they seek from the investments have been realised.[7]

The statement made by Mark Morgan, Raymond Levitt, and William Malek in *Executing Your Strategy* represents a typical example of this assumption error.[8] The trio argued that 'transition is the crucial final step in realizing the benefits of strategic projects and programs' and defined transition as the hand off that takes place between the project management organisation and the on-going (IT operations and maintenance) organisation.[9] The trio further trivialised the operationalization and the realisation of benefits from the outcomes of programmes and projects by stating that 'benefit realisation does not require a costly, long-drawn-out initiative.'[10] And that benefit realisation can be carried out by 'simply looking at the last ten projects the organization has undertaken and comparing the actual results and outcomes with what was expected when the projects were initiated.'

Enterprises totally overlook all the work that is required to translate IT capabilities or systems into business-relevant IT services or operational systems that will be used to deliver value to the enterprise and the work required to support and protect the systems and services in order to ensure that they are always available throughout their economic life cycle. This is a clear indication that enterprises are confusing the success of IT investment projects with the success of IT investment projects *management*; while the former extends further into the operationalization of

IT systems and to benefit realisation, the latter ends when IT systems are handed over to the users or business sponsors.[11] It is therefore clear that the benefits of strategic IT investment projects are not realised by IT and project staff alone, but instead calls for the action of IT operations or services manager (IT staff) in cooperation with the project staff, as well as the business staff who are responsible for realising the expected benefits of IT investments.[12,13]

The role of IT operations or service management is to optimise the benefits of the IT systems or services that are delivered by projects. According to Maggie Kneller, in an OGC Best Management Practice White Paper, 'For an IT investment to provide benefit, the resulting IT service must be well planned, well designed, well managed, and well delivered,'[14] and the responsibility for all these activities belongs to the IT operations or services manager.

Solving the IT Operationalization Challenge: Managing IT as a Service

Enterprises and their managers should be aware that it is the provisioning of IT services, which means doing something for internal or external customers that delivers value, and not the availability of IT capability (the ability to do a thing) or IT systems (a component of IT capability). It is for these reasons that the concept of IT service management (ITSM) emerged to help enterprises cope with the translation of the IT capabilities or systems delivered, deployed, and transited to users at the *IT execution step* into a portfolio of IT services in a structured and predictable way.

According to most literature, the goal of ITSM is to advance best practices in IT service delivery and support. Following the emergence of the ITSM concept, the UK Office of Government Commerce (OGC) documented a collection of best practices, a methodology called IT infrastructure library (ITIL) to industrialise the concept.[15]

It is also for these reasons that Forrester Research advocated for enterprises to make IT-as-a-service (ITaaS) their strategy by refocusing their IT organisation around the provisioning of *services* instead of the provisioning of disjointed components of hardware, software, products, activities, and so forth.[16] Forrester Research further advocated strongly that in order to implement the ITaaS model, the IT unit of enterprises must translate their disjointed portfolios of strategic IT capabilities (hardware/software and activities) into unified IT services, and they must aggregate them into a consolidated portfolio of business-relevant services in order to create a connection between business demand and IT supply.

Enterprises should follow the creation of a unified portfolio of IT services with the implementation of a unified governance process that establishes the explicit link between portfolio of business services and the resources—that is, portfolio of IT services required to deliver them in order to align ITaaS with business strategy.[17] In conclusion, Forrester Research recommended that enterprises shift their focus from creating IT capabilities to delivering IT services and from managing IT in silos to governing IT holistically.

Similarly, Joe Peppard, a professor at Cranfield University, extends his support for managing IT-as-a-service. He argued that by adopting a service orientation and managing IT as a portfolio of services—that is, managing IT-as-a-service—organisations might be able to engage business managers and users in IT activities because this level of involvement has been found to be a critical ingredient for success with IT, even though it has proven difficult to achieve.[18] The premise of his argument was based on the idea that the adoption of a service-oriented approach to managing IT systems, infrastructure, and processes will provide the much-needed language/perspective for carrying out a more meaningful and understandable dialogue between IT and business, which can improve the total contribution of IT to enterprise performance considerably. OGC supported this premise in its Best Management Practices White Paper written by Valerie Arraj.[19] The organisation asserted that adopting a service-orientation approach to IT systems operationalization helps to build a true partnership between business and IT, with the benefit of being able to negotiate a realistic level of service that will deliver value at an acceptable cost and risk.

Managing IT-as-a-service or the adopting of a service-orientated approach to managing IT, or just simply adopting IT service management, also helps enterprises to do the following:

1. Support the alignment of IT operations with business needs or the linking of IT services with business services[20] and, by implication, adopting a service orientation to enable the linking of IT and business capabilities through services.[21]

2. Enable enterprises to negotiate better service levels,[22] which can lead to improved availability and reduced downtime, consequently leading to increased profits and revenue that will result from improved customer satisfaction and increased IT services utilisation.[23]

3. Enable IT services chargeback, or providing a charging mechanism for IT services delivered.[24]

4. Enable enterprises to identify opportunities for strategic sourcing of IT services and facilitate the making of IT outsourcing decisions.[25]

5. Facilitate IT services unit cost identification, allocation, and benchmarking,[26] or enable enterprises to measure the unit cost per IT service, which provides the information that enterprises can use to review and enhance IT value for money, or to communicate IT's value.[27]

6. Change enterprise perception of IT as a cost centre.[28]

7. Improve the quality of IT services delivery.

Therefore, if the translation of strategic IT systems into a unified portfolio of business-relevant strategic IT services is critical to the operationalization and use of strategic IT systems and to the generation of maximum value, what then is a service or an IT service? And what does IT operationalization capability entail? And how can enterprises develop their ability to manage IT services effectively and efficiently?

What Is IT Service?

According to the OGC, 'A service is a means of delivering value to customers by facilitating outcomes customer want to achieve without the ownership of specific costs and risks.'[29] The OGC went further to offer a very descriptive definition of IT service, they defined IT service as 'a service provided to one or more Customers by an IT Service Provider',[30] and that, 'an IT service is based on the use of Information Technology and supports the Customer's Business Processes.'[31]

Due to the descriptive nature of these definitions, we defined an IT service from a capability-oriented approach as the use of an enterprise IT capability (people, processes, information/application services, and infrastructural services) to do a thing or to carry out repeatable activities that support or enable the operations of an enterprise or the delivery of business services. According to Joe Peppard, enterprises deliver IT services via the portfolio of applications that are deployed on their technology platform,[32] which corroborates the application and infrastructural services mentioned in the IT service definition provided in this book. The OGC corroborated the capability-oriented approach adopted in the definition of IT services presented in this book by stating that an enterprise IT service consists mainly of people, processes, and technology/enterprise applications software and infrastructures (IT capabilities).[33] Forrester Research also corroborated this view by pointing out that the design of IT services is usually motivated by the needs of the business and, to fulfil these needs, IT services must integrate internal and external capabilities.[34]

Along with the definition of IT services, this book will leverage the Capgemini Integrated Architecture (IAF) Framework to explicate the concept of *service-orientation* within the context of the architecture of an enterprise using the four major components of the IAF framework, called aspect areas: business, information, information systems, and technology infrastructure.[35] The first aspect area is *business service (BS)*, which is an activity or a thing that is undertaken by the business in order to achieve a well-defined goal. The second aspect area is information or *business information (BI) service*, which represents the information that business service uses to achieve its goal; therefore, business information service is also a business service, or a thing that a business does. The third is *information systems (IS) services*, which are the application components or IS systems that must be bought, built, or customised to provide business information services. The fourth is the *technology infrastructure (TI) services*, which are the user interface, communication, storage, system software, management, and generic application services that are needed to support the IS service.

Typical examples of enterprise IS/IT services are payroll, e-mail, manage customer information, manage sales information, update employee record, order processing, lead creation, claim payment, payment processing, transaction authorisation, office network service, storage service, printing service, security services, and so forth.[36]

What Is IT Operationalization Capability?

We now move from the previous high-level definition of IT operationalization to a lower, more detailed definition. This book defines IT operationalization capability as the availability of the right enterprise resources—that is, the availability of the right governance architecture (organisational structure filled with competent people), processes, information, systems/tools, and other resources that are necessary for identifying, planning, sourcing, provisioning, and monitoring IT services. IT operationalization also includes the capability for operating, protecting, supporting, and maintaining the portfolio of enterprise applications and technology platforms upon which the IT services are deployed. According to Forrester Research, 'IT enables the business to be successful through systems it supports, services it provides, and projects it conducts.'[37]

Recall that the governance architecture aspect of IT operationalization capability is the design of effective IT operationalization governance architecture, which was the subject of the first chapter of this book. The remaining three key components of IT operationalization capability—people, processes, and information—is the focus of this chapter.

IT operationalization has three main goals. The first is to ensure that the strategic IT capabilities-cum-services delivered to an enterprise are closely aligned to its needs. The second goal is to ensure that the delivered IT services continue to be available to the end users in the enterprise at the specified level of quality and cost. The last goal is to ensure that the services are effectively utilised by the users throughout their entire life span.

The Evolution of the IT Operationalization Capability Model

Following an enterprise's need to align its IT capabilities with business capabilities, the need to improve the delivery and support of IT services, and the need to improve the availability, continuity, protection, and their utilisation of IT services, is the need to have a structured and formal process for meeting these needs. Consequently, the concept of IT service management (ITSM) was conceived by an unknown entity to help enterprises deliver and support IT services that are aligned to the needs of the enterprise. According to Wikipedia, 'No one author, organization, or vendor owns the term "IT service management" and the origins of the phrase are unclear.'

The Rick Leopoldi suggested that one possible origin of ITSM is in the historical IT systems management functions and services carried out in the mainframe-computing era, refined over the years to a certain level of maturity that now includes examples of services such as disaster recovery, issues resolution, change management, high availability management, configuration management, and so forth.[38]

ITSM has evolved to a methodology that is based on the IT Infrastructure Library (ITIL), which is a compilation of IT service management best practices developed by the OGC. The only difference between the two is that while ITIL compiles the best practices, ITSM puts them to use in the real world.[39] ITSM consists of five main steps: assessment, architect and designing, planning, implementation, and support for executing the two main functional areas of the methodology (IT services delivery and support). These two main functional areas consist of eleven (11) sub-processes.[40]

The first category, IT services support, consists of the following:[41]

1. Configuration management
2. Change management
3. Release management
4. Incident management
5. Problem management
6. Service desk (function)

The second category, IT service delivery, consists of the following:[42]

1. Availability management
2. IT service continuity
3. Capacity management
4. Service level management
5. Financial management for IT services

Following the evolution of ITSM, the OGC published a compilation of IT services management best practices called ITIL that consists of five (5) service life cycle stages: service strategy, service design, service transition, service operation, and continual service improvement.[43] Each of the ITIL service life cycle stages or disciplines consists of numerous service management processes that are meant to guide enterprises in their effort to design, transit, and operate IT services (see Figure 5.0).

THE FOURTH RATIONAL STEP: IT OPERATIONALIZATION

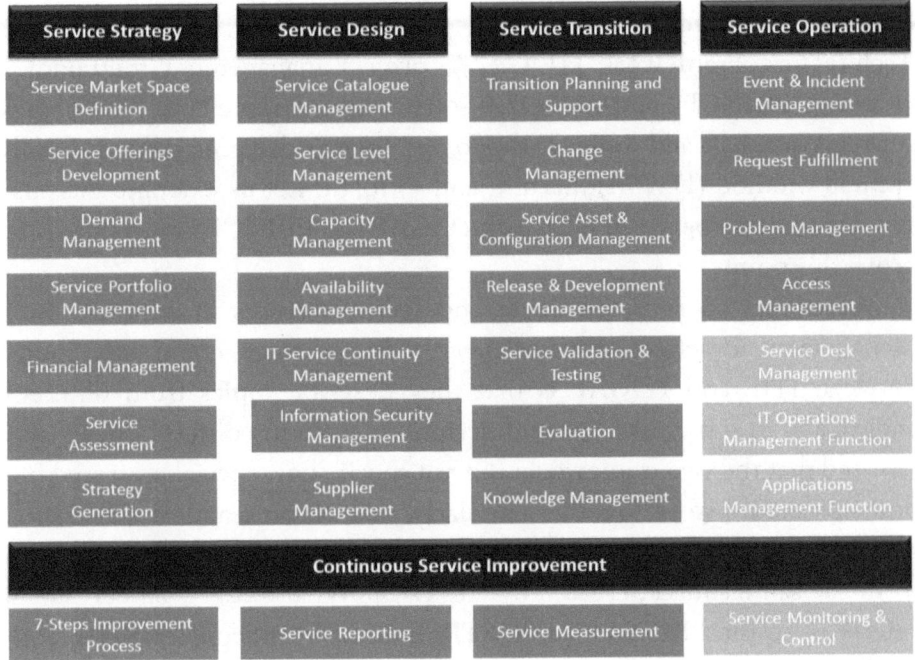

Figure 5.0 ITIL Service Management Processes

Rational Steps for IT Operationalization

The ITIL framework is comprehensive and all encompassing, making it a complex topic. Because of this complexity, the adoption of the framework might be costly and require a lot of time to complete, which might make the realisation of benefits from ITIL difficult.[44] In addition, because the framework is complex and requires a considerable amount of time to implement, the framework might not be seen as good value; as a result, the probability of the implementation of ITIL being abandoned midway, before the benefits are realised, is very high.[45]

Another limitation of the ITIL framework is that the framework was developed without considering other frameworks or methodologies. Thus, ITIL does not integrate seamlessly with other popular IT management frameworks and methodologies such as strategic IT planning frameworks;

enterprise architecture management frameworks (e.g., The Open Group Architecture Framework [TOGAF]); project management methodologies (e.g., PRINCE2 and PMBOK); software development methodologies such as Waterfall; and Agile methodology such as dynamic systems development method (DSDM), Scrum, and so forth. Let us examine the possible integration between ITIL with TOGAF and PRINCE2 as examples to prove this point.

According to Tom van Sante and Jeroen Ermers in an OGC Best Management Practices White Paper, 'What is most commonly found between ITIL and TOGAF is that they describe topics from different angles, and in some cases those descriptions seem to conflict.'[46] They also stressed that the two frameworks did not specify how specialists from both domains should work together. Similarly, there is no seamless integration between the ITIL framework and PRINCE2, even though they are both from the same source, created by UK OGC. What exists is an occasional reference to the PRINCE2 in the ITIL framework documentations, coupled with the fact that the framework did not give any details on the integration between the two.[47]

Another major drawback of the framework is in its perception of IT service as something that is tangible, something that is built, created, or procured, which totally contradicts the generally accepted notion of service as something that is intangible. The Software Engineering Institute (SEI) at Carnegie Mellon University defined a service as 'a product that is intangible and non-storable.'[48] This idea of the tangibility of IT services was clearly demonstrated in the OGC's description of the ITIL framework, even though the OGC itself regarded services as 'delivering something of value to a customer that is not goods (physical things with material value).'[49] The OGC later described an IT service as something that has to be designed with considerations for service availability, capacity, security, and continuity, after which they are created by being built or procured, followed by their transition and operation, all of which is initiated by the formulation of a service strategy.[50] Strategy consists of the portfolio of services to be created and their design, transition, and operations requirements.

In addition to this misconception, the OGC's ITIL framework perceived a service as something that is created through the availability of a particular capability, and when an enterprise does not have the capability to create and deliver a service, and if the service does not already exist in its service portfolio pipeline, then *a new service is created*.[51] One would have thought that upon the non-availability of the capability to create or deliver an IT service, the next logical step would have been to contact the segment of the enterprise whose responsibility it is to develop new IT capabilities for the creation and delivery of IT services. It is understandable that a service can be procured from a service provider; however, the building of a service or the development of a capability to create and deliver a service belongs to the domain of strategic IT planning—called IT solutioning—and that of the portfolio, programmes, and projects management office (called IT execution) and not of ITSM. However, the ITIL framework did not make any effort to explain these distinctions or relationships, thereby causing a lot of confusion in the adoption and implementation of the framework.

Because of these limitations, this book has developed a simplified capability framework for IT service management called the rational IT operationalization capability framework (see Figure 5.0).

Rational IT Operationalization System or Capability Model

The rational IT operationalization capability model consists of six (6) key capability phases or steps (see Figure 5.0 below), each with its own goal or purpose, owner, input, processing activities, supporting systems, and output that contributes toward the operationalization of IT systems. The goal of this model or framework is to guide enterprises in developing their IT operationalization capability. Subsequent series of this book will provide detailed descriptions of this model.

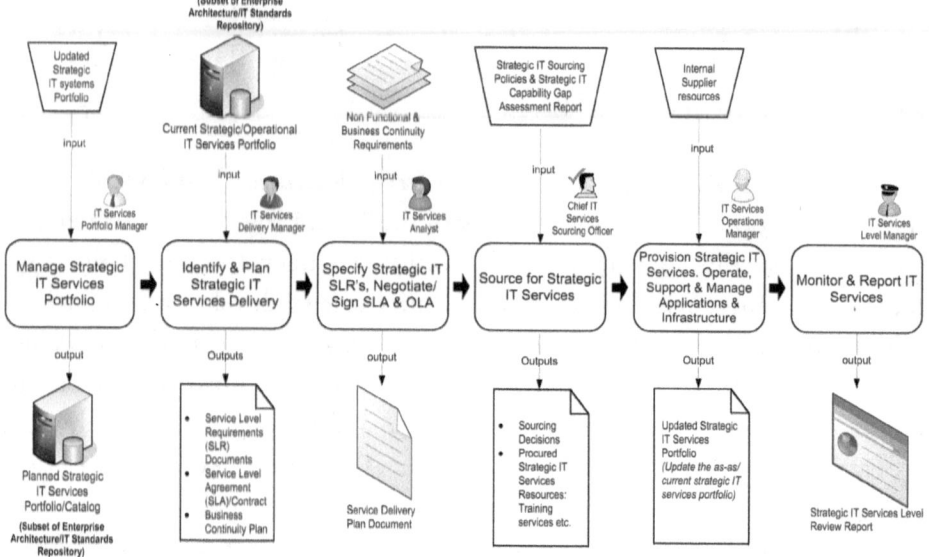

Figure 5.0 Rational IT Operationalization Capability Model

Summary

IT operationalization capability is critical to the management and generation of maximum value from IT investments and for succeeding with IT in general because it helps to ensure that an enterprise is provisioning the right IT services at the right level of quality and cost to support the delivery of business services that create value for its customers.

This capability represents the ability of an enterprise to translate the strategic IT systems delivered at the IT execution step into a business-relevant portfolio of strategic IT services or *operational systems* that will be used to support or enable the delivery of business services. This capability also includes the ability of an enterprise to maintain the usability, availability, protection, and continuity of those IT systems or services throughout their economic life cycle.

NOTES

1. Weill, P., & Broadbent, M. (1998). *Leveraging the New Infrastructure: How Market Leaders Capitalize on Information Technology*. US: Harvard Business School Press, p. 8.
2. Brainy Quote. (n.d.). *Peter Drucker Quotes*. Retrieved February 7, 2012, from Brainy Quote Web Site: http://www.brainyquote.com/quotes/authors/p/peter_drucker_2.html.
3. Delone, W. H., & McLean, E. R. (2003). The Delone and McLean Model of Information Systems Success: A Ten-Year Update. *Journal of Management Information Systems, 19*(4), 9-30, p. 1.
4. Symons, C., Leaver, S., & DeGennaro, T. (2009). *Programs, Not Projects, Delivers Business Value*. US: Forrester Research Inc, p. 1.
5. IBM Global Services. (1998). *Improving systems availability*. US: IBM, p. 1.
6. Hunter, R., & Westerman, G. (2009). *The Real Business of IT: How CIOs Create and Communicate Value*. US: Harvard Business Press, p. 24.
7. Ibid.
8. Morgan, M., Levitt, R. E., & Malek, W. (2007). *Executing Your Strategy: How to Break it Down and Get it Done*. US: Harvard Business School Press, p. 213.
9. Ibid.
10. Ibid., p. 231.
11. Cook-Davies, T. (2002). The real success factors on projects. *International Journal of Project Management*, 185-190, p. 185.
12. Ibid., p. 187.
13. Peppard, J., Ward, J., & Daniel, E. (2007, March). Managing The Realisation of Business Benefits from IT Investments. *MIS Quarterly Executive, 6*(1), 1-11, p. 3.
14. Kneller, M. (2010, September). Executive Briefing: The Benefits of ITIL. *OGC Best Management Practice*. UK: The Stationery Office, p. 3.
15. Office of Government Commerce. (2010). *Introduction to the ITIL Service Lifecycle*. UK: The Stationery Office, p. 3.

16 Peters, A., Symons, C., Cullen, A., & Worthington, B. (2008). *Five Essential Best Practices for The IT-TO-BT Transformation: CIOs Must Prepare IT For its Future Role As BT Enabler.* US: Forrester Research Inc.
17 Ibid., p. 6.
18 Peppard, J. (2003). Managing IT as a Portfolio of Services. *European Management Journal, 21*(4), 467-483, p. 467.
19 Arraj, V. (2010, May). ITIL: The Basics. *OGC Best Management Practice.* The Stationery Office, p. 4.
20 Kneller, *Executive Briefing: The Benefits of ITIL*, p. 4
21 Peters, A., Symons, C., Cullen, A., & Worthington, B. (2008). *Governing The Business Technology Service Portfolio: BT Portfolio Management Requires Demand-Supply Governance.* US: Forrester Research Inc, p. 3.
22 Arraj, *ITIL*, p. 4.
23 Hunter & Westerman, *The Real Business of IT*, p. 51.
24 Weill, P., & Ross, J. W. (2004). *IT Governance: How Top Performers Manage IT Decision Rights for Superior Results.* US: Harvard Business Press, p. 102.
25 Broadbent, M., & Kitzis, E. (2005). *The New CIO Leader: Setting the Agenda and Delivering Results.* US: Harvard Business School Press, p. 180.
26 Ibid., p. 193.
27 Hunter & Westerman, *The Real Business of IT*, p. 49.
28 Kneller, *Executive Briefing: The Benefits of ITIL*, p. 4.
29 Office of Government Commerce. (2010). *Introduction to the ITIL Service Lifecycle.* UK: The Stationery Office, p. 5.
30 Ibid., p. 199.
31 Ibid.,
32 Peppard, *Managing IT as a Portfolio of Services*, p. 467
33 Office of Government Commerce, *Introduction to the ITIL Service Lifecycle*, p. 199.
34 Peters et al, *Governing The Business Technology Service Portfolio*, p. 2.
35 Wout, J., Waage, M., Hartman, H., Stahlecker, M., & Hofman, A. (2010). *The Integrated Architectural Framework Explained: Why, What, How.* Germany: Springer
36 Ibid.,

37 Scott, J., Cullen, A., & An, M. (2009). *Business Capabilities Provide The Rosetta Stone for Business-IT Alignment: Capability Maps Are a Foundation for Business Architecture.* US: Forrester Reseach, Inc, p. 3.
38 Leopoldi, R. (n.d.). *IT Service Management General Information.* Retrieved February 11, 2012, from IT Service Management Portal: http://www.itsm.info/ITSM.htm
39 Ibid.
40 Ibid.
41 Ibid.
42 Ibid.
43 Office of Government Commerce, *Introduction to the ITIL Service Lifecycle*, p. 150.
44 Tudor, D. J. (2010). *Agile Project and Service Management: delivering IT services using ITIL, PRINCE2 and DSDM Atern.* London: The Stationery Office, p. 27.
45 Ibid.
46 Sante, T., & Ermers, J. (2009, September). TOGAF 9 and ITIL V3 Two Frameworks Whitepaper. *OGC Best Management Practice.* UK: The Stationery Office, p. 8.
47 Bordewijk, M. (2005, June 6). *ITIL and Prince2 - Change Using Project Management.* Retrieved Frebruary 12, 2011, from An IT Business Edge Site: http://www.itsmwatch.com/itil/article.php/3510161/ITIL-and-Prince2--Change-Using-Project-Management.htm.
48 Software Engineering Institute. (2009, February). Improving Processes for Better Services. *CMMI for Services, Version 1.2.* US: Carnegie Mellon University, p. 495.
49 Office of Government Commerce, *Introduction to the ITIL Service Lifecycle*, p. 213.
50 Ibid., p. 158
51 Ibid.

CHAPTER 6

THE FIFTH RATIONAL STEP: IT BENEFITING
HOW-TO HARVEST THE EXPECTED BENEFITS OF IT SERVICES IN FULL

IT BENEFITING

*The technology, the software, it doesn't
do anything—it enables people do things they
didn't think they could do...*
—Steve Ballmer, CEO of Microsoft[1]

The four (4) IT investment management capabilities that have been developed to manage IT investments and generate maximum business value are outlined below:

1. The capability to make effective IT alignment and investment decisions (IT governance).

2. The capability to *identify* the *right* strategic IT investment initiatives and to translate the initiatives into technically, financially, and business feasible strategic IT solutions through the design of effective solution architectures (IT solutioning).

3. The capability to choose and deliver the *best* strategic IT solutions-cum-projects, or IT investments with the highest potential to deliver value (IT execution).

4. The capability to provision, protect, support strategic IT systems-cum-services, as well as to operate and maintain the underlying IT infrastructure (IT operationalization).

The assertions of Richard Hunter and George Westerman in *The Real Business of IT* helped to further consolidate the credibility of the five rational steps or capabilities for managing IT investments and generating maximum business value, four of which are summarised above.[2] The duo stated that, aside from managing the IT function well, effective IT executives also assist business executives to carry out their responsibilities in making good IT investment decisions by designing effective IT governance architecture, by putting effective IT oversight mechanisms in place for their business peers so that they can understand what is happening in IT.[3] The duo further stated that by helping business executives make sense of their business applications needs and decide on the best IT initiatives that will get investments, and by executing the initiatives-cum-projects successfully and ensuring that the projects deliver the benefits they promised, the IT organisations create a systematic process that visibly helps to generate maximum value from IT investments.[4] The duo succinctly summarised all the steps or capabilities that are the core of this book, and outlined above; these capabilities were described as the critical factors for managing and generating maximum value from IT investments, except for one step that is not included in their assertion: the IT operationalization capability.

The fifth and final IT investment management capability that enterprises must develop in order to manage and generate maximum value from their IT investments is the IT benefiting capability, which is required to realise or harvest the value promised by strategic IT investment projects or by their business sponsors. IT benefiting is the last step in the IT investment management life cycle because it is the point in time where the rubber meets the road, the point where the value promised by IT investment projects is realised and reviewed by the *business change* or *benefit realisation manager*. Marianne Broadbent and Ellen S. Kitzis, in *The New CIO Leader*, argued that 'having a benefits-management or value realization process in place is one of the big differences between those who do and those who don't realize value from their initiatives.'[5]

Given the significance of value realisation to the success of IT investments, one might assume that enterprises would have developed a matured capability for harvesting value from their investments in IT; on the contrary, the IT benefiting capability of most enterprises is not mature enough to completely harvest or review the benefits they are expecting from their investments in IT. According to a 2006 Cranfield University School of Management study, 65 percent of the IT managers of the one hundred European organisations studied said that their organisations were not okay or confident in their ability to identify all the benefits that are available or attainable from an IT investment project.[6] From the same study, 69 percent of the IT managers admitted that they did not quantify the benefits adequately, nor did they place value on them. Therefore, if the IT managers of an organisation cannot identify and quantify all the benefits that are attainable from their IT investment project, it is almost impossible for them to harvest the expected benefits of the investment project in full because benefit identification and quantification are necessary conditions for benefit realisation.

Another study revealed that only 25 percent of enterprises regularly review the expected benefits of their IT investment projects at the end of delivery,[7] which has resulted in a major issue for both business and IT executives. In *Achieving Business Value From Technology*, Tony Murphy pointed out that 'obtaining business value from IT investments continues to be among the top concerns of CIOs and CEOs, as evidenced by Gartner's annual survey of business and information technology executives.'[8] The reason why top executives are having this concern, Murphy explained, is that they are not sure when or if their investments in IT projects will generate any form of return. So, if IT benefiting or the realisation of value or benefits from IT investments is critical to achieving success with IT, what type of value are enterprises seeking from strategic IT investments, and how can enterprises achieve or realise this value?

What is Value?

Before discussions on the types of IT value, the challenges associated with IT value realisation, and their possible solutions, one needs to understand what exactly business value or even just value is, and to understand the relationship between value and benefit, as they are often used interchangeably in most literature, including this book.

Having a clear and unambiguous definition of value will help us to understand the reasons why enterprises are concerned with obtaining value from their investments in IT and to understand the kind of value they are hoping to generate. The IT Governance Institute (ITGI) defined 'value as the total life-cycle *benefits* net of related costs, adjusted for risk and (in the case of financial value) for the time value of money.'[9] While the *Oxford Advanced Learner's Dictionary 8th Edition* explained value as 'how much something is worth compared with its price,' it also defined value as 'the quality of being useful or important.' The same dictionary also indicated that value is synonymous with benefit, which means value has the same or nearly the same meaning as benefit.

Gerald Bradley, in *Benefit Realisation Management*, defined benefit as 'an outcome of change which is perceived as positive by the stakeholder.'[10] He further elaborated that benefits are measurable outcomes that are of *value* to an enterprise and its stakeholders. The *Oxford Advanced Learner's Dictionary* also defined benefits as 'an advantage that something gives you; a helpful and useful effect that sth [something] has.' Based on Bradley's definition above, it is tempting to say value and benefit are the same, but this is not so because the necessary and sufficient condition for anything to be valuable is when the benefits—the advantage that something gives you—outweigh the costs and risks of possessing that thing.

Therefore, if the benefit of a thing does not outweigh the cost of its acquisition and the risk associated with it, the thing cannot be said to be of value. From a benefit-realisation point of view, the ITGI corroborated the view maintained in this book about value or business value by stating that 'benefit realisation further ensures that the realisation of business benefits is unfolding at levels of return sufficient enough to merit the resources being expended to achieve the benefits.'[11]

What Is IT Benefiting Capability?

The aim of this section is to answer the question that was posed in the previous section of this book; that is, how can enterprises realise the value that is promised by IT investments? And the answer to this question is simple and straight forward: enterprises can generate maximum value or realise full benefits from their investments in IT by developing the capability that is necessary and sufficient for realising or harvesting all the benefits promised by IT investments (by developing IT benefiting capability).

IT benefiting capability is the availability of the right combination of enterprise resources that are required to plan and carry out all the actions or changes that are needed to harvest the benefits promised by IT investments. In other words, IT benefiting capability is the availability of the right governance architecture (organisational structure filled with competent people), processes, information, and systems to harvest the expected benefits of IT investments.

The Evolution of the IT Benefiting Capability Model

In order to develop the model that is necessary and sufficient to aid the development of the ability of enterprises to harvest or realise the full benefit of their investments in IT, we began by identifying the challenges that enterprises are facing regarding the realisation of benefits from IT investment projects. Second, we identified the factors that are responsible for these value-generation or benefit-realisation challenges, after which this book identified the factors that are critical to the successful harvesting of value or benefits from IT investment projects, or those factors that can help to overcome the benefit harvesting challenges identified earlier.

The Benefit Challenge

Like any other type of capital investment project, an enterprise invests its scarce resources in information technology (IT) assets in order to make good returns on its investments, a return/benefit that is expected to outweigh the cost and the risk involved in carrying out the investments and a return that is better than those offered by competing investment opportunities.

Unfortunately, the finance director or chief financial officers (CFOs) of enterprises hoping to receive positive returns on their investments in IT are extremely frustrated by the huge investments they are making in IT that are not yielding any direct or measurable benefits.[12] Peter Weill, a research scientist at MIT, and Margrethe H. Olson, a professor at Bentley College, affirmed earlier assertions by stating that enterprises invest in IT with the hope of making a real return. But contrary to their expectations, investments in IT have not yielded any real or direct return and, if they have, little direct evidence exists to prove it.[13]

Further compounding CFOs' dilemma is the admission by 20 percent of all US IT managers or chief information officers (CIOs) that their existing IT investments have failed to generate positive returns for their enterprise; another 25 percent admitted that they are only mildly convinced that their investments in IT had delivered a good or positive return.[14] It is surprising that IT executives admitted to not delivering good returns on IT investments; one can only imagine what the results will be if business executives were the ones surveyed. Corroborating these appalling statistics, the Standish Group reported in 2009 that only 32 percent of IT investment projects are considered successful, meaning they are delivered on time, on budget, and with the required functionalities; 44 percent of projects are challenged; and the remaining 24 percent fail or are cancelled prior to completion, or they are delivered and never used.[15]

Reasons for the Value/Benefits Challenge

Although many explanations have been given to justify the reasons why enterprises' investments in IT assets are not yielding good returns, this book has identified five major factors that are deemed to be responsible for this benefit realisation challenge.

Challenge 1: Financial Justification

The approach chosen by enterprises to calculate the return of investment (ROI) of their IT investments is one reason why enterprises are not able to generate maximum value from their investments in IT or for the failure of IT investments to deliver maximum value or deliver their full benefits to an enterprise. Research indicates that enterprises tend to focus more on reducing IT cost by manipulating the denominator when they are calculating the cost-benefit ratio of their IT investment projects, rather than focusing on how IT will be used to generate significant benefits (the numerator).[16]

Challenge 2: Business Case Challenge

Another explanation that was given for why IT investment projects do not deliver their benefits in full is that in many organisations, the availability of a business case is mandatory for the approval of IT investment projects, which in itself is a good practice. However, during the development of the business case, the benefits of IT investment projects are often exaggerated: the cost of the project is underestimated or the benefits are overestimated in order to get the projects selected or to get the investment proposals approved[17,18] so that they can move to the next IT investment management step—execution. Since these expected benefits are exaggerated, most enterprises do not even bother to review them—that is, to assess whether the expected benefits are being realised from the delivered IT systems. According to a 2003 Kellogg School of Management survey of 130 CIOs of major US enterprises, 68 percent of the CIOs surveyed do not care to carry out a post-investment benefit review (i.e., to assess whether the investment projects actually delivered the expected benefits) as part of their performance review.[19]

Challenge 3: IT Investment Life Cycle Management

The naïve assumptions enterprises make when they invest in IT is yet another explanation that accounts for the inability of IT investments projects to deliver maximum value or deliver their full benefits. Enterprises assume that once an IT investment project is delivered on time, within budget, with the required features and functions, and within the specified technical constraints, benefits will begin to roll in.[20] This is a classic case of confusing IT investment project *management* success with IT investment project *success*. According to Richard Hunter and George Westerman in *The Real Business of IT*, 'Some CIOs, and many other IT professionals, act as if they believe that their jobs are finished when the technology is installed.'[21] From the point of view of business executives, however, the job of the CIOs and other IT professionals is finished only when the benefits that an enterprise seeks from investing in IT are realised.[22]

Challenge 4: IT Benefit Measurement

Another major reason why enterprises could not realise the full benefits of IT investment is that a large percentage of the benefits delivered by IT investments are not easily quantifiable as they are mostly qualitative benefits rather than quantitative benefits; as a result, traditional performance metrics such as ROI, NPV, IRR, and payback period are not adequate.[23] According to the old adage, 'What you cannot measure, you cannot manage.' So, if an enterprise cannot measure the expected benefits of investments in IT, how likely is it that the same enterprise will be able to manage the realisation of these immeasurable benefits. Because these intangible benefits are not easy to measure, most enterprises tend to ignore them and, hence, set to zero.[24]

Challenge 5: IT Benefit Harvesting or Realisation

Last, the lack of an effective benefit realisation management process—that is, the process for planning, executing, reviewing, reporting, and making benefit realisation management become deep-rooted in the DNA of the enterprise—was also found to be responsible for the inability of enterprises to generate maximum value from their investments in IT.[25]

Critical Success Factors for IT Benefit Realisation

Enterprises that desire to generate maximum value from their investments in IT must consider the following critical factors when developing processes, plans, strategies, methodologies, frameworks, approaches, or capabilities that will be used to harvest or realise the full benefits of their investments in IT:

1. Provide an effective mechanism for governing strategic IT investment programmes, including the provision of governance architecture for benefit realisation or the availability of a business sponsor to own the benefit realisation process and be accountable for its performance.[26] According to Tony Murphy in *Achieving Business Value from Technology*, 'Without clear accountability, the business value of IT investments cannot be fully realized, if realized at all.'[27]

2. Make available general IT benefit realisation principles to guide a benefit realisation plan, process, or approach and to guide business case development.[28]

3. Ensure that every major IT investment project is accompanied by a business case with the exception of mandatory projects.[29,30]

4. Every strategic IT investment *programme* should have a benefit realisation strategy or plan, and every strategic IT *project* should have a benefit review plan.[31,32]

5. Perform a periodic post-investment benefit realisation review.[33]

6. Perform a post-implementation review (PIR).[34,35,36]

Effective Governance of Benefit Realisation Activities or Processes

Ensuring that strategic IT investments deliver their expected value is very long and tedious,[37] a process that usually begins when the business need for a strategic IT system is established or when strategic IT investment opportunities are identified—that is, starting from solutioning (where business cases are created), transiting through execution, operationalization, and benefiting. Because this process is very long and cuts across many domains with multiple stakeholders' involvement, it must be governed and managed effectively for its successful performance.[38] According to the duo Peter Weill and Marianne Broadbent in *Leveraging the New*

Infrastructure, 'Governance processes are an important part of achieving business value from information technology investments.'[39] They further stated that having transparent governance processes in place to govern the realisation of value from IT provides enterprises with clear paths for engaging, involving at different levels, and distributing decision rights and responsibilities among different stakeholders in the enterprise with the intent of making effective IT benefit realisation decisions.

Governing the IT investment benefit realisation process entails designing the right governance architecture, which is, selecting or arranging the right governance building blocks—organisation structure, competent people, processes, systems, and communications mechanisms—for making effective IT benefiting decisions and for managing the risk associated with benefit realisation. A detailed description of how enterprises should design effective IT benefit governance architecture is provided in the chapter on IT governance.

In *The New CIO Leader*, Marianne Broadbent and Ellen S. Kitzis suggested that the business unit head whose function is dependent on the new IT investment project should be appointed as the sponsor of the benefits management or value realisation process.[40]

Availability of general IT benefit realisation principles

Three notable professors—two from the Cranfield School of Management and the other from the Open University—suggested five key principles that should form the basis of an enterprise plan, processes, approach, and decisions for the realisation of benefits from its investments in IT[41] and for the development of business cases. The first principle points out that IT alone does not confer any benefit or generate value; IT only enables the creation or generation of value. Unlike other investments, such as diamonds, a house, and so forth, the value of IT is not in its possession or the possession of its product: information, the value of IT, is in its exploitation or effective utilisation. The rest of the principles are listed below:[42]

- *Principle 2:* Benefits emerge when IT enables or supports an enterprise to do things in a more effective or efficient way.

- *Principle 3:* Only business managers, end users, customers, and suppliers can realise the expected benefits of IT investment projects; as a result, line-of-business managers acting as business sponsors should be held accountable for benefit realisation.

- *Principle 4:* All IT investment projects can either have positive or negative outcomes; enterprises must identify the negative outcomes and avoid them, while maximising positive outcomes.

- *Principle 5:* Benefits do not occur automatically, so enterprises must actively manage benefit realisation across the entire life cycle of IT investment projects in order for them to be realised.

Ensuring Every Major Strategic IT Investment Project Is Accompanied By a Business Case

The creation and utilisation of a business case is one of the most important tools, if not *the* most important tool, for generating maximum value from IT investments.[43] It is essential input to almost all of the IT investment management (ITIM) process steps.[44] First, the business case is the essential tool for identifying the right IT investment opportunities (IT solutioning) and for evaluating and selecting the best IT investment projects to fund (IT execution).[45,46] Second, a business case is also an essential tool for executing or delivering IT investment projects.[47] Therefore, the creation and use of the business case is the first among the seven themes of the PRINCE2 project management methodology.[48] Finally, the business case is the essential component for harvesting the value of IT investments (IT benefiting). The business case is the only document that exists throughout the entire life cycle of IT investments.

Although, it might make perfect sense to a typical chief financial officer (CFO) and might also seem rational to the chief executive officer of an enterprise that all IT investment initiatives should have a financial justification or business case, there are situations in which it is practically impossible to develop a business case for IT investment opportunities or initiatives. IT investment initiatives that are foundational or infrastructural, which will provide a shared IT services foundation to be used by multiple application software (e.g., networking, middleware technologies, and security technologies), and those that are mandated by government regulations, do not require a business case; they should be considered exceptions.[49]

In addition, the benefits of some IT investment opportunities, such as strategic and infrastructural IT investment opportunities, are hard to quantify as the benefits they deliver to enterprises are mostly intangible; these types of IT investments typically have long payback periods.[50] This apparent difficulty in quantifying the benefits or estimating the net cash flow of strategic and infrastructural IT investments in advance, led researchers, including Peter Weill and Marianne Broadbent in *Leveraging the New Infrastructure,* to recommend using alternative approaches in justifying these types of investments.[51,52] Weill and Broadbent argued that 'most strategic and many infrastructural investments require other approaches.'[53]

Given the significance of the business case to the generation of maximum value from IT investments and to enterprise success with IT, what then is a business case? And how should an enterprise go about developing an effective business case document? Last, at what stage of the IT investment management life cycle should a business case be developed and by whom?

What is a Business Case?

A business case is a living document (not a static document that is created once and left alone) that contains all the information required to justify potential IT investments—that is, to judge whether an investment opportunity is *desirable* (has the best potential for value), *viable* (will deliver expected products), and *achievable* (will deliver the expected benefits).[54,55,56]

To be effective in justifying potential IT investment initiatives, a business case document must provide the following information:[57,58,59,60]

1. *What* initiative is needed to achieve strategic business objectives, to solve strategic issues, or to exploit emerging opportunities.

2. Reasons *why* the investment should be done, stating the specific benefits to be derived from the investment opportunities.

3. A description of *how* it should be done by giving solution options and their architectural descriptions, sourcing strategy, funding strategy, project management and software development/implementation methodologies, and so forth.

4. *What* is required to get it done and realise benefits from it: actions/enterprise changes, costs/resources, and timescales.

5. *Who* will be responsible for realising the benefits promised by the investments or who will own or sponsor the investment opportunities.

In order to *give reasons why the investment should be done*, the business case usually contains information that is in line with the criteria for evaluating and selecting the best investment project, which was pre-determined at the IT governance stage. Other information contained in the business case will be outlined in subsequent sections.

How to Develop a Business Case

The first step to creating an effective business case is to ensure that it contains all the information that is required by all concerned stakeholders in the enterprise—that is, IT portfolio managers, programme/project managers, IT service operations manager, business change managers, and so forth—to make effective IT investment decisions or to carry out their individual assignments.

In order to be an effective tool for generating maximum value from IT investments, enterprises or the responsible stakeholder should ensure that the final document of a business case contains the following information:

1. Strategic business capability assessment report (enterprise analysis report): provides the strategic context for strategic IT investment opportunities[61]

2. Alternative solutions and analysis: identifies options and alternatives to the proposed strategic IT solution; further analysis of potential options should be performed to identify the preferred solution[62]

3. Selected strategic IT solution options, their architecture, and sourcing strategy: provides solutions context by detailing the product description and scope, assumptions, and constraints and provides answers to the *what* question[63,64]

4. The expected benefit (tangible and intangible) and high-level statement of how they will be realised, together with a statement of what constitutes a successful outcome

5. The expected dis-benefit

6. The estimated cost: initial and on-going costs of operations and maintenance

7. Funding strategy: statement of how the project will be funded

8. Risk assessment: statement of major risks and any proposed responses

9. Cost/benefit analysis or investment appraisal

10. Non-financial benefit analysis

11. Risk/return analysis

12. Estimated timescale

13. The enterprise (business and technology) changes needed to create additional value or business process impact or impact assessment[65]

14. Business sponsor/benefit realisation accountability

When should a business case be developed and by whom?

The first type of business case to be developed by the enterprise is called the initial programme concept business case or preliminary project proposal,[66,67] which involves nothing more than conducting a technical and commercial feasibility analysis on IT investment opportunities in their embryonic stage.[68]

The initial business case should contain just enough information to assess the viability of the strategic IT initiative-cum-solution concept, or the proposed investment project, and to determine whether it merits the development of a full or detailed business case.[69] Initial business cases are usually mandatory for large IT investment initiatives.[70] Where the development of a detailed/full business case requires substantial commitment of financial and human resources; therefore, in order not to waste these resources, enterprises are obligated to first assess the viability of large IT investment opportunities before major resources are committed to the development of a full business case.

The initial business case is developed or created at the earlier stage of the IT investment management life cycle (i.e., at the IT solutioning step), the point where IT investment opportunities are identified and translated into technically and commercially feasible IT solutions, while the detailed/full business case is developed at a much later stage of the IT solutioning process.

The development of an initial business case should be a joint collaboration between IT function and the business management that is most affected by the IT solution[71] because it is primarily created to assess the technical feasibility of a potential IT solution, followed by the assessment of the business and financial feasibility of the said solution. This is an indication that an IT solution must first be technically possible to realise before it is assessed for financial affordability to assess whether the enterprise can afford the proposed IT solution, and business possibility to assess whether the proposed IT solution is aligned with business strategy, and if the business has the capability to deliver the solution.[72] The IT Governance Institute (ITGI) advocated that the technical aspects of both the initial and detailed business case—that is, the outcome of the technical feasibility assessment—should be approved and signed off by the CIO,[73] while both the initial and detailed business case should be approved and signed off by the business sponsor.[74]

Peter Weill and Jeanne W. Ross in *IT Savvy* also supported this view by stating that 'the lines of business prepare a business case detailing the specific business benefits of a new initiative, while the IT group provides input on costs, technology options, alternative approaches, and time frames.'[75] Mark D. Lutchen, author of *Managing IT as a Business*, corroborated this view by stating that 'the ultimate responsibility for making the business case rests with the various functional and business-unit leaders.'[76]

It is now overwhelmingly clear that the line-of-business manager acting as business sponsor should own the business case document for specific strategic IT investment solutions/projects; however, he or she can choose to delegate the development of the business case to a team that consists of the following people:[77,78]

- An enterprise/business analyst working on behalf of the business sponsor to assess the commercial feasibility of the IT solution, and

- An enterprise solutions architect working on behalf of the CIO to assess the technical feasibility of the proposed IT solution, assisted by

- Financial specialists

Forrester Research supported this conclusion by stating that 'every investment proposal that [has] a business case document[s] must have a named sponsor who will take overall accountability for the business case.'[79] Forrester Research further asserted that a committee, an IT steering or investment review committee, that is made up of both business and IT executives should be the manager and owner of the process, templates, guidelines, and standards for developing business cases.[80]

Following the development, review (that is, determining if the initial business case is strong enough to be assessed at the portfolio level), and approval of the initial business case by the business sponsor or other decision makers, enterprises can commence the development of full/detailed business[81,82] using the same set of resources that created the initial business case.

How to Improve the Effectiveness of a Detailed Business Case

In order to increase the effectiveness of their business cases, enterprises should consider the following recommendations during the development process as they represent some of the reasons why business cases do not yield the best IT investment projects:

- Properly estimate the on-going IT operations cost
- Consider both tangible and intangible benefits (use an IT Balance Score Card if necessary)
- Use different criteria or approaches to review IT investment categories
- Identify who owns each benefit and will be accountable for its delivery
- Identify links between each benefit and the required changes, and identify the stakeholder who will be responsible for ensuring that each change is successfully made[83]
- Baseline current financial or operational metrics of the enterprise and the metrics that are the target of IT investments—before and after metrics[84]
- Agree on business value indicators or evaluation criteria and responsibilities[85]
- Develop or use a standardised business case template with a consistent table of content[86]

Existence of Benefit Realisation Strategy and Plan

The existence or availability of a comprehensive benefits realisation strategy or plan is critical to realisation or generation of maximum value from IT investment programmes because it lays down a structured approach for governing, planning, and executing the enterprise/business changes, or changes to the enterprise's ways of working, that are required to secure the benefits promised by IT investments.[87,88]

Typical examples of enterprise changes required to realise the value of IT investments are as follows: training, policy change, business process redesign, management systems/incentives (introduction of reward system or performance appraisal systems), introduction of new roles/structure, and so forth.

Rational Steps for IT Benefiting

After all that has been said about the challenges enterprises face in realising value from their investments in IT systems, or the fact that IT investment projects often do not deliver their expected value, and the reasons why these challenges exist and continues to exist, organisations are now seeking ways to overcome these challenges. Luckily, so many principles, frameworks, methods, and tools already exist or have been proposed for overcoming these challenges. A few of these principles, methods, and tools will be discussed in this book.

In his book *Achieving Business Value from Technology*, Tony Murphy, a former Gartner VP of Consulting, proposed a framework for realising the business value of IT investments called the five pillars of benefit realisation, which are simply criteria for evaluating and approving potential IT investment projects. The framework proposed by Murphy consists of three elements: pillars, process, and people. The pillar consists of five benefit realisation factors that assess the (1) strategic alignment, (2) business process impact, (3) architecture impact, (4) direct payback, and (5) risk of IT investment opportunities.[89]

Joe Peppard, a professor at Cranfield University, on the other hand, proposed five principles for realising benefits through IT (see previous section). He also asserted that there is a relationship or link between *enterprise change management* and *benefit realisation*.[90] Following up on his proposals and assertions, Peppard recommended the development of a benefit realisation plan based on his aforementioned principles to realise the full benefit of IT investment projects. In order to develop this plan, Peppard suggested enterprises should answer the following seven (7) questions:[91]

1. Why must the enterprise improve?

2. What improvements are necessary or possible?

3. What benefits will be realised? How will each benefit be measured?

4. Who owns each benefit and will be accountable for its delivery?

5. What changes are needed to achieve each benefit? (link benefit and required changes)

6. Who will be responsible for ensuring that each change is successfully made?

7. How and when can the identified changes be made?

Although proven principles, processes, and methodologies exist for realising the expected value of IT investment projects to the fullest, this book has decided to contribute to the existing body of work and knowledge in this area by presenting a capability-oriented model for realising the value of IT investment projects called the rational IT benefiting capability model (see Figure 4.0).

The Rational IT Benefiting Capability Model

The rational IT benefiting capability model consists of five (5) key capabilities phases or steps (see Figure 4.0 below), each with its own goal or purpose, owner, input, activities/tasks, and output that contributes toward the achievement of the overall goal of strategic IT benefiting, which is to realise the full benefits promised by strategic IT investments initiatives.

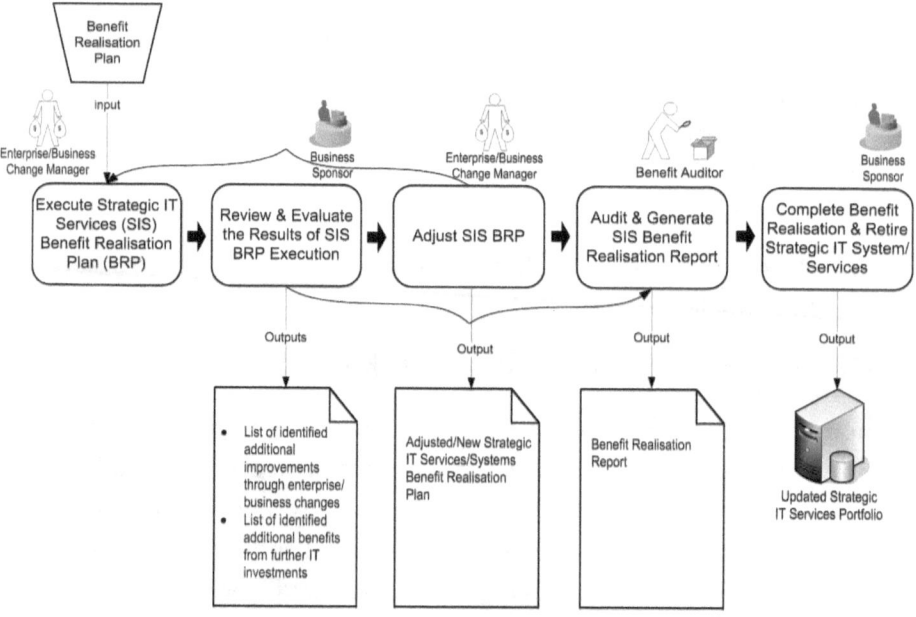

Figure 4.0 Rational IT Benefiting Capability Model

Critical Input for the Rational IT Benefiting Capability Model

The major input for the rational IT benefiting model is the *benefit realisation plan* developed at the IT execution step—that is, during strategic IT programme management.

Critical Output for the Rational IT Benefiting Capability Model

- List of identified additional improvements through enterprise/business changes

- List of identified additional benefits that requires further IT investments

- Adjusted or new strategic IT services or systems benefit realisation plan

- Benefit realisation report

- Updated strategic IT services portfolio

Summary

Enterprises must develop the capability or ability to harvest the full benefits promised by strategic IT capabilities and services (IT investments) in order to generate maximum value from their investments in IT and to succeed in leveraging IT for their success. This capability will help to ensure that enterprises have a plan for realising the benefits of their investments in IT and a plan for reviewing the implementation of their IT investment projects. It also helps to ensure that these plans are executed well, which consequently helps to ensure that enterprises get the benefits they expect from their IT investment projects.

NOTES

1. Ballmer, S. (2005, February 17). *Steve Ballmer: AACIS Unlimited Potential Grant Announcement.* Retrieved February 25, 2012, from A Microsoft Corporation: http://www.microsoft.com/presspass/exec/steve/2005/02-17aacis.msp
2. Hunter, R., & Westerman, G. (2009). *The Real Business of IT: How CIOs Create and Communicate Value.* US: Harvard Business Press, p. 11.
3. Ibid., p. 20.
4. Ibid., p. 11.
5. Broadbent, M., & Kitzis, E. (2005). *The New CIO Leader: Setting the Agenda and Delivering Results.* US: Harvard Business School Press, p. 139
6. Ward, J., Daniel, E., & J., P. (2008). Building Better Business Cases for IT Investments. *MIS Quarterly Executive*, 1-15, p. 2.
7. Ward, J., & Elvin, R. (1999). A New Framework for Managing IT-enabled Business Change. *Information Systems Journal*, 197-221, p. 198.
8. Murphy, T. (2002). *Achieving Business Value from Technology: A Practical Guide for Today's Executive.* US: John Wiley & Sons Inc, loc 112.
9. IT Governance Institute. (2008). *Enterprise Value: Governance of IT Investments, The Val IT Framework 2.0.* US: The IT Governance Institute, p. 10.
10. Bradley, G. (2006). *Benefit Realisation Management: A practical Guide to Achieving Benefits Through Change.* England: Gower Publishing Limited, p. 84.
11. IT Governance Institute, *Enterprise Value: Governance of IT Investments, The Val IT Framework*, p. 14.
12. Bradley, *Benefit Realisation Management*, p. 84.
13. Weill, P., & Olson, M. H. (1989, March). Managing Investments in Information Technology: Mini Case Examples and Implications. *MIS Quarterly, 13*(1), 3-17, p.13.

14 Peppard, J., Ward, J., & Daniel, E. (2007, March). Managing The Realisation of Business Benefits from IT Investments. *MIS Quarterly Executive*, 6(1), 1-11, p. 1.
15 The Standish Group International. (2009). *CHAOS Summary 2009*. US: The Standish Group, p. 1.
16 Peppard et al, *Managing The Realisation of Business Benefits from IT Investments*, p. 1.
17 Ibid., p. 2.
18 Weill, P., & Broadbent, M. (1998). *Leveraging the New Infrastructure: How Market Leaders Capitalize on Information Technology*. US: Harvard Business School Press, p. 212.
19 Bitterli, P. R. (n.d.). Retrieved 03 1, 2012, from Bitterli Consulting Web site: http://www.bitterli-consulting.ch/deutsch/files/EuroCACS09ITGovernanceHardFacts.pdf
20 Peppard et al, *Managing The Realisation of Business Benefits from IT Investments*, p. 2.
21 Hunter & Westerman, *The Real Business of IT*, p. 24.
22 Ibid.,
23 IT Governance Institute. (2005). Measuring and Demonstrating the Value of IT. *IT Governance Domain Practices and Competencies*. US: IT Governance Institute, p. 7.
24 Clemons, E. K., & Weber, B. E. (1990). Strategic Information Technology Investments: Guidelines for Decision Making. *Journal of Management Information System*, 7(2), 9-28, p. 14.
25 Kohli, R., & Devaraj, S. (2004). Realizing the Business Value of Information Technology Investments: An Organisational Process. *MIS Quarterly Executive*, 3(1), 53-68, p. 53.
26 IT Governance Institute, *Enterprise Value: Governance of IT Investments, The Val IT Framework 2.0*, p. 18.
27 Murphy, *Achieving Business Value from Technology*, loc 1247
28 Peppard et al, *Managing The Realisation of Business Benefits from IT Investments*, p. 3.

29 IT Governance Institute. (2005). Optimising Value Creation From IT Investments. *IT Governance Domain Practices and Competencies.* US: IT Governance Institute, P. 13.
30 Gliedman, C., Leganza, G., Visitacion, M., Cecere, M., & Brown, A. (2004). *Key Elements In An IT Business Case.* US: Forrester Research Inc. p. 1.
31 The Office of Government Commerce. (2009). *Managing Successful Projects with PRINCE2.* UK: The Stationery Office, p. 218.
32 IT Governance Institute, *Enterprise Value: Governance of IT Investments, The Val IT Framework 2.0*, p. 18.
33 Hunter & Westerman, *The Real Business of IT*, p. 164.
34 Weill Broadbent, *Leveraging the New Infrastructure*, p. 250.
35 Weill, P., & Ross, J. W. (2009). *IT Savvy: What Top Executives Must Know to Go from Pain to Gain.* Massachusetts: Harvard Business Press, p. 52.
36 Hunter & Westerman, *The Real Business of IT*, p. 163.
37 Weill & Ross, *IT Savvy*, p. 53.
38 Hunter & Westerman, *The Real Business of IT*, p. 160.
39 Weill & Broadbent, *Leveraging the New Infrastructure*, p. 253.
40 Broadbent & Kitzis, *The New CIO Leader*, p. 139.
41 Peppard et al, *Managing The Realisation of Business Benefits from IT Investments*, p. 2.
42 Ibid.,
43 IT Governance Institute. (2006). *Enterprise Value: Governance of IT Investments, The Business Case.* US: The IT Governance Institute, p. 11.
44 Ibid., p. 13.
45 Gliedman et al, *Key Elements In An IT Business Case*, p. 1.
46 IT Governance Institute, *Enterprise Value: Governance of IT Investments, The Val IT Framework 2.0*, p. 13.
47 Ibid.
48 The Office of Government Commerce, *Managing Successful Projects with PRINCE2*, p. 17.
49 Weill & Ross, *IT Savvy*, p. 48.

50 Bardhan, I., Bagchi, S., & Sougstad, R. (2004). Prioritising a Portfolio of Information Technology Investment Projects. *Journal of Management Information Systems, 21*(2), 33-60, p. 34.
51 Ibid.
52 Weill & Broadbent, *Leveraging the New Infrastructure*, p. 213.
53 Ibid.
54 The Office of Government Commerce, *Managing Successful Projects with PRINCE2*, p. 21.
55 Paul, D., Yeates, D., & Cadle, J. (2010). *Business Anlaysis*. UK: British Informatics Society Limited, p. 223.
56 IT Governance Institute, *Enterprise Value: Governance of IT Investments, The Business Case*, p. 10.
57 Cadle, J., & Yeates, D. (2008). *Project Management for Information Systems*. UK: Pearson Education Limited, p. 31.
58 IT Governance Institute, *Enterprise Value: Governance of IT Investments, The Business Case*, p. 12.
59 Feld, C. (2009). *Blind Spot: A Leader's Guide To IT-Enabled Business Transformation*. US: Olive Press
60 Gliedman et al, *Key Elements In An IT Business Case*, p. 3.
61 Cullen, A., Symons, C., Scott, J., & An, M. (2010). *Using Business Capability Maps To Guide IT Investment Governance*. US: Forrester Research Inc., p. 2.
62 Cardin, L., Cullen, A., Symons, C., & Belanger, B. (2007). *The Components Of A Quality Business Case: Don't Let Your Business Cases Tell Only Part Of The Story*. US: Forrester Research Inc., p. 2.
63 Ibid.
64 Paul et al, *Business Anlaysis*, p. 230.
65 Ibid., 235
66 IT Governance Institute, *Enterprise Value: Governance of IT Investments, The Val IT Framework 2.0*, p. 18.
67 Broadbent & Kitzis, *The New CIO Leader*, p. 135.
68 Paul et al, *Business Anlaysis*, p. 223.
69 Broadbent & Kitzis, *The New CIO Leader*, p. 136.
70 Ibid.,

71 Cardin, L., Cullen, A., Orlov, L. M., & Belanger, B. (2007). *Who Owns The IT Business Case?* US: Forrester Research Inc., p. 1.
72 Paul et al, *Business Anlaysis*, p. 227.
73 IT Governance Institute, *Enterprise Value: Governance of IT Investments, The Val IT Framework 2.0*, p. 69.
74 Ibid., p. 79.
75 Weill & Ross, *IT Savvy*, p. 48.
76 Lutchen, M. D. (2004). *Managing IT as a Business: a survival Guide for CEOs*. US: John Wiley & Sons, Inc., p. 18.
77 The Office of Government Commerce, *Managing Successful Projects with PRINCE2*, p. 22.
78 Paul et al, *Business Anlaysis*, p. 11.
79 Cardin et al, *Who Owns The IT Business Case?*, p. 1.
80 Ibid., p. 3.
81 IT Governance Institute, *Enterprise Value: Governance of IT Investments, The Business Case*, p. 11.
82 Broadbent & Kitzis, *The New CIO Leader*, p. 135.
83 Peppard et al, *Managing The Realisation of Business Benefits from IT Investments*, p. 4.
84 Hunter & Westerman, *The Real Business of IT*, p. 159.
85 Weill & Broadbent, *Leveraging the New Infrastructure*, p. 247.
86 Cardin et al, *Who Owns The IT Business Case?*, p. 3.
87 Paul et al, *Business Anlaysis*, p. 241.
88 Peppard et al, *Managing The Realisation of Business Benefits from IT Investments*, p. 3.
89 Murphy, *Achieving Business Value from Technology*
90 Peppard et al, *Managing The Realisation of Business Benefits from IT Investments*, p. 3.
91 Ibid.,

ABOUT THE AUTHOR

SOLOMON BABA is the founder and chief architect of Rational Steps Inc., a global IT investment management (ITIM) consulting, research, and training company. He has more than a decade experience, knowledge, and skill in helping enterprises to manage their IT investments successfully and generate maximum business or organizational value. Prior to founding Rational Steps Inc., Solomon was enterprise and solutions architecting consulting manager at Oracle Corporations. Solomon has a postgraduate degree in business technology consulting from the prestigious Henley Business School at the University of Reading, a programme delivered by Henley in conjunction with enterprise architecture experts from Capgemini UK. Solomon currently resides at the boundary between London Borough of Lewisham and Greenwich. He may be reached at:

Tel: +44 (0) 7778 266 305
E-mail: solomon.baba@rationalsteps.com
Website: www.rationalsteps.com

INDEX

application infrastructure, 40-41
application platform framework, 39-41
application platform framework
    decisions, 40
application platform infrastructure
    software
  decisions:
    about, 40
    applistructure, 40
Architect strategic IT solutions, 127,
    132, 139, 142

benefit realisation:
  critical success factor, 220
  management process, 220
  manager, 56, 179-180, 214
  plan, 69, 179, 181, 231-233
  principles, 221-222
  process, 221-222
  report, 233
benefit review, 219
benefit review plan, 183, 221
blueprint, *see IT architecture blueprint*
board of directors (BoD), 20, 23, 28, 64
business analyst, 75-76, 228
business architecture, 138
business capability, 73, 128-130, 135

business capability gap assessment report, 130
business case:
  about, 224
  conceptual business case, 47
  content of business case, 225
  develop business case, 225
  full business case, 227
  initial business case, 227-229
Business change manager, 56, 179, 180, 225
business continuity:
  about, 55
  decisions, 60
  plan, 68
  requirement, 55
Business information analysis and
    integration
  technique (BIAIT), 108
business information control study
    (BICS), 107, 108
business Service, 5, 10, 68, 193, 198
business sponsor, 60, 214, 221, 223
business Strategy, 11, 38, 49, 122, 125
business systems planning (BSP), 107, 108
business value, 5, 10, 215, 221

capability, 8, 92, 99
capability model, *see IT governance capability model*
capability orientation, 8, 92
capability-oriented approach, 8, 199
capital investment approval and budgets, 27
change management strategy, 181
Charan, Ram 19, 129, 164, 166
chief enterprise architect, 58, 103, 134,
chief executive officer (CEO), 29, 34, 117, 223
chief financial officer (CFO), 218, 223
chief governance officer, 29
chief information officer (CIO), 92, 134, 147, 218
chief operations officer (COO), 72
Cigna, 23
clarify business strategy, 132
COBIT, 6
Commonwealth of Virginia, 145
conversion effectiveness, 5, 13, 63
Critical Success Factor (CSF) Method:
    about, 108, 117
    Key result areas (KRAs), 118, 119

decisions, 31, 34
Deloitte, 21
Department of Defense Architecture Framework (DODAF), 114
Discretionary IT investments, 9
doing the right things, 5, 51, 100, 102, 143

effective IT governance system, 24
enterprise analysis, 107, 108, 114, 115, 226
enterprise architecture, 6, 111, 114, 182, 204
enterprise architecture (EA) repository, *see repository*
enterprise change management plan, 68, 179, 181
enterprise IT architecture, 27, 31, 39, 48, 173
enterprise IT infrastructure, 31, 34, 36, 42
Enterprise IT principles, 31, 34, 36
enterprise IT standards decision, 41
enterprise modeling, 108, 110, 111
enterprise programme management (EPM), *see enterprise programme management office*
Enterprise Programme Management Office (EPMO), 53
enterprise requirements, 146
enterprise solution architect (ESA), 139
enterprise Solution Architecture, 12, 93, 106, 174
evaluation criteria:
    architecture compliance, 28, 51, 67, 175
    internal rate of return (IRR), 51, 67, 220
    IT standards compliance, *see architecture* net present value (NPV), 51, 67, 220

return on investment (ROI), 47, 51, 173, 218
strategic alignment, 51, 67, 114, 230
strategic fit, *see strategic alignment*
execution, 165
external IT service provider, 46, 48, 54, 65

failure of IT investment, 22, 219
feasibility assessment:
　decisions, 50, 59
　business feasibility analysis, 50
　financial feasibility, 125, 227
　technical feasibility, 125, 227, 228
Federal Enterprise Architecture (FEA), 114
financial justification, 218, 224
formulate IT strategy, 11, 127, 132, 137, 142
framework, 4

generate maximum value, 4, 6, 114, 167, 172

Hess Corporation, 143

Integrated Architecture Framework (IAF), 114
investment, 3
IT and business alignment, 92
IT Architecture, *see enterprise IT architecture*
IT architecture blueprint, 38, 42, 48, 63
IT audit committee, 27

IT benefit measurement, 220
IT benefiting, 222, 223, 230, 233
IT benefiting capability:
　about, 216
　Evolution, 217
　Input, 232
　Model, 232
　Outputs, 233
IT benefiting decisions, *see IT benefiting*
IT budget, 48, 65, 105
IT Capability, *see capability*
IT execution:
　about, 166
　decisions, 32, 44, 50, 51, 59
IT execution capability:
　about, 167
　Evolution, 168
　Model, 184
IT exploitation archetypes, 34, 36
IT funding decisions, 46, 47, 58
IT funding model, 47
IT funding policy, 142
IT funding strategy, 182
IT governance, 19-24
IT governance architecture building blocks:
　about, 25
　communications, 28
　structure, 19, 26
　processes, 27
　styles, 25-26, 36, 57-59
IT governance Process, 27-28
IT governance structure, 19, 26

IT governance styles, 25-26, 57
IT governance system, 7, 19, 22, 24-25
IT investment, *see investment*
IT investment committee, 27
IT investment decisions, 36-37, 43-45, 98, 146
IT investment life cycle, 219
IT investment management:
　capability, 20, 74
　principles, 7
　process, 4, 10, 20, 45
　systems, 7
IT investment review board (ITIRB), 27, 174
IT leadership, 27
IT operationalization:
　about, 193
　decisions, 33, 44-45, 54, 60
　governance, 34, 200
IT operationalization capability:
　about, 193, 198, 200
　Evolution, 201
　framework, 205
　Model, 205
IT Planning, 6, 32, 98, 101
IT portfolio managers, 102, 225
IT programme manager, 76
IT project manager, 104
IT project portfolio management (ITPPM), 124, 172-173, 177, 180
IT services:
　about, 199
　core IT service, 48

informational IT service, 9
infrastructural IT services, 9
　management, 7
　non core IT services, 48
　portfolio, 68, 126, 233
　strategic IT services, 9, 12
IT service infrastructure library (ITIL), 196, 201-205
IT service management (ITSM), 196, 198, 201, 205
IT service provider, *see external IT services Provider*
IT solutioning:
　about, 91-93, 99
　capability, 11-12,
　decisions, 44, 50, 59, 66
　Evolution, 100-127
　Input, 128
　Model, 127
　Output, 142
　process, 49
IT sourcing decisions, 47, 49, 59, 65
IT sourcing governance decisions:
　multisourcing, 47, 49
　netsourcing, 48
　outsource, 47-48, 64, 65, 94
　public cloud, 48
　selective outsourcing, 48-49, 59
　single outsourcing, 47
　insource, 48, 65
IT sourcing strategy, 48, 64, 142, 182
IT standards, 27, 38, 41-42, 63-64, 115
IT steering committee, 26-27
IT Strategy, 21, 65, 91-93, 106-107

IT strategy committee, 27, 75
IT strategy formulation:
    Strategic IT initiative, 91, 93, 96, 103, 106
    Strategic IT objective, 142, 148, 163-164, 172
    Strategic IT plan, 6, 32, 50, 100-101
    Strategic IT solutions, 103, 107, 125, 139-140
    Strategic IT Solutions Architecture, 142
    Strategic IT Solutions Road Map, 142
    strategic IT Sourcing Strategy, 142
IT Strategy Formulation Framework, 138

Kredietbank ABB Insurance CERA (KBC) Bank, 70

low conversion effectiveness, 5

manage strategic IT solutions portfolio, 127, 140, 142
middleware, 39-42, 224

non functional requirement, 96, 183

operational IT plan, 104, 126
organisation structure, 222
Oxford Health Plans, 22

Portfolio, 9
post implementation review (PIR), 221
post IT investment decisions, 44

pre IT investment decisions, 43
PRoject IN a Controlled Environment (PRINCE2), 33, 171, 183, 204
Project management body of knowledge (PMBOK), 33, 204
Project management methodology, 53, 223

Rational IT benefiting capability model, 231-233
Rational IT execution capability model, 184-185
Rational IT operationalization capability model, 205-206
Rational IT solutioning capability model, 127, 131

service level agreement (SLA), 55, 68, 74
service level requirement, 55
service orientation, 110, 197-199
service strategy, 202, 204
service-oriented approach, 9, 197
software development life cycle (SDLC), 7, 33, 53, 109
solution architect, *see enterprise solution architect*
Solutions Architecture, *see enterprise solution architecture*
strategic agility, 42
strategic business capabilities, 119
strategic business capabilities gap assessment report:
    about, 119, 130, 137

current strategic business capability (cSBCs), 137
required strategic business capability (rSBCs), 137
Strategic business initiative, 119, 129-130, 137
strategic business unit (SBU), 26, 31, 58, 71-72
strategic information systems planning, 97, 104, 107, 110
strategic IT capabilities (SBCs), 106, 120, 172, 178-179
strategic IT capabilities gap assessment report:
  about, 120
  current strategic IT capabilities (cSBCs), 106
  required strategic IT capabilities (rSBCs), 106
strategic IT funding policy, 142
strategic IT investment project, 125, 168-170
strategic IT planning methodology, 50, 117
strategic IT programme, 125, 168, 172, 177
strategic IT programmes mandate, 117
strategic IT project manager, 117, 180-181, 225
strategic IT project portfolio manager, 102, 176, 225
strategic IT projects portfolio, 174, 185
strategic IT service, 12, 175, 182, 193, 198
strategic IT services portfolio, 68, 126, 233
strategic IT solutions portfolio, 125, 127, 142
strategic IT solutions portfolio manager, 140
Strategic IT solutions repository, 132, 142
strategic IT system, 54-56, 178-184, 195, 213
strategic IT systems portfolio, 175, 183,

tactical IT plan, 104, 126
Tactical IT planning, 103, 123-124, 126
The open group architecture framework (TOGAF), 114, 117, 204

US General Accounting Office (GAO), 19
user requirements, 97, 182

Val IT, 6
value, 215, 218
value generation, 217
Virginia Information Technologies (IT) Agency, 145

Weill, Peter, 13, 19, 26, 112

Zachman framework, 114

www.ingramcontent.com/pod-product-compliance
Lightning Source LLC
Chambersburg PA
CBHW020739180526
45163CB00001B/281